W9-ACO-361

2 ov

GERMANY'S ROAD TO RUIN

Kiel Week 1900
H J M the German Emperor

Kiel Week 1900

H.J.M. the German Emperor

GERMANY'S ROAD TO RUIN

THE MIDDLE YEARS OF THE REIGN OF THE EMPEROR WILLIAM II

BY

KARL FRIEDRICH NOWAK

TRANSLATED BY

E. W. DICKES

NEW YORK

THE MACMILLAN COMPANY

1932

PRINTED IN GREAT BRITAIN

3780

Contents

vii

For a detailed list of authorities
see pages 337 to 353

Illustrations

ix

ILLUSTRATIONS

¶ *The illustrations in this book are reproduced by permission from originals in the private collection of Kaiser Wilhelm II. The Publishers desire to express their grateful acknowledgments for the use of the pictures and for the descriptive titles in the Kaiser's own handwriting. These are printed in facsimile.*

GERMANY'S ROAD TO RUIN

Chapter I

THE UNRAVELLING OF
THE ALLIANCES

Leo von Caprivi, the second Chancellor of Imperial Germany, had not the magic of a great name, the glamour of heroic achievement, that were Prince Bismarck's. He had come from the army, where in spite of an exceptionally brilliant career he had had many times to suffer for his over-sensitiveness. At Mars la Tour, as a young staff officer, he had determined the course of the engagement by his nerve and coolness. Yet when he went at the end of the war, worked to death, to Field Marshal von Moltke to ask for leave, Moltke had merely said:

'What is your war record?'

For that wounding inquiry he never forgave the Generalissimo. Another he remembered with even more bitterness against Marshal Count Waldersee. A matter in which Caprivi was concerned had come before Waldersee, who had asked absent-mindedly:

'Caprivi—who is he?'

For all that, the young officer had steadily advanced to high military rank. He was already General in Command of a Division at Metz when he received his entirely unexpected appointment as head of the Admiralty. He knew nothing of the navy. The appointment was welcomed by the army, in which his reputation stood high; his own satisfaction was not so great.

Caprivi obeyed the summons, for he was a Prussian officer. At that time the German navy had no Admiral who could have performed the duties of head of the Admiralty. Caprivi's predecessor had been Stosch, a General like himself. The navy had not been particularly enthusiastic over Stosch and the all-too-numerous 'Stoschites' whom his nepotism had busily pushed forward, and gave Caprivi a warm welcome on the strength of the esteem in which he was universally held. He himself took over his new duties with no undue exaltation, and not without the howlers natural to the novitiate of an Admiral Landlubber. At times he had to leave his papers and visit the fleet, and a lot of little vessels amid which he found it no easy matter to steer straight. He would arrive on board and find the orderly officer standing rigidly at attention to report in accordance with regulations. At first he had little or no idea of the correct procedure —he did not as much as know, for instance, what 'four bells' or 'eight bells' meant. But he wasted no time in laughter over these little apprenticeship incidents; he returned to his desk, where he worked unremittingly on his papers.

When he left the Admiralty he had himself created out of nothing a great technical organization. He had found the navy with no clearer idea of strategy than that if war came its job was just to sail out and shoot all round; he left it endowed with a developed plan of offensive. With Commander von Tirpitz he had perfected a system of torpedo warfare. Thanks to him, also, the navy at last had a mobilization plan. As head of the Admiralty he had shown a clear and masterly grasp of the broad lines even of things quite remote from his own profession. He had shown himself to be an organizer with long views, great capacity, and a strong will of his own, not to be thwarted. He was at all times meticulous and entirely self-sacrificing in his devotion to duty; he was no less meticulous and, indeed, obstinate in insisting on the full measure of his rights and authority. Only once did Emperor William issue a direct command to the navy over his head. Caprivi immediately asked to be relieved of his post. He went to Hanover as General Commanding.

He was without private means; his officer's uniform was his whole fortune. Subordinates found him pleasant to deal with; but in ordinary intercourse he was reserved, with an inconspicuous but perceptible haughtiness. He went little into society, burying himself in his studies. His spare time was spent with English and French books. He had been in Russia and France. He was reputed a man of absolute loyalty to the King, a General who scrupulously carried out every command. He was prepared to resist wrong in any form, though he envisaged resistance reluctantly, almost tragically; but, once wrong was done or an encroachment attempted, he was immediately up in arms. Prince Bismarck, a few months before his resignation, had recommended Caprivi to the Kaiser should an emergency come 'in which only military leadership can make good the harm done by civilians.' The Prince had been thinking of a change in the Prussian Premiership—of an Iron General to strike terror into the populace, prepared, if occasion called for it, even to shoot in face of 'Socialist imbecilities.' He had not for a moment thought of Caprivi as his own successor.

3

The Prince, and those who took their cue from him, did less than justice to the General; even his loyalty demanded a King in the right. The Kaiser, when he decided to make Caprivi Chancellor, saw qualities in the General which had escaped Prince Bismarck. He was aware of Caprivi's sensitiveness. He knew that he could be stubborn, 'obstinate to the point of rudeness.' But he also knew that there was no question of his uprightness and discretion; that he had attained through much reading to a definite outlook on the world; that he had considerably broadened it when the building up of the navy had led him to consider the influence of their environment on the maritime peoples. Britain was not the enigma to Caprivi that she was to most of his German contemporaries. Prince Bismarck had described him to the Kaiser as 'inexperienced in politics.' But the Kaiser had seen the work of the organizer who had gone, entirely inexperienced in his new sphere, to Kiel. He knew of no other General, no other statesman who was fitted to step into Prince Bismarck's place as Chancellor. It would, perhaps, only be a holding of the fort for the true successor. But whoever entered now into that succession would be bound to seem a small figure while men's minds were still full of the thought of the Titan, a poor and pitiful figure in the eyes of Germany and Europe, and a hateful one in those of the disgruntled Titan, departed now for Friedrichsruh, and of his large following.

The General had occupied only a single room in the Chancellor's residence; Prince Bismarck, meanwhile, had been in no hurry at all to get his property

4

and documents packed and brought away. On one occasion only, one day in March, Prince and General had spoken of Bismarck's departure. Caprivi merely said:

'If in an engagement I am at the head of my 10th army corps, and I receive a command, and if I have reason to fear that, if I carry it out, it will bring final disaster on the corps, and in the battle, and on myself, and if I have no success in representing my considered objection, then I have nothing left to do but to carry out the command and perish. What in the end does it all amount to? A man overboard.'

Prince Bismarck had been hurt by the new Chancellor's laconic comment. He had been hurt, too, at his having no questions to put—at his failing to realize 'that the transfer of a lease demanded a certain amount of consultation between the outgoing and the incoming lessee.' But at that trying moment the General had had no other resource than his rather dismal soldier's philosophy. It is true that he shook it off at once at the sound of the battle cries as he took up his new post. There he had definite decisions to make, and no reason for melancholy.

With Prince Bismarck's departure there had come a sudden rending of the thick veil which had lain over Germany's true situation, concealing it even from her ruler: the news that there existed a secret treaty with Russia, unknown even to the Kaiser until a few days before, and that the decision had now to be made whether or not it should be renewed, had brought sudden but alarming enlightenment. Count Herbert Bismarck, shortly before resigning office as Secretary of State, had made use of this treaty, and of the procedure for its renewal, as a means of bringing strong

5

pressure to bear on the Kaiser to compel him to retain the Count and his father in office. He had informed the Kaiser in writing that the Tsar's instructions to his Ambassador in Berlin, Count Shuvalov, required the negotiation and sealing of the renewed treaty to be exclusively in the hands of Prince Bismarck; and that, as the Prince had been dismissed, the Tsar was now dispensing altogether with a renewal. But on the very same day Count Shuvalov had sent a report to the Russian Foreign Minister, de Giers, in which he convicted the Secretary of State of having given incorrect information. Count Lambsdorff, the Assistant Minister, noted in his diary 'this manœuvre' of Count Bismarck's 'to make use of the negotiations as a means of maintaining himself in power,' and quoted the actual words of Shuvalov's report:

'What I actually said to Count Bismarck was that, in view of what had just happened, I had decided to suspend the negotiations which had been begun a few days before with his father. In view of the fundamental change in the situation, and of the change of personnel, it was entirely natural that I should want first to see how matters now stood. That was the main reason why I decided to seek fresh instructions before continuing the negotiations which had so suddenly been interrupted by events.'

On Count Bismarck's report, with its startling news that the Tsar was withdrawing from the negotiations, the Kaiser had written an astonished 'Why?' The Kaiser saw in the treaty a national concern, not one merely of Prince Bismarck's. He had at once sent for the Russian Ambassador. Then he learned that he had been misinformed.

However, it was the treaty that mattered, in the Kaiser's view, rather than this final effort of Count Bismarck's to preserve his father's power and keep him in office. Emperor William declared to the Russian Ambassador that he was ready to renew the secret treaty without delay, even without studying its contents, to which until then he had been a stranger—if the Tsar would tell him that he wanted his signature as an express and personal pledge and guarantee of lasting friendship. If the Tsar did this, he would be binding himself by his personal honour as Monarch and gentleman, and proving that he did intend sincerely and loyally to maintain the alliance, with no ulterior idea or reservation. If the Tsar hesitated, then at least time would have been gained, and would bring the opportunity of seeing clearly. The existence of this agreement, totally unknown to him until its sudden production from the archives, seemed to Emperor William to throw a vivid light on Germany's situation amid the Powers. He saw her enmeshed in the toils of European entanglements in every conceivable direction. He put no trust in the Tsar's personal commitment. But, for all that, the thing that mattered now was to insist on one of two things: either the Tsar must be committed or the entanglements cut away.

Only Prince Bismarck had imagined that the security of the German Empire could be assured by a secret treaty concluded behind the back of his ally and against his ally's supreme and vital interests. He had overlooked, or disregarded, the fact that the Austro-Hungarian Monarchy could not for a moment permit Russian guns, Russian money, Russian priests to

7

infiltrate either into Bulgaria or along the border of the orthodox Kingdom of Serbia. On Prince Bismarck's theory they must all be left free to push on through Roumania, in constantly increasing strength. He took no account of the suffocating, mortal grip on the Monarchy which that would imply, from Poland and Galicia through Bulgaria and Serbia as far as Montenegro and the Adriatic. If, moreover, 'the key of the Straits' came into the hands of the Tsar, as was contemplated in the treaty, Russian ships would be able at any time to appear in the Adriatic. Clearly, too, Prince Bismarck had entirely ignored Italy's vexation if she heard of his encouragement to the Tsar to march on Constantinople, the gateway into the Mediterranean. The Mediterranean agreement between Britain, Italy, and Austria-Hungary was aimed against any Russian advance into the Balkans. Prince Bismarck had been the most active supporter and promoter of that agreement between the three Powers. Yet, the moment Germany's allies learned of the strange conception which the Prince had of loyalty to treaties, they would be lost to her. The European grouping of the Crimean war would then suddenly reappear, with Italy added to the western combination. In that situation the Tsar, for all his power, had already once gone under. If Germany joined him, her fate too would be uncertain. For Britain would then be fighting for her life, with all the allies and vassals that she could summon or tempt in or force in on her side. On that basis the world war would have flared up in the last decade of the nineteenth century.

At times the Prince had regretted the impossibility,

in view of the Tsar's insistence, of publishing the treaty. Perhaps he did not actually realize that the public sacrifice of the Triple Alliance—which was what publication would amount to—would mean disaster. Certainly he was not entirely aware of the reasons why Tsar Alexander III was insisting on utter secrecy.

Emperor William II had had more than one disillusionment in regard to Tsarist sincerity; Prince Bismarck had had little else but disillusionment. On the impulse of the moment Alexander III could be lavish in professions of friendship, warmly worded and even sincerely meant. After the thorough clearing up between Tsar and Prince of the question of the Bulgarian forgeries, Bismarck had felt convinced that he had recovered the Tsar's confidence. Yet when William II told the Tsar the story of the Chancellor's fall, Alexander assured him of his sincere and sympathetic approval. The Tsar's moods, indeed, were incalculable. Even those who stood closest to him went in terror of some sudden outburst or malevolent impulse. Those, wrote Count Lambsdorff in his diary, who credited the Tsar with 'absolute sincerity' and who placed faith 'in his justice and his power' were quite 'mistaken': Alexander III was rough, high-handed, contemptuous. William II sent him by way of compliment a picture of a march past the Russian Embassy; the Tsar made a grimace at it. Prince Bismarck wrote to him about a journey to England which Count Herbert Bismarck had made; the Prince was concerned to remove any apprehensions from the Tsar's mind. The journey, he wrote, had been a courtesy visit rather than a political one. The only political

9

element had been a desire to secure British help against America in the Samoa question. The Tsar wrote on the margin of the letter: 'Here is this super-blockhead trying once more to steal a march on us. He is just throwing sand in our eyes with his story of Samoa and the Americans. That won't wash.'

In one thing only the Tsar had never changed—his deep and insuperable mistrust of Prince Bismarck. He had hated and feared him, as a dangerous intriguer, from the moment when the Prince had brought the Russians to the Berlin Congress as a friend and advocate of their aims. The Prince had had no choice but to leave the Russians in the lurch; he had been unable to prevent Disraeli's and Andrassy's triumph over Russia. But that was not the whole depth of his offence. He had been so indiscreet as himself to convey Disraeli's ultimatum to Russia to Prince Gortchakov, and to recommend that Russia should give way. In his 'Letters' to two sisters Disraeli wrote exultantly of 'my victory!' The Tsar never forgave Bismarck for that piece of advocacy, and when, in spite of it, the Reinsurance Treaty was signed in June 1887, the Tsar was the very last of its celebrants.

The only deeply-rooted loyalty of the Tsar was for Russia's people, for the Slav nationalism of the countless millions whose absolute lord he considered himself to be, but whose feelings, for all that, he must allow to determine his own if he was to maintain his arbitrary power in security. But scarcely a soul among those Slav millions had any affection for Germany and the Germans. Nor were they merely indifferent to the Empire beyond their border; all classes and all parties

were filled with dislike or hatred of it. Alexander III
was well aware of this. It had not been his idea, when
the Three Emperors' League expired in 1887, to conclude a new secret treaty with Prince Bismarck. He
had had no great opinion of the old agreement, and
had been reluctant to see a new one come into being.
Count Peter Shuvalov, brother of the Russian Ambassador in Berlin, had made the suggestion in Berlin of
a fresh agreement between Russia and Germany entirely on his own initiative. Austria was to be excluded
—and enmeshed. Constantinople was to be conquered. In all of this the Germans were counted on
as willing accomplices. All that was offered in
return was that Russia should remain neutral if
France attacked the Germans. But the Tsar had refused to consider the proposal or to look at the Ambassador's first draft. De Giers, the Russian Foreign
Minister, had accordingly wriggled out of the matter.
He knew, equally well with the Assistant Minister,
Count Lambsdorff, that the Tsar looked more kindly
on France than on Germany. The divergence of view
on this subject between Tsar and Minister sometimes
brought such plain signs of Imperial displeasure that
the Foreign Minister expected any day to be dismissed.

De Giers was not entirely the 'poor old man'
that he seemed to Count Kalnoky in Vienna. He had
plenty of persistence, for all his feeble health. He was
shrewd, in spite of the impression of entire absence of
pretensions which he often made on his visitors. He
never had any trouble in conveying on two successive
days two quite contradictory impressions of his views
on one and the same question. His tone was usually

filled with resignation, but that did not prevent the play of an obstinacy which wrested from his opponent a generous measure of the main thing in dispute as the equivalent of any small concessions wrung from him. That done, he would at once begin to relegate to oblivion the main object sought by dwelling on the minutiæ yielded. He had at once seen in the secret treaty with Germany the means of undermining the Triple Alliance. He spoke pathetically of the isolation of Russia, but he saw and had in mind the isolation of the Germans. For that he fought in connexion with the treaty, silently, tenaciously, until the day should come for him to give his consent to it.

The absence of Katkov, the Pan-Slav leader, who had great influence with Alexander III, and Grand Duke Vladimir's advocacy of the German case, enabled the Foreign Minister at last to win over the Tsar. Alexander himself could not but realize the opportunity which he was getting for entrapping and strangling Austria. In any case, Russia would be able to move more freely in the Balkans. The glittering prize of Constantinople was brought closer. All these aims were easier to attain one day with Germany's help than in the face of her enmity—and there need be no actual payment of the price in the sacrifice of France. The Tsar began to see advantages on which he could count, provided that he could conceal the agreement and avoid popular discontent. Moreover, he saw how Prince Bismarck would be entangled in a mass of agreements and conventions amid which no genius in all the world would be able to stand unseared if the conflagration came. Not even Prince Bismarck. Alexander III accepted the treaty, but

asked that, out of consideration for Russian susceptibilities, it should be kept secret. He had, in any case,
another reason for secrecy in regard to this new commitment. For he knew more than Prince Bismarck
knew.

Russia's relations with France already amounted to
something not far removed from an alliance. In
January 1887 three Bulgarian envoys had visited
Flourens, the French Foreign Minister, to represent
to him the anxieties of the Principality in regard to
Russia; the Foreign Minister had candidly advised
them to show more consideration for Russian feelings
and to make concessions to the Russians, and from
that date secret but more and more substantial ties
had bound France and Russia. In the very month of
January in which the first draft of the Reinsurance
Treaty was put on paper in Berlin, Count Shuvalov,
the very man who had suggested it, had received
instructions from St. Petersburg to make inquiries
at the Foreign Ministry concerning Count Herbert
Bismarck's unfriendly attitude towards France—
inquiries actually made at France's instance. It was
the time of General Boulanger's push for military
preparedness, and his erection of barracks along
the Franco-German frontier. The Russian Ambassador, while actually working on the agreement between Russia and Germany, had had
himself to report to France the Russian overture in
her favour. Prince Bismarck had refused to accept
any reassurance in regard to Boulanger's activities;
and, a few days after Count Shuvalov's effort at mediation, he had sent General von Schweinitz to the
Tsar, and demanded outright that Russia should

13

remain neutral in the event of a Franco-German war. Evidently the Chancellor was beginning to be quite clear as to the Tsar's real feelings. The Tsar had replied by reminding General von Schweinitz that the Prussians had waged three successful wars, against Denmark, Austria, and France, while he had kept his own troops and guns idle, regardless of his own interests. He most certainly would not now promise neutrality in regard to France; Russia would be guided by her own advantage. In the months that followed, Prince Bismarck had watched impatiently over the progress of the new treaty, which was at last to bring an improvement in Germany's relations with Russia. But it could not be said that Russia was in any hurry. And all the time the intimacy between Russia and France had been steadily growing; in spite of the ultimate conclusion of the new secret treaty—and more than ever after it came into existence.

It had, indeed, been growing visibly in the sight of all the world, when those readily granted loans showered French gold upon Russia—gold that Prince Bismarck had banned from Germany. On one occasion when a French Government fell, Baron Mohrenheim, the Russian Ambassador, who was already busily wooing France on the Tsar's behalf, had threatened time after time to demand his recall, until in the end a Cabinet came to power under a Premier to Russia's taste. While on holiday in Munich in July 1886, Baron Mohrenheim had drafted a memorandum in which he set forth the necessity of Franco-Russian co-operation and the advantages which it offered. Count Osten-Sacken, then Minister in the Bavarian capital, had had no enthusiasm at all

for Baron Mohrenheim's projects. He advised him
not to submit the memorandum to de Giers:

'You are risking displeasure, even dismissal.'

Baron Mohrenheim was risking nothing of the sort.
The memorandum was submitted to the Tsar. Alexander sent for the Ambassador. Mohrenheim had got
no further than the anteroom when he learned exactly
what the Tsar thought. Count Dimitri Tolstoy, the
Minister of the Interior, was waiting there. He too
had read the memorandum, and gave the Ambassador
a warm greeting:

'At last that rarity in our diplomatic corps, the voice
of a patriot!'

The Tsar loaded Baron Mohrenheim with proofs
of his high favour. The Ambassador went on working
in Paris. There, at the end of the 'eighties, Ministers
came and went incessantly, though sometimes they
merely changed seats. The Goblet Ministry gave place
to that of M. Rouvier. Rouvier was succeeded by
the President of the Chamber of Deputies, M.
Floquet, a Radical who once had given bitter offence
to the Russian Ambassador of the day—in 1865, when
he had shouted at him: 'Vive la Pologne, Monsieur!'
Now, however, the Ambassador and the President of
the Chamber met at a reconciliation dinner on the
eve of Floquet's taking office. Freycinet became
Minister of War; the Russophil Flourens became responsible for foreign policy. But whoever the new
men might be, whatever their antecedents, Baron
Mohrenheim, assured of the Tsar's approval since his
audience in St. Petersburg, collaborated with them in
the forging of the Franco-Russian bond. Five weeks
before the signing of the Russo-German secret treaty,

15

the President of the French Republic declared to Jules Hansen, a confidant of the Russian Ambassador:

'Obviously France and Russia have a common interest in preventing any further growth of Germany's power.'

The golden millions of French loans were quickly followed by half-a-million guns, supplied by the French to the Russians. The French Minister of War made it one of his main concerns to push forward a general technical assimilation between the Russian and French weapons. Russian staff officers came to France to learn the latest improvements in commissariat and army transport. Russia was openly at issue with Bulgaria; she had no chargé d'affaires at Sofia. The Minister of the Republic at Sofia became the Tsar's privy ambassador; Flourens sent for exhaustive reports from Bulgaria, and these went on at once to Baron Mohrenheim for transmission to St. Petersburg.

Thus, Tsar Alexander III was thoroughly alive to the reasons why the new secret treaty with Germany must at all costs be kept secret. The main reason had nothing to do with popular susceptibilities in Russia: the main reason was France. In the end the Tsar had given his assent to the conclusion of the treaty in Berlin. But when General Schweinitz, on Prince Bismarck's instructions, asked for Russian neutrality in the event of war with France, the Tsar had rejected the request out of hand:

'To-day,' he had added, 'it is more than ever Russia's duty to watch over her own interests. She cannot always be helping Prussia. Besides, Prussia is the ally of Emperor Francis Joseph, and that makes it impos-

1405

H. M. Yacht "Hohenzollern" Hernösand

sible for Russia to attempt a war against Austria with any prospect of success.'

Now Alexander III had Emperor Francis Joseph's Prussian ally in the toils. To make quite sure that they should not be observed, Prince Bismarck might be glad to seize the occasion of the advance of Russian troops into Galicia to offer renewed assurances of friendship in Vienna, in such a form as to remove all apprehensions. Thus the Austro-Hungarian Ambassador in Paris was able unhesitatingly to assure M. Valfrey, in a confidential interview at the French Foreign Ministry, that there was not the slightest question that 'if war broke out between Austria and Russia, Germany would be bound, in compliance with her treaty obligations towards Austria, to place army corps along the Russo-German frontier in order to comply with the principle of armed neutrality.' The Austro-Hungarian Ambassador had not the smallest idea that he was playing the part of a dupe. Tsar Alexander III and Prince Bismarck were seated in the boxes, both smiling at the spectacle before them—the Prince, at Austria; the Tsar, at the Prince.

Both were protected by the obligation of secrecy. But even of this the Tsar, or the Russians, had their special conception.

The Russian Emperor had insisted that the knowledge of the existence of the secret treaty should be confined to a very small number of people. It was intended that only the actual signatories should be fully acquainted with its contents. Prince Bismarck went so far as to keep even Emperor William II in complete ignorance of the intimate relations which now existed

B 17

between the Empire and Russia. But in St. Petersburg they came to the knowledge of Sir Robert Morier, the British Ambassador, who was no friend of Germany or of Prince Bismarck. In London Count Ignatiev, the Russian Ambassador, passed on in confidence some indication of them. It was not clear whether he had his information from Count Shuvalov or from the Russian Foreign Minister. What is quite clear is that, very soon after the exchange of signatures to the treaty, Lord Salisbury learned of the fact. It mattered little whether it was de Giers, the Foreign Minister, himself or Count Lambsdorff who informed Prince Lobanov, the Ambassador in Vienna, of the existence of the secret treaty. In any case Prince Lobanov knew about it. He had been Ambassador in London for three years, and had many close ties with England—and he was anything but uncommunicative. A day came when General Schweinitz called in alarm on the Foreign Minister: could it be true, he asked, that Prince Lobanov had actually been let into the secret of the treaty?

'In quite general terms,' de Giers admitted.

'Quite enough,' Prince Bismarck wrote on the margin of the General's report of the interview.

But Lord Salisbury was still in the dark. He had often found Count Ignatiev a magnificent liar. He knew that Morier had never forgiven Prince Bismarck for the charge brought against him of carrying on espionage for France in the war of 1870. Yet the hints came from many quarters—never with definite details, but always conveying the central fact that Germany was now allied with the Russians. Lord Salisbury was determined to get to the bottom of the matter. There might be a possibility of bringing Germany over to Britain's side. The Mediterranean agreement had done useful work in preparing the way for a *rapprochement* with the Triple Alliance. Lord Salisbury began with Count Hatzfeldt his many conversations about the 'assurance' which Germany might be able to offer him in regard to the contingency of an Anglo-Russian war. If Prince Bismarck would agree to give this 'assurance,' the way would be opened for fruitful negotiations. But Prince Bismarck did not agree. He could not possibly; he was bound fast by the secret treaty. Prince Bismarck found many fine phrases to cover his refusal. At Europe's open window he spoke at length on the moral considerations which alone could induce the Germans to go to war. Lord Salisbury, however, knew now all that he needed to: Prince Bismarck did not want Anglo-German co-operation, or it was no longer within his reach. That was enough: it tallied with the rumours.

Neither Prince Lobanov nor Count Ignatiev nor anyone else spoke of the details of the treaty. They were all careful to say nothing in London either about the German agreement with Russia concerning Constantinople or about her turn towards France. But if they did no more than let out all sorts of mysterious hints, 'in quite general terms,' it was enough to win a good point for Russia: the gateway to London was double-locked against Prince Bismarck. The Tsar had Germany's support in the Straits. He had Austria in shackles. With France, against whom the Prince had sought protection, the Tsar was on terms of friendship that grew daily in cordiality. Prince Bismarck himself, indeed, sometimes had the gravest doubts whether Russia would remain neutral in the event of war coming between Germany and France. And from Britain the Tsar had cut him off.

The secret treaty was of great value to Russia. To Germany it brought only the risk of grave unforeseen complications and an entirely unprecedented defencelessness in the face of all Europe.

A memorandum setting forth the good and the evil in the secret treaty had been prepared by Count Berchem, Under Secretary of State. Chancellor von Caprivi took the memorandum as the basis of the discussion—urgently pressed for by *Geheimrat* von Holstein—which he had with the Under Secretary, with *Vortragender Rat* Raschdau, and with Baron Holstein himself, before the final pronouncement was to be made by Emperor William. In the memorandum Count Berchem had estimated the effects of the treaty all over Europe. Everywhere he saw Germany compromised and imperilled. 'As the late Chancellor often declared,' Germany would be 'compelled, in spite of everything, to fight for Austria-Hungary if she got into difficulties, and that would mean our breaking faith with the Russians.' The Under Secretary was opposed to the renewal of the treaty 'if only on account of the suspicion abroad—a suspicion not entirely without foundation—of our felony.' In his view the treaty was irreconcilable with the obligations entailed on Germany by the Triple Alliance treaty. Count Berchem reviewed all the various complications that might involve Germany in war: each and all of them brought the German Empire into an impossible situation, in regard both to Austria-Hungary and to Roumania, if the day were to come for the fulfilment of the obligations incurred under the secret treaty. Even in regard to Turkey the Germans would stand convicted of double-dealing, since they had only just advised her to resist and arm herself against that very Russia for whom they were now once more to make easier the capture of Constantinople. Over against all these entanglements Count Berchem failed to see the most insignificant advantage for the Empire:

'The treaty does not safeguard us against a French attack; on the contrary, while it extends to Russia the right of offensive against Austria on the lower Danube it prevents us from taking the offensive against France—and all this quite apart from the fact that the tendency of the treaty is difficult to reconcile with the German-Austrian alliance.'

Plainly, the Under Secretary of State had no knowledge whatever of the real relations which for some time past had bound France and Russia together. He was entirely unconscious of the vast menace which for years had been towering up against Germany, and could only have been averted by co-operation with Britain. But the confusion arising from Prince Bismarck's treaties of alliance was enough in itself for Count von Berchem's finding:

'So complicated a policy, the success of which has in any case been problematical at all times, cannot possibly be persisted in by us after the departure of a statesman who was able to go to work with the advantage of thirty years of success and an absolutely magnetising influence abroad.'

Count Berchem had been Prince Bismarck's right hand. Every day he had seen the great magician

21

continually throwing his lassoes from end to end of Europe, entangling friend and enemy alike in them, and imagining that all would dance in response to the ends which he held in his grip. The magician had been spared the awakening out of his legerdemain. He left the arena before any time of testing came. Count Berchem, however, knew that he could neither cast a noose like Prince Bismarck nor muster that strength to betray which, for the Prince, was an element in statesmanship, and, when the ultimate catastrophe was at hand, might be the alliance-maker's only means of escape. Half frightened, half indignant, with a courtierly obeisance to the Bismarckian strategy in the very act of tearing it up, Count Berchem came in his memorandum to the conclusion that the renewal of the secret treaty could not be recommended.

On that point Baron von Holstein had made up his mind before ever he read the Berchem memorandum. Were the treaty renewed, Prince Bismarck would still remain firmly implanted in the life of the State. He might be brought back any day from Friedrichsruh. At any moment of clouded relations with Russia, if the prospect was darkening and influence had to be brought to bear on Tsar Alexander, the Tsar's supposed sole trust in the Prince, on which the ex-Chancellor had so often banked, might again be a dominant consideration. Baron von Holstein's register of the vulnerable points in his contemporaries did not extend to the secrets of St. Petersburg, or extended only to those of the members of his own Embassy. The real thoughts and feelings of Alexander III were a closed book to him; he knew nothing of the mistrust that alienated the Tsar from Bismarck. Baron Holstein shared the general belief in the Tsar's faith in Prince Bismarck—whom he himself hated, and not only on account of the ill-odoured mission on which the Chancellor had sent him to Count Arnim in Paris long years before. So long as Prince Bismarck had been in office, Holstein's only path to power had been underground. The Chancellor had monopolized all power himself. He had exercised it with a despotism which for decades had stifled all opposition; and, finally, he had established his dominion exclusively for himself and his family.

'Bismarck is a Wallenstein,' Baron Holstein had declared to Prince Radolin as early as 1885, when Count Herbert Bismarck was nominated to the Secretaryship of State—'his ambition is to found a Bismarck dynasty.'

Now at last Baron Holstein meant to establish his own dominion. In a nightmare vision he imagined the Prince still in possession of the bridge of his friendship with the Tsar; he saw the bridge brought into perfect repair, even newly underpinned, and the Prince able at any moment to cross it with his heavy, awe-inspiring tread, back to the Chancellor's palace. Rather than that, away with the bridge! General Caprivi's succession to the Chancellorship had no sooner been definitely settled than he had informed the General about the Reinsurance Treaty; and had made no secret of his own view of it. He knew, moreover, that this was the way of approach to the Kaiser, who up to then had not had the slightest inkling of the whole matter. When the Kaiser's indignation burst forth, Holstein hurried forward the decision.

23

No successor had yet been nominated to Count Herbert Bismarck. Whoever the new Secretary of State might be, he should find himself faced with a settlement of the issue which he might approve or not but could no longer influence. Nothing was more urgent than to have Prince Bismarck firmly nailed down in Friedrichsruh.

Quite apart from his feelings towards the old Chancellor, Baron Holstein had the excuse for precipitancy that on the merits of the case he was firmly convinced that the treaty must not be renewed. For he fully realized the soundness of Count Berchem's arguments. He may even, indeed, himself have put them into the Count's head. There could be no doubt that the Triple Alliance was undermined by the treaty. No one knew better than Baron Holstein how much that is secret can be learned from incautious tongues. Baron Holstein was himself powerful only if Germany was powerful. From that point of view at all events he was a great patriot, as, indeed, in spite of his hunger for power, no one could deny him to be. It needed only one person to betray the contents of the secret treaty, in Vienna, or in Rome or London, for the Triple Alliance to be destroyed and Britain ranged with Germany's enemies. Leaving Austria-Hungary entirely out of consideration, the secret treaty was a plain piece of treachery towards Italy, to whom, under her treaty with the Empire, Germany was bound to communicate every agreement made with any other Power. Here again Prince Bismarck had broken faith with the signed pledge of the Empire. Everything in the wide sweep of this treaty seemed to Baron Holstein to be dangerous. The Russians had

laid the mine very skilfully under Germany's firmest
friendships. He would not give it any further chance
of exploding. Baron Holstein was strenuously opposed
to the renewal of the Reinsurance Treaty even on
quite impersonal grounds.

He agreed entirely with the view expressed by
Vortragender Rat Raschdau that Bismarck's whole
treaty arrangement with Russia was just as unfortunate and untenable as it could possibly be. The
Vortragender Rat shared Baron Holstein's apprehension as to the exposure of Germany before her
allies if any of the Russians were to gossip out of
school. He assumed that Prince Lobanov had
'learned of the fact (not the contents) of the treaty';
here he was in error, for Prince Lobanov knew its
exact provisions. But this one case of a Russian outside the stipulated circle of those authorized to know
of the treaty being acquainted with it, was sufficient
to lead the *Vortragender Rat* to attach special importance to the question of Russian discretion.

His scepticism was increased by his recollection of
a report which Prince Reuss, Ambassador in Vienna,
had sent to Prince Bismarck, which had made Bismarck himself alarmed for all his treaties and their
inter-reactions. Prince Reuss reported a conversation
which he had had with Count Kalnoky, the Foreign
Minister, on Balkan affairs. The Minister had shown
the Ambassador, a little bitterly, how since 1866 the
only field of activity remaining to Austria-Hungary
had been the Balkans, and now Prince Bismarck was
warning her against venturing to cast her eyes in that
direction. Raschdau had no belief in the Russian toler-
ance suggested in Count Peter Shuvalov's statement

that it would be possible for Austria to make
herself mistress of Serbia the moment the Russians
had come into Bulgaria. Far from it—he was convinced that the Russians would never tolerate any
dominant Austro-Hungarian influence in orthodox
Serbia. Nor could he see how to reconcile the granting to the Russians of a right to march through Roumania with Germany's obligation to protect that
country against any attempt at aggression. The *Vortragender Rat* saw also, or divined fairly accurately,
how much that was unavowed had been going on in
recent years between France and Russia. Since the
days of Alexander II, since the humiliations that the
issue of the Berlin Congress had brought the Russians, since the German alliance with Austria in 1879,
he felt that Russo-French relations had been growing
'continually more intimate, so that for the purpose
which it has in view there is scarcely any need now for
that intimacy to be confirmed by any particular document.' The main question, however, was whether
Russia would really move a step to help Germany,
and of that he doubted very much: for 'our great
statesman himself repeatedly expressed his grave
doubts whether the provisions of the Reinsurance
Treaty would be carried out.'

Accordingly *Legationsrat* Raschdau, like the three
others, pronounced against the renewal of the Reinsurance Treaty—so far as concerned the actual
policy to be followed; though he had other ideas as to
the attitude to be adopted towards it as a matter of
form, and for the time being. As a matter of form he
was for agreeing to renewal—subject to modifications.
He offered his own suggestions to the Chancellor and

the Under Secretary of State as to the modifications to be proposed. They were so devised as to secure that, in the conversations concerning the modifications, the Russians should be led on from step to step until in the end they would themselves have destroyed the treaty. The young *Legationsrat* was aiming at the same final result as the others and only proposed a different method. But he was outvoted. Baron Holstein was in a hurry, both on general and on personal grounds. He was against any modification, any concession, any delay in bolting the door. He was on thorns until he could send to Count Philipp Eulenburg —the Kaiser's friend, so important to him, so attentively cultivated, and already initiated by him into this secret of state—a telegram announcing the final disposal of the matter:

'Russian business quashed.'

It must be absolutely and finally quashed. Especially as Chancellor von Caprivi was himself against the treaty. Caprivi shared the view that it was not straight dealing. If Bismarck had some affinity to Tsarism, something of the Russian in him that made him himself Caesarian, a devotee of absolutism, a standard-bearer of princely prerogative, contemptuous of the common herd, if it was Prince Bismarck's unshakable conviction that every act, every decision rested with the Monarch (except in so far as he himself made use of that symbol of power to maintain his own power)—the General, once he had exchanged soldiering for statesmanship, was inclined both by conviction and temperament to take exactly the opposite view. The new Chancellor believed that modern wars are made and waged not by kings but

27

by their peoples. It was, therefore, for the peoples to choose their alliances, and certainly it was their elementary right to know about them.

Caprivi had almost as great a distrust of Russia as the Tsar had of the Germans. He preferred to look towards England: there the horizon seemed brighter, and he himself would do nothing to dim it or darken it. But above all he meant to see honest dealing, not craftiness and treachery on all sides. If alliances were concluded they must be observed in the spirit and not only the letter—and not with the old hairsplitting in the treaties as to who was carrying on a 'war of aggression' and who not, or whether the *casus fœderis* arose in this case or that—

'It is possible to exasperate an opponent with pinpricks until he hits out; does the *casus fœderis* then arise?'

Caprivi resolved that in future, so far as he was concerned, treaties should be open. In whatever decisions he might take in his time, he would leave no room for terror whether the Russians could be trusted to hold their tongues. He too saw in the Reinsurance Treaty an incendiary bomb rather than any protection or service.

Before the time came for him to go to the Kaiser to give his opinion, Baron von Marschall, the Minister for Baden in Berlin, was appointed to succeed Count Herbert Bismarck as Secretary of State. He had been a lawyer, a public prosecutor. The Grand Duke of Baden had sent him to Berlin, where his advice had often been sought during the critical period preceding Prince Bismarck's retirement; and now the Grand Duke had recommended him to the Kaiser as Secre-

28

tary of State. The new Secretary had had little past experience of affairs of state. He bowed now to the opinion of the four. General von Caprivi's view found loyal support also from the accommodating General Schweinitz, who happened to have come back from the Embassy in St. Petersburg for a ceremonial occasion in Berlin. The Kaiser had asked his view of the secret treaty, and the Ambassador had promptly replied:

'It would be lovely—if it were practicable. But it carries a very great risk.'

Yet General Schweinitz must have felt the desire, natural to any Ambassador, to be of service to the Court and Government to which he was accredited. But the General was not a man of very great independence either in action or thought. His letters and diplomatic reports were masterpieces of unfailing amiability, but every word was swathed in wadding and everything unpleasant apparently entirely banned. General Caprivi had put backbone into his concurrence in the refusal to renew the treaty. The Ambassador did not want, moreover, to be responsible for another Chancellorship crisis, and Caprivi had made it quite plain to him that if it was decided to renew he would resign.

Chancellor and Ambassador, Secretaries of State and *Räte*, all agreed that the secret treaty with Russia must not be renewed.

Emperor William was waiting for news from the Tsar. The message that he had sent to Alexander III through the Russian Ambassador, Count Shuvalov, must have been transmitted to St. Petersburg by the Count on the same day. Yet the Tsar had sent no reply.

29

Recollections of Brest-Litovsk came into the Kaiser's mind. There Tsar Alexander had displayed his guns before him. He had shown him how Russian troops could storm a position. Prince William had had a message to convey from Prince Bismarck; the Russian Emperor had met it with overbearing, wounding replies. The Russian officers' corps had taken not the slightest trouble to conceal from their guest their antipathy to Germany. Then there had come the recent years of nervousness over Russia's continually increasing armaments, her unceasing reinforcement of the frontier garrisons. Prince Bismarck might have faith in the Tsar's friendship; the Kaiser was filled with doubts of it. And his judgment did not mislead him. When at last the reply came, he read in it cold, outworn, oft-reiterated stock phrases of empty politeness, where he had asked for a personal pledge and a personal guarantee.

Count Lambsdorff had drafted the Tsar's message, not as a direct communication from Emperor Alexander to Emperor William, but as an instruction to Count Shuvalov 'to convey the Tsar's thanks to the Kaiser and to say that the Tsar had never had any doubt of the unalterable devotion of his friend and ally to the principles and traditions of a great past, which was the best guarantee of peace.' The Tsar had wriggled out.

'Alexander III has steadily diverted Russian policy into a fresh course, and is preparing an alliance with France'—so Hansen, Baron Mohrenheim's confidant, declared in these very weeks of the spring of 1890. He added: 'Bismarck lost Russia's friendship mainly because Russia was unable to forgive his ingratitude

30

for the services rendered by Russia to German policy.' Alexander's preparations were not being paraded before Emperor William. But he could guess what the Tsar was thinking of when he wrote of 'the principles and traditions of a great past': even if he had not preserved a vivid memory of Brest he needed only to recall the Berlin Congress. Never, so long as Alexander III lived, could there be any hope of real sincerity or real friendship.

The Chancellor urged that the Reinsurance Treaty should be allowed to lapse. He pictured to the Kaiser the endless confusion that might be produced by the treaty. The Kaiser agreed. At that moment Philipp Eulenburg telegraphed. He had had Baron Holstein's telegram. But he was still dominated by Prince Bismarck's statesmanship. He advised against letting the treaty go. The Kaiser threw the telegram away.

The breakaway from the treaty began. However it was to be effected, it was bound to give offence to the Russians. They learned first that, on instructions which had come still from Count Herbert Bismarck, the negotiations were not to be conducted by the new men in Berlin but by General Schweinitz in St. Petersburg—he had been familiar with the matter from the outset. The Ambassador was returning, they gathered, with plenary powers. The Russian Foreign Minister expressed his gratification. The Tsar assented, indifferently.

'His Majesty,' General Schweinitz reported shortly after his arrival in St. Petersburg, in his account of a conversation with the Foreign Minister—'His Majesty has never taken much interest in the treaty at any time.'

Count Lambsdorff was the only one who suspected trouble when it was learnt that the General was entrusted with the conduct of the negotiations. Light broke, however, on all the Russians when, in spite of the message from Berlin, the Ambassador arrived without plenary powers. But the Russian Foreign Minister and his assistant did not give up the fight for the treaty. If the Tsar wanted an alliance with France, that could be arranged in spite of the secret treaty with Germany. Indeed, it would only be then that Germany would really be in the toils. On top of that, the Triple Alliance would be crippled; and still there would be Germany's guarantee in regard to the opening of the Straits. The Russians had themselves proposed long before to do away with the secret protocol to the treaty, with its crude and undisguised mention of the conquest of Constantinople and of the setting up of Russian dominion over the Balkans. All that they now wanted to save was the broad lines of the treaty, unchanged in sense but at least a little less shameless in expression. Three times the Foreign Minister conferred with General Schweinitz. If the renewal of the treaty was not secured, it would be enough to have 'an exchange of notes—perhaps of letters between the Monarchs.' The General allowed himself to be talked over. Gone was the firmness with which he had advised the Kaiser in Berlin. He urged the Chancellor not, after all, to let Germany refuse to take 'the Tsar's hand,' which he was now, perhaps, holding out for the last time.

In these May days the Tsar was in excellent spirits. The French Government had arrested a number of Russian anarchists, and was handing them over to

Aalesund 1900
The rejoycing citizens welcoming
the German Emperor

the Russians—a thing which, in a country like France, with its conceptions of the right of political sanctuary, was incredible only to those who knew nothing of the Franco-Russian intimacies of recent years. In June 1890 the Russian Foreign Minister was still struggling at least to 'preserve the essentials of the understanding' in some sort of 'formula.' Now, however, the Tsar, the 'master who finds such difficulty in making up his mind,' was ready at last to give freer expression to his feelings. He laid down that if the matter was to come up again at all it must no longer be Russia but Germany who must make the next overture. He added that there must be no more discussion of the matter in his name.

But it was no longer possible to save the secret treaty, or even fragments of it, in any form or by any formula. The longer the passage of time, the more incensed was the Kaiser at the Tsar's frigidly official reply to his own warm plea, touched almost with romance, for chivalry and the pledged word of a friend. At the same time, it was no small satisfaction to him that he had been right in his judgment of the true attitude of the Tsar towards Germany. Emperor William looked out on a future full of anxieties. But he was at least freed from the burden of uncertainty concerning his own ally. He had sent to Emperor Francis Joseph on April 4, 1890, a full account of the breach with Prince Bismarck; now he sent a further letter on the Chancellor's retirement:

'It is better so, and better also for our relations with one another, as in view of the independence and with it the secretiveness of the Prince I should, unhappily, not have been in a position to know, quite

c　　　　　　33

freely, what courses he might be entering on in our foreign policy without my knowledge, and how these could be justified to my allies.'

The Tsar, too, was relieved when, about the middle of June, everything fell through:

'For my part, I am very glad,' he wrote on the margin of a written report which his Foreign Minister had sent him, 'that Germany has taken the initiative in refusing to renew the treaty, and I do not greatly regret that it will no longer be in existence.'

The Tsar may have felt discomfort on his side in his liability to protect Germany against a French attack. For he was himself seeking an alliance with France.

In August, while Emperor William was on a visit to the Tsar, the Russian Foreign Minister tried once more to save the mine under the Triple Alliance; but this effort too failed—so much so, that in the end the Russian Embassy Counsellor, Count Muraviev, had to answer for suggesting the effort. Chancellor von Caprivi, who had accompanied the Kaiser, was no longer prepared to move a finger in the matter.

Needless to say, in spite of the termination of the partnership there was no lack of reassuring declarations from the spokesmen of the two Empires, both during the negotiations and after their cessation. It was perfectly true that Emperor William wanted neither war nor enmity. He did really want so to conduct his policy that Russia should have no ground either for complaint or concern. What the Tsar's future plans might be for Constantinople and the Balkans, for France and against the Triple Alliance, for war or peace—all this lay in obscurity. The Kaiser

34

admitted to himself that the turn of affairs was bound to leave the Tsar a little sore, for all his professions of entire satisfaction. But there was no other way out of the Bismarckian maze. It was just that soreness that *Vortragender Rat* Raschdau had feared when he proposed working for time, keeping the door still open in regard to the treaty until ultimately the Russians lost patience. The Kaiser had been afraid of his allies' suddenly finding out about the treaty, especially if there had to be three months of dallying with it and then three more of negotiation and correspondence. As to that risk he might have been unduly apprehensive; but the Russians would have been just as offended if Germany had made one objection after another and finally rejected every proposal. The bitterness over the ultimate breach was bound to come, however tactfully and adroitly Ambassador Schweinitz might draw out the conversations, and however tender might be his consideration for the other party up to the last moment. One thing especially needed to be borne in mind about the Russians: if the negotiations had dragged on interminably, the day might have come when in exasperation they would explode the mine while there was yet time. They might have done it either from Vienna or Rome. For Raschdau's plan had been to go on and on with the negotiations, prepared, ostensibly at all events, at any time to sign the agreement afresh behind the back of Germany's friends. At any time those tactics might be ended and revenged by an exposure of the negotiators.

At last, in the early summer of 1890, two years after his ascent of the throne, Emperor William had found his freedom. At last he was able himself to have a say in the settlement of the course which Germany should pursue. Since Prince Bismarck's departure he had been crippled by the apprehension that the disclosure of the legacy of the secret treaty might wreck Germany's own alliances, and Germany one day find herself completely isolated. The ending of the treaty was deeply wounding to the Russians. But if there was any possibility at all of recovering the Tsar's trust, it could only be after the atmosphere had been cleared. The Tsar must himself be aware that both he and Prince Bismarck had been engaged in furtive moves that might mean destruction to neighbour States: that Prince Bismarck had been guilty of sharp practice, betraying an ally, and he himself equally so, deluding the Prince with a hypocritical treaty which aimed at splitting Germany off from the Triple Alliance and bringing her, in her sudden isolation, under his own sway. Once an end had been made of disingenuousness, of the continual need for the dissembling of everything on all sides, of the universal spinning of secret intrigues against everyone, it might become possible to build up genuine friendships, to feel and inspire genuine trust—even towards Russia.

Now, however, Kaiser and Chancellor deliberately and resolutely smashed the secret treaty. General Schweinitz was replaced by General von Werder, an Ambassador with great influence over Tsar Alexander, for whom Alexander had himself asked, and to whom Emperor William always, on that account, listened carefully; and the anxieties and apprehensions of the former Ambassador gave place, under the direction of the Chancellor, to very plain language and very independent criticism. Russia could rest assured of Germany's pacific intentions. But there were to be no more genuflections every time the Tsar knitted his brows, and there was to be an end of the old smartness and overreaching on both sides. If Russia feared the Triple Alliance, the Alliance would only recover real power after its members had recovered faith in one another. Italy was dependent and always would be dependent on Britain, on account of her vulnerable coastline. Austria had never within human memory been anything but a friend of Britain. Prince Bismarck had been aware that the only natural extension of the Triple Alliance would be towards Britain. But everything English had had for him the repulsiveness of the unfamiliar. His method of ruling in Germany and Prussia had in itself been evidence enough of the gulf which separated him from British ways of political thinking. He had had an inveterate hatred of 'the Englishwoman,' Empress Frederick. His obstruction of the marriage of Prince Alexander of Battenberg with Emperor William's sister and his whole attitude towards it—in order to serve the Tsar's purposes—had deeply offended Queen Victoria, the Prince of Wales, and the whole British court. Again and again Lord Salisbury had sounded Count Hatzfeldt in London on the subject of an 'assurance,' but the Prince had had no 'assurance' to offer. But all this was now old history: there was no longer any commitment to Russia. It might be that a way of approach to Britain would now be discoverable. If a rapprochement were achieved, and were to grow into friendship, there would be peace in the world for all time. General von Caprivi was temperamentally inclined towards Britain rather than Russia. Not only that, but he had a

37

thorough understanding of Britain. Emperor William himself was 'half an Englishman.' Kaiser and Chancellor determined to make the effort.

For Kaiser and Chancellor alike realized that, even if the ground were cleared and a new crop of friendship were to grow to fruition, Russia was in any case no safe refuge.

Chapter II

THE WOOING OF BRITAIN

Lord Salisbury and his colleagues in 'Her Majesty's Government' naturally regarded Prince Bismarck's retirement as a very important turn in affairs, with great potential significance for British-German relations. Prince Bismarck's statesmanship had produced nothing but exasperation in England, or at least deep annoyance and concern. When, in the 'eighties, the Prince embarked on Germany's first efforts at colonization, he had been keen to arrive, if possible, at any sort of arrangement with the most powerful colonial empire and the greatest sea power in the world, and he had confidently expected some sort of result. Undoubtedly Britain had met his overtures quite in the wrong way. Whether it had been a discreet or timely move on Germany's part to initiate a colonial policy, with the possibility it involved of friction with Britain, was another question. Once, however, Prince Bismarck had embarked on the new course he was unwilling to proceed without a discussion with the Power that was everywhere dominant; and Britain should have agreed to the discussion. But she had remained silent for two years. Finally Prince Bismarck had laid claim to the territory which he wanted to secure for Germany by landing troops there.

The sensitiveness over Germany's entry into the

39

colonial sphere might soon have entirely disappeared, since Prince Bismarck had ended by taking what he wanted, the British had accepted the position, and the British statesmen had themselves realized the mistakenness of their attitude. But now Prince Bismarck himself inflicted one annoyance after another on Britain, although she too was seeking a rapprochement and he was actually trying to arrive at something like an alliance with her. He wanted to divert France's thoughts from the Rhineland. Wherever he could he supported the plans of the French colonial party—against British and none but British interests. One day Count Herbert Bismarck gave M. Barrère, the French Counsellor of Embassy in Stockholm, the friendliest of advice as to the way in which they needed to work against Britain—forgetting that the conversation would be reported not only to Paris but equally as a matter of course to London. Soon after his rejection of Lord Salisbury's overtures in regard to a rapprochement—overtures which the secret treaty with Russia had made it impossible for him to accept, —Prince Bismarck had attempted to set the crown on his system of alliances by proposing to the British a defensive alliance against France. Lord Salisbury had long felt that the Prince was hostile to Britain; now he got the unpleasant impression that on top of all his pin-pricks the Prince was making fun of him. It was certainly possible that one day France would attack Germany in order to recover her lost provinces. But that the idea should ever come into a French head to land troops on an island protected by the strongest navy in the world, was more than either the Marquis or the Prince could seriously suppose. The Chancellor had offered worthless goods at a high price. 'Bismarck,' declared Lord Salisbury when the offer came up for discussion, ' is offering us ten per cent and asking a hundred.'

The British Prime Minister was suspicious enough by nature. The Prince's proposal might have been much less transparent and would still have been received with the greatest caution. On top of all this there was the painful memory of Prince Bismarck's attitude towards Prince Alexander of Battenberg, a direct rebuff to Queen Victoria and her whole Court. Lord Salisbury knew definitely that Germany was more or less on terms of alliance with the Russians. In any case, Prince Bismarck had thoroughly capped the British blunder in regard to Germany's oversea aspirations.

Lord Salisbury breathed a sigh of relief when the news came of the Chancellor's downfall. A better time might now perhaps be dawning for Britain and Germany.

There were, at least, at once plenty of indications of it. Emperor William paid quite unaccustomed attentions to the Prince of Wales, who happened at the moment of Prince Bismarck's retirement to be staying in Berlin. In addition to the distinctions showered upon him, Prince Edward noticed this time with satisfaction something almost approaching cordiality in his nephew's manner towards him; though it was almost impossible to imagine two men more utterly different in body and soul than the Prince of Wales and the Kaiser.

There was not a shred of romanticism in Queen Victoria's shrewd son and heir, though he was full of ambition to get a great deal done for which, so far, he had had virtually no opportunity at all. The Prince of Wales was twenty years older than Emperor William. He was the pattern of a well-groomed man of the world of the 'eighties, dressed by his own choice in the broad frock-coat, the fancy waistcoat, the hand-made tie, and the matt square bowler, all of which, with the very cut and the striped or check pattern of trousers and the particular model of shoes, he had gradually grown accustomed to imposing on the gentlemen of England. (Emperor William preferred the eagle-helmet of his cuirassiers.) Prince Edward's face might have been carved out of a copy of Queen Victoria's; the almond-shaped eyes had a rather sleepy, far-away expression, but one that, unlike his mother's, suggested a quiet contentment with the day and confidence in the morrow, a suggestion gently reinforced by the round beard of the period.

Everything about him seemed to convey entire aversion from the stiff formalities and the whole world of ideas amid which his nephew lived. Prince Edward had grown up amid German influences, and had a perfect mastery of the tongue. He rolled his R's with un-English ease, and his English never had the perfection of his nephew's—Emperor William had drunk in Prince Edward's mother-tongue with his own fostermother's milk. The Prince of Wales had been exposed to all the storms of life: he had knocked about a great deal, all over the world, while Prince William had stayed at home, or had been confined to the little journeys permitted by his grandfather's meagre favours and rigid soldier's outlook. Prince Edward, if the civil list ran dry, had borrowed.

Prince William had had no experience of women. Prince Edward's experiences with women filled one diary after another, volumes of them. Often Prince William, in disgust at the dullness of his thesis or with the Professor's methods of instruction, had thrown the thesis to the winds. The Prince of Wales had learnt everything to the lees: love, good living, life and politics. Fate had brought the nephew early to the throne. The uncle had reached middle age, and was still shut out of every public activity natural to the heir to a throne. The nephew learned early to command and to rule. If the uncle did so much as to venture his opinion concerning a peer in the public eye, he received a short and sharp rebuke in a note from his mother:

'Let this subject drop now.'

The Queen kept a tight hold over him, alike in business of state and in pocket. But she could have no hold over the personal doings of the grown man. On one solitary occasion Prince William had spent a few days in Paris. From the balcony of the Hotel Mirabeau he had looked across the Rue de la Paix and found surprising initiation into the mysteries of the Ateliers Worth opposite. Prince Edward had not been used to surprises at all that distance. He knew all the mysteries of Paris toilettes. He also knew the city's loveliest *cocottes*. He had a captivating way with them all: they all hung round him, made love to him, spoiled him, adored him. In London he never went outside the most elegant and exclusive clubs, and he only left town for country house, shooting box, or yacht. In Paris he would feed in the nearest decent restaurant. Any café would do. At night he would

43

play with anyone who knew the game, who had money, and who had nothing else against him.

'People always put faith,' complained one of his friends and defenders, 'in the picture the gossips paint of the Prince of Wales—a sort of elegant vagabond.'

But Prince Edward made quite a serious study of this life. He listened to the talk at the next table in the café, remembered the things said to him in the heat of the game. Everything he noted down. He was as particular in recording the conversations with his *cocottes* as in registering his political annoyances at home. What he did not learn from his many men friends, or from the diplomats, his women friends confided to him. Most things he knew much sooner and much more accurately than the British Ambassador. Many things he learned that never reached the Ambassador's ears.

Though he was heir to the throne, he never had any money. It might cost him a couple of days of running all over Paris to get a loan of a thousand francs. That taught him the value of money. He was fond of thoroughbred racing, of lively evenings with light music and pretty American women and clever Jews. He was always ready for any possible compromise; in that he had inherited his royal mother's good, homely common sense. Aggressiveness or insistence to the point of a breach were foreign to his nature. Many people set him down as a keen man of business, though he left the demonstration of that quality in him mainly to the clever Jews who, by dint of manipulative artistry, maintained some sort of order in the enormous mass of debt that the Prince managed to run up in the very earliest years of his heirdom.

44

He often came to Germany—every year to Bad Homburg. There, as everywhere else, he lived the life of a quiet, distinguished *grand seigneur*, free from all ostentation, scarcely more than an ordinary visitor like the rest. He took his meals in his hotel, well-arranged little dinners and breakfasts to which he usually invited a dozen gentlemen, distinguished friends passing through, people from South Africa, industrialists or brewers, who had to pay a thousand guineas for the honour of the invitation. The less exotic guests also paid for their own breakfasts: the *maître d'hôtel* stood at the door with the bill when the gentlemen rose from the table. No one was able to take offence: the matter was always tactfully arranged, if it was a little unusual.

Prince Edward was accomplished in all the arts of good living. They were arts entirely strange to Emperor William. So great was the difference between the two men in every respect that they repelled one another if they merely stood alongside one another. The Prince found the Kaiser's morals too rigid. The Kaiser found the Prince's too lax. They never exchanged an acid or a hostile remark. Up to now they had never exchanged a word on matters of state. They loaded one another with friendly attentions wherever they met. But wherever they met they felt that they could hardly endure one another. As soon as they had parted they overflowed with harsh judgments of one another. The Kaiser's entourage learned what Prince Edward had said to his own entourage, and passed it on to the Kaiser. Through the same channels the Prince learned things that the Kaiser had said of him. Without ever coming to a direct issue with one another, Kaiser and Prince were two hostile camps, or at the least two different worlds.

There came at the end of the 'eighties, to crown all this superfluity of incompatibilities, one incident which was bound still more to alienate uncle and nephew. Statements that the Prince was alleged to have made repeatedly were retailed to the Kaiser—that Emperor Frederick, had he been on the throne instead of his son, would certainly have been ready to restore Alsace-Lorraine to the French, and to make concessions to the Danes in Schleswig. After that the nephew left the friendly letters that came from his uncle unanswered. And when Emperor William went to Vienna to visit Emperor Francis Joseph, the German Ambassador in Vienna, Prince Reuss, informed the Foreign Minister, Count Kalnoky, and the British Ambassador that the Kaiser did not want to meet the Prince of Wales—who had also come to Vienna. That was a message unique in all the long history of the relations between Courts or their representatives. Lord Salisbury wrote a memorandum on the incident for the Queen and Ministers. For the first time the Prince definitely turned against the Kaiser. He told his brother-in-law Prince Christian of Schleswig-Holstein that he was demanding an explanation. If the Kaiser failed to give one, he would pay no further visit to him, and if he should think of coming to England he would ignore him.

Various things now came out. What the Prince had said with regard to Emperor Frederick proved to have been something quite different. In the course of a conversation with Count Herbert Bismarck, Secretary of State, he had asked whether it was true that a rumour to that effect concerning the views of the late Kaiser was current in Germany. This question, according to the heir to the British throne, had then been passed around in its twisted version. As for the Kaiser, he declared that the allegation that he had objected to meeting the Prince in Vienna was a pure invention. What had actually happened was that Prince Reuss had made the unfortunate remark to the British Ambassador entirely on his own initiative, in connexion with a message from Count Berchem warning Germany's ally Austria-Hungary of Prince Edward's supposed habit of passing on things told him in confidence, and his dangerous curiosity in regard to military matters. Emperor William had at least ample occasion, as Count Berchem's communication showed, for annoyance over all sorts of habits of his uncle's. The German Ambassador actually declared to Emperor Francis Joseph that 'the presence of the Prince of Wales would have a disturbing effect on the spirits of Emperor William.' It is uncertain whether Prince Reuss simply read into Count Berchem's message an indication of the step which he should take, and thus acted quite on his own initiative, or whether he was influenced by the knowledge that Count Berchem's message had been sent at the instance of Prince Bismarck himself. What is certain is that by a gross blunder he formally made to the British Ambassador a communication which was an indubitable insult to the heir to the British throne, without considering the probable and even inevitable consequences.

The Kaiser's declaration cut them short, however;

Prince Edward expressed himself satisfied with it. But the incident did not increase the uncle's liking for his nephew. Friendlier feelings did not come until during the visit to Berlin just at the time of Prince Bismarck's retirement, when Emperor William exerted himself in his reception of Prince Edward to efface the unpleasant memory entirely. He took every possible opportunity of making much of his uncle. Now of all times he did not want to offend him.

But at the moment there was not the slightest question of that.

Emperor William raised his glass in a rousing toast to Queen Victoria. And long live her heir! The Kaiser drank to the old comradeship in arms that had united the English with Prussia. He recalled the days of Waterloo, a glorious tradition, as was only natural, in England, as it was also in his own country and its royal palaces.

Emperor William was resolved thenceforward to cultivate the rather rusty friendship with England in every way he could. British naval officers should come to Germany. He spoke in words full of admiration of Britain's glorious navy. In the past it had been on board British ships that German naval officers had pursued their earliest studies. He awoke to a new sense of his essential Englishness. Besides, he wore the blue full dress of an Admiral.

He certainly meant to remain at peace with the Tsar. But the Triple Alliance needed strengthening— even if the Tsar were to take alarm; even though he were saying to General Werder in St. Petersburg all sorts of things about the new turn in German policy which it was really not for him to say. The very point

Lofoten, Digersnälen Summer 1900
The "Hamburg" and a Cruiser.

of an indestructible friendship with Britain was that it would make an end of the dependence on Russia.

Chancellor von Caprivi looked along the same lines into the future; but with a soberer outlook—particularly in view of his military knowledge and his lately won insight into the questions of sea power. For him Russia was the only menace that seriously threatened the Empire. He saw Germany as liable, in any hostilities which might affect her, suddenly to find herself involved in a war on two fronts. Consequently the army must be made as strong as it possibly could be. Important as this was for Prussia, it was a consideration that had long been neglected. Many defects had crept in and become firmly rooted. The Chancellor was determined to extirpate them as rapidly as possible. Then, with the aid of the allied armies, he would feel that even a war on two fronts could be faced.

But the Chancellor saw yet further into the future: he saw the part that a blockade would play in a future war. A collision might come between the two groups of Powers in Europe, and yet bring neither victory nor defeat. But if Germany's enemies were to blockade her, that would bring defeat. It was thus on Britain that Germany's future depended—and on Britain alone. Germany's main objective in her foreign policy should, he considered, be an understanding with Britain.

No colony in the world, in the Chancellor's view, was worth a quarrel with Britain. It was characteristic of the changed outlook and policy at which the Chancellor had arrived, that in the first agreement which he made with Britain her gains seemed greater than Germany's. In exchange for Heligoland, for the

D

coastal trading centres of German East Africa, and for a narrow strip of land in South-west Africa, he ceded to Britain the wide territories of Vitu, Uganda, and Zanzibar. The Chancellor at once became the target for sharp criticism: 'A bathroom for the two kingdoms of Vitu and Uganda!' Bitter comment came also from Friedrichsruh, from the mouth of Prince Bismarck. In Zanzibar, in the old ex-Chancellor's estimation, a jewel had recklessly been thrown away, a transhipment port of inestimable value in trade with Africa. No doubt the ex-Chancellor had taken only a casual glance at the map, or none at all: it was naturally of more advantage to load and unload goods coming from and into the interior of the continent in the actual coastal ports, instead of first shipping them to the island and there unloading and reloading them for their ultimate destination.

Chancellor Caprivi stood unmoved by the attacks: 'There should be no dallying with the idea of pushing any dispute over colonies to the point at which it might lead to a breach with Britain. There can be no question that the material value of our colonial possessions is very far from being enough to outweigh the cost of a war, with the utterly shattering effect which that would have on the well-being of both combatants. Not only should actual war be avoided, but there should be no estranging of the nations, no embittering of opinion among large numbers of the investing classes, no diplomatic feud for the sake of our colonial possessions. We are keenly concerned to carry forward into the future our long-standing good relations with Britain.'

The Kaiser and Caprivi saw in the possession of

Heligoland advantages which the opponents of the agreement failed to realize. The island could be made into the only real defence of the Hansa towns in any naval war of the future. The Prince of Wales was, perhaps, the only one who realized the ultimate purposes and effects of the exchange. After the conclusion of the treaty, Queen Victoria had sent for the German Ambassador, Count Hatzfeldt. As the Ambassador left the Queen the Prince offered him his congratulations:

'You have carried out your commission very cleverly. But I will tell you one thing: if I had known anything about it I should have prevented the agreement!'

A yet more important gain at the moment than the possession of the island was the marked brightening of the atmosphere, the visible irradiation of the relations between the two countries with a new and friendlier spirit. The old resentments seemed to have been buried. Queen Victoria, who had refused to cede Heligoland at Prince Bismarck's suggestion, had now agreed for Emperor William's sake, since he seemed to be making very friendly approaches to Britain, and since he had pressed for Heligoland as the gratification of one of his fondest wishes. For all her shrewdness and the insight born of long experience, the old Queen was peculiarly attracted towards her grandson. She was not blind to the Kaiser's foibles. Sometimes she was sharp enough in her criticism of him—when the bursts of imperial oratory came hot on one another's heels, when he cut short the Court mourning for his father, or when he went banquetting or sabre-rattling with his garrisons. Yet

51

she was—there is no other word for it—decidedly
proud of him. She was captivated by his youth and
his impetuous onslaught on every obstacle that stood
in his way. If he was going to employ his energy and
enterprise in the conquest of Britain's friendship,
so much the better. The only source in Germany now
of bitterness and ill-humour was the Empress
Frederick. She left her son without a shred of good in
him. She had something new to tell in every letter.
The old Queen made never a word of reply so far as
her grandson was concerned. She had willingly given
him Heligoland. And she was genuinely pleased and
delighted when, only a few weeks later, he came to
England to see her.

Brighter and brighter grew the atmosphere of
British-German relations. Almost it seemed that the
British statesmen were the more concerned for Germany's security. The Triple Alliance had fallen due
for renewal. Rudini, the Italian Prime Minister, was
hesitant; he was more drawn towards France. British
advice brought him round: Italy renewed the alliance.
Roumania too was not quite sure. Britain offered her
services in keeping Roumania on the side of the alliance. All this was not by any means merely the outcome of Queen Victoria's pride in her grandson, or of
any sudden discovery of Lord Salisbury's that the
Germans were charming fellows. The agreement over
Heligoland was the least of Britain's anxieties; she
had, indeed, come out of it not at all badly. But Russia
was a source of anxiety, and France another. Constantinople and the Dardanelles, Syria, Egypt, were
all clouds on the British horizon. The Russian ambition, dating from the will of Peter the Great, to seize

Constantinople, was never absent from the thoughts of St. Petersburg. The French were working to secure control of the Ottoman Bank. They were doing all they could, moreover, in Constantinople to Gallicize the young pashas, to destroy the last vestiges of British influence among them—and the old pashas had all been Anglophils. The French, too, did not conceal their dislike of the thoroughness with which the British in Egypt had been protecting the interests of the Powers after the misgovernment of Ismail Pasha which had first brought them into Egypt. In Constantinople the French were disturbers of the peace.

Moreover, Admiral Gervais was preparing to take the French fleet to Kronstadt to visit the Tsar. The British knew little or nothing of the secret history of the alienation of Germany from the Russians; but it was plain to all the world that there had been a change. What was going on between the French and Russia was equally a mystery as yet, but once more it was plain enough to the British that there was a good deal going on, or had been. No one knew how long it would be to the day when the clouds would be rent by lightning. The growing friendship with Germany was beginning to be of importance. Caprivi was not Bismarck. He did not seem to be a man whose every move must be suspect. Lord Salisbury forgot the German rebuff of the 'eighties. The air seemed to have been cleared. He made a fresh attempt at an understanding—cautiously and tentatively as before. Germany had had experience of British reasonableness over Heligoland. Britain had assisted in the maintenance of the Triple Alliance. Lord Salisbury

indicated to Baron Marschall, the Secretary of State,
all his troubles. He still spoke in veiled language; but
having explained his difficulties to the German
statesman, he hoped for a return for his confidence
which would carry matters a stage onward. Then it
would be time to discuss what would be due from
Britain if Germany lent support to her interests.

The Secretary of State replied promptly and in
plain terms. He began by placing Germany's needs
before Lord Salisbury. He then asked that Britain
should support her with Italy. He asked her advocacy
of German interests with Roumania. Finally, he
showed how Britain stood in regard to her own problems. He pointed out how negligible was her influence in Constantinople. He went on to give some
advice as to her best line of action in Egypt. Lord
Salisbury had grown even more carefully measured,
more soft-stepping and hesitant in his approach since
Prince Bismarck's rebuff; his hints at the possibility
of co-operation had been scarcely perceptible: he now
had from the Secretary of State a prompt and plain
reply, and one which he felt to be unmistakably inspired by manly sincerity. Germany, said the Secretary of State, could not bind herself.

Baron von Marschall's answers were all prompt and
plain and manly. This lawyer from Baden was open
and downright by nature, never hesitating to call a
spade a spade, and, indeed, rather taking pleasure in
doing so. He said what he thought straight out, even
in front of foreign statesmen, feeling that his direct-
ness and firmness must make an impression; the impression that it did make was of rudeness and arrogance. As a lawyer and an ex-public prosecutor he

attached real value only to the written word. He had no great sense of fine distinctions. This big and burly statesman tended, without knowing it, to exaggerate the significance of the tangible thing-before-his-nose, and to fail to appreciate the finer and subtler issues. He was a great eater, an incessant smoker of his big cigars, and no contemner of the deep draught of strong wine. Amid the cigars and the wine, in the intervals of office and business of state (in all of which he leaned on the judgment of *Geheimrat* von Holstein) he was always ready to talk at length on the most varied subjects, far countries and their peoples, problems of the day, scientific issues—to the real advantage of his listeners, for he had always been a man of great industry, always a thorough student of every subject in a way which the world has not yet learnt to make its own. His outspokenness was not softened by his gift of humour, of which he was inclined to be a little vain. It was not a humour of the infectious sort which the Swabian Kiderlen-Wächter could bring into play, enabling him so often to pass off his natural roughnesses, and to maintain his dignity and worth as *Vortragender Rat* in attendance on the Kaiser, by a hearty laugh that cleared the air.

Even Baron von Marschall, in his conversations with foreign statesmen, made no use of the strong language which had come into use and had found such favour at home since Count Herbert Bismarck's day. The habit had grown of making use at every turn of full-blooded phrases not generally admitted into Society, in an appreciation of ruddiness for its own sake, even without wine. But it was answer enough when the Secretary of State gave Lord Salisbury's overtures a short and sharp dismissal. That was all he had been able to do toward the realization of the desires of the Kaiser and Chancellor for a rapprochement. Unfortunately the Chancellor did not go thoroughly into details. As a rule, indeed, he learned nothing about them. The diplomatic routine work was handled by Secretary of State and *Geheimrat*. In London the Secretary was free to display his diplomatic gifts. Lord Salisbury was driven back, frozen out at every delicate advance with an icy answer. The Baron made no very favourable impression on Salisbury. Perhaps he really had failed to appreciate how powerfully the whole situation was pushing Britain into Germany's arms, or the profit that could, with careful management, be extracted from it.

'Diplomacy will always be a sealed book to him,' wrote General Schweinitz of Baron von Marschall, 'for he knows nothing either of the places or the people with whom one has to reckon in this business.'

This much Lord Salisbury had to admit—that it would still be a long time before the doors of the house in which British-German friendship could dwell were really thrown open. He had had one more try at the door, but it had only banged to again in a gust of winter wind.

Then, in the early summer of 1892, Lord Salisbury and the Conservatives went out of office. Their place was taken by a Liberal Ministry under Gladstone, now a frail old man, whom Salisbury had not credited with the strength to govern any longer. Lord Rosebery went to the Foreign Office. Gladstone made no secret to anyone of the fact that his inclinations and those of various members of his Cabinet lay in the direction of France. Lord Rosebery went to work in almost entire independence of Gladstone's control. He himself had a closer regard for the Germans than the French. But there was so much opposition in the Cabinet to any markedly friendly policy towards Germany that he was obliged to go cautiously in his negotiations with her, especially in any discussion of mutual commitments.

The whole trend of the times of itself brought him closer to Germany. Lord Salisbury's disappointments had no effect on him: he had not lived through them. In his talks with Count Hatzfeldt he was brought into contact with the ideas of a distinguished *grand seigneur* who certainly had no desire to make difficulties for him. Count Paul Hatzfeldt, scion of an old Hessian family, was a man of striking presence, the outward expression of real qualities. His fine intellect had been tempered amid the busy activities of a long life and sharpened by a wide and varied experience. For nine years he had had as tutor Ferdinand Lassalle, who restored for his mother the ruins of a fortune almost destroyed by his father's extravagance. The young aristocrat listened to the flaming postulates of the apostle of the people, but without letting his own pride, his own outlook or his career be caught in them. He went with Lassalle through the short weeks of the revolution of 1848, weeks in which the emanations of the Jacobinism which had long played around the house of the old Countess had lit up the Rhineland. A few years later he had decided on a diplomatic career; he had at once come under the notice of Prince Bismarck and had rapidly gained promotion. In the days of Versailles Count Hatzfeldt had been at Prince Bismarck's side, and the Prince had employed the very able young man as a sort of *préfet* in occupied cities, where his brilliant command of French and his discretion carried him extremely well, with never an incident, through his dealings with their hostile population. He was no enthusiast for work: '*Paulchen ist faulchen*'—'Our little Paul likes his little laze,' said Prince Bismarck good-humouredly. The Prince frequently employed the Count on special missions abroad; finally he moved into the Foreign Ministry as Secretary of State, with his knowledge and experience, his great shrewdness, his pride and his many debts.

But he was not to pattern. He was unique, among his colleagues in that office and that profession, in his private life—always in difficulties, queer in one way and another. The American woman whom he had married lived apart from him. The fight with his creditors never ended. In Court ceremonial and Court etiquette he was an awkward problem: a Secretary of State who lived like a Bohemian, whose financial straits were always making him talked about, could not be shown at Court. Prince Bismarck sent him as Ambassador to London.

There he continued to live the life of a man not to pattern. Queen Victoria approved of his intelligence, his knowledge of the world, and the fine manners of this elegant, slender, almost emaciated *grand seigneur*. She was unable equally to approve of an Ambassador being accredited to her Court who was living apart from his wife. Hints of this reached the ears of the Count, ears resolutely schooled to pass in and out with a cool and lofty indifference whatever society and the world might say of him. He was highly thought of by the heir to the throne and all the British Ministers and diplomats. They were all aware that his reports and recommendations carried great weight with the Kaiser and the German Foreign Ministry. He fell a victim to disease while yet young, spent most days in bed, often had to take flight to the milder air of Brighton, and would only get up out of bed if he had to visit the Queen or her Ministers; all this added to the difficulty of communication and the conduct of business with him. No other German statesman, however, except *Geheimrat* von Holstein, had his wide grasp of world affairs. But while the *Geheimrat*, out of hatred or the gambler's passion, out of hunger for power or some evil caprice, set out resolutely to bend them to his will, Count Hatzfeldt frequently vacillated under the influence of his sorely tried nerves. The Ambassador had certainly some affinities with the school of Bismarck. He had not the old Chancellor's tone or his ruthless, completely amoral pursuit of undisclosed aims; but he had the Bismarckian belief in the virtue of elasticity in statesmanship, though unlike the Prince he set limits to it. Count Hatzfeldt had from his early years been almost as familiar with English life as with French. Above all he won admiring appreciation in London for his never-failing tact. He accurately gauged Lord Rosebery's difficult position in the Cabinet. He had learnt, moreover, that in England it was best never oneself to broach the subject on which one had aims in view. He put no pressure on Lord Rosebery, who gratefully recognized the fact and came to the subject of his own accord.

For Gladstone's liking for France gave Britain no protection from unpleasant experiences with the French. The friction of recent years continued unabated; new causes of friction were added to the old ones. Plainly France had recovered from the war. Everywhere she put to the test her newly regained strength. Since 1891 the French had been at issue with the British East African Company in Uganda. Cardinal Lavigerie had founded in that African kingdom the order of the Frères Blancs for the conversion of the heathen. It was not for that that Britain had come to terms with Germany over Uganda. The White Brothers came into conflict with the British colonists. Captain Lugard intervened with a display of armed force. The French retired, but the dispute left a sting behind in Paris and London. In Madagascar the French were putting pressure on the native queen. They were entirely within their rights, but they were taking such thorough advantage of them by means of new and prohibitive duties that British trade, against which these had been aimed, was being destroyed. On top of this there came never-ceasing controversies over fishery rights, now off Newfoundland, now in the New Hebrides. The more awkward for the English the question of the evacuation of Egypt became, the more frequently the French raised it. In Constantinople their capitalists outbade the British in the competition for railway concessions. France had, in fact, strung together a whole bundle of questions each more troublesome than the one before. From Africa, especially, there was some new vexation every day. Uganda and Madagascar were bad enough; next the French occupied Dahomey. Then they marched on Timbuctu. They invited the Russians to a naval cruise in the Mediterranean; there they could settle down for good. On top of all this, the situation suddenly grew acute in Siam.

The French had occupied the left bank of the Mekong. Siam was wedged in between British and French possessions, a perfect buffer state, preventing the confusion or jeopardising of the spheres of interest of the two European owners. Now the French had come right up to the British: they had simply annexed by force of arms the strip of Siamese territory needed to bring them alongside them. Astonishing effects proceeded at once from this inconvenient and intolerable neighbourhood. British gunboats lay off Bangkok. The French blockaded the port. Into the peace of an English week-end there burst the blatantly irregular news that the Senior Officer in charge of the gunboats had been requested by the French, without periphrase, to get up steam and leave Bangkok.

Lord Rosebery had for some time already reached the limit of his patience. War with France hung by the slenderest of threads. Days before this, when Lord Rosebery received Count Hatzfeldt, the Ambassador had found him upset and depressed. France was making life a burden for Britain. Rosebery 'suggested' that Germany's 'interest in the question would increase in the event of a war between Britain and France, since that eventuality would offer the opportunity of bringing the Quadruple Alliance into being.'

Geheimrat von Holstein wired now at once from Berlin. He saw that the time had come for action. He did not first make his usual formal recommendation to the Secretary of State: he replied himself. Lord Rosebery, he considered, had a peculiar idea of how to pave the way for a Quadruple Alliance: he was proposing to begin by bringing Italy into the threatening conflict between Britain and France. Then Italy's war would automatically become the concern of the whole Triple Alliance.

'Germany's part,' concluded *Geheimrat* von Holstein, 'is clearly marked out for her. We are bound to support Italy in a war against France. Under our treaty the fact of war is all that matters: its cause is beside the question. The only proviso is that the declaration of war or the first act of war must come from France.

'We are, therefore, directly interested in seeing that Italy's relations with France do not worsen unless we have tangible or treaty assurance of British support.'

Britain must be made to guarantee the completion of the Quadruple Alliance. Neither Italy nor either of the other Triple Alliance Powers must move a finger until that was done. Britain must first give the undertaking, in return for Italian support, that would pledge her to the reality of the Quadruple Alliance. Suppose Italy were to help the British in the Mediterranean with no prior guarantee—later, if the British drew back, Italy would be the conductor for the lightnings of French vengeance. The *Geheimrat* placed no trust in Britain: he meant to see her firmly tied down. His message showed a shrewdness and definiteness and prevision that it would be difficult to overreach. Lord Rosebery had 'suggested' an 'eventuality': the *Geheimrat* replied through the Ambassador, Count Hatzfeldt, with a stern demand for a guarantee and instructions to see that it was got. Unfortunately, his Lordship had no chance to learn of this imposition of a new order of things— an order of things to the possibility of which ' in the event of a war between Britain and France' he had only referred under the burden of his anxieties.

The ill-omened telegram from Bangkok had arrived on a Sunday morning. When he reached Downing Street Lord Rosebery found no one in the Foreign Office but 'an old woman' who was on duty for any emergency. The members of the Cabinet were out of town. He sent a messenger to Mr. Gladstone. On his own responsibility he instructed the Senior Officer that he was of course to reject the French demand. He informed the Queen by telegram of the ominous incident, and went back to bed.

Queen Victoria turned to Emperor William, her guest at the moment in Cowes. She asked what would be his and Germany's attitude if war broke out between Britain and France. She also asked the Kaiser to receive Lord Rosebery in audience in the matter. It was instantly clear to Emperor William that a service of far-reaching importance could be rendered to Britain, either by declaring neutrality or by offering mediation. As for any prospect of an immediate sealing of the Quadruple Alliance, of the securing of it before war had actually broken out, he did not believe in it. Nor did he believe that war was going to break out.

He sent for Kiderlen-Wächter, who accompanied him on his journeys as *Vortragender Rat* representing the Foreign Ministry. He spoke to the *Vortragender Rat* of the desirability of showing an accommodating and reassuring attitude towards Britain. He was willing to receive Lord Rosebery. The Queen, he said, had been informed accordingly. He had no desire to leave her in any doubt of his readiness to assist.

The *Vortragender Rat*, however, dissented. He at once adopted the warning, half menacing tone towards the Kaiser which continually recurred when the Foreign Ministry had advice on points of statesmanship to give him through any official. The *Vortragender Rat* warned the Kaiser. On no account must he show accommodation towards the British. They were only 'panicking,' and wanted German help cheaply. Naturally they turned to the 'English grandson.' The British admiral's uniform was most useful for such purposes. What the Kaiser ought to do was to 'steer midway between Paris and London.' Then he could dictate to both.

'You need not,' the Kaiser replied, 'bring me this nonsense as the wisdom of Berlin. I will see first what Rosebery has to say; and then Hatzfeldt. He knows Britain better than the Wilhelmstrasse does.'

Lord Rosebery came—grave and a little anxious, and strangely preoccupied. After his Sunday experience he had woke up rather astonished to hear nothing of the coming, inescapable war, of which he alone had known in London on the Sunday. The Senior Officer's telegram must have been a mistake. No doubt the French were thinking twice before declaring war. Perhaps they had put it off. The breach, at all events, was no longer a question of hours or days. Lord Rosebery breathed again—all the more

Copenhagen Summer 1905
The German Emperor and Prince Waldemar
of Denmark.

''

confidently on the strength of the Kaiser's assurances, for which the Queen thanked her grandson.

They had done no more than provide a little encouragement for British-German friendship. With the disappearance of the war cloud Lord Rosebery let the question of the Quadruple Alliance lapse. But the Foreign Ministry in Berlin was not ready to lose sight of it. Italy had certain moral obligations towards Britain in the Mediterranean. Germany, in Baron Holstein's view, became automatically bound to go to the assistance of Italy if she were involved in a war, no matter for what reason. It might, he thought, be possible yet, with a little pertinacity, to engineer the Quadruple Alliance by a consideration of Italian participation in a Franco-British conflict. But the real issue, Quadruple Alliance or no, was not put again to Lord Rosebery at all. The menacing professions of German friendship got no farther from Baron Holstein's room than to Count Hatzfeldt's. The Ambassador recommended that the question of the Quadruple Alliance should still be presented once more, in plain and unambiguous terms, to Lord Rosebery. 'But,' writes Professor Erich Brandenburg, 'the question was not actually put. France gave way at the last moment and a conflict was avoided. Marschall drew from this experience the conclusion that it was impossible to rely on Britain.'

Baron von Marschall's logic was decidedly random. The Kaiser described the whole statecraft of the Foreign Ministry as a sort of *Bierphilisterpolitik*—the politics of the Private Bar.

For a while Lord Rosebery remained friendly and interested. He had advanced from Lord Salisbury's search for 'assurances' in Bismarck's days as far as to pronounce the words 'Quadruple Alliance.' But before they could be translated into action France had, for the time, visibly recoiled. There was plenty of time for Britain's formal signature if clear gain or plain necessity should drive her into the alliance. Lord Rosebery was at a loss to discern what France was after. The first gunshot, whether from France or Britain, would be bound to bring the alliance, for all that the Cabinet was still plainly against it.

'The best beginning'—so Chancellor von Caprivi wrote on the margin of one of Count Hatzfeldt's enquiries from London—'The best beginning, so far as we are concerned, of the next great war will be for the first shot to be fired from a British ship. We shall be certain then of being able to expand the Triple into a Quadruple Alliance.'

The Chancellor had scarcely seen more than this one communication from Hatzfeldt. All the others went, as addressed, between the Count and *Geheimrat* von Holstein, who drafted every syllable of the letters, Baron von Marschall signing them as they stood. The Chancellor was beginning to be absorbed in the difficulties of internal affairs in Germany. The Secretary of State and his staff were acquainted with the broad lines of his policy towards Britain and of his foreign policy in general; they must carry on on the lines indicated. Even if there were incidents with Britain they would pass over. Under Caprivi's guidance the general trend of policy was in the direction of friendship with Britain; when the incidents passed, the threads could be taken up again.

But *Geheimrat* von Holstein was enraged with

Rosebery. He could not wait, and in any case he had no intention of waiting. He had long since gained full control of affairs. He exercised his control regardless of the Chancellor's views—through the manipulation of the organization of the Ministry, which was firmly in his grasp. His room in the Ministry represented all Germany—a section of the world which was in his thrall. That Britain failed to realize this, that Britain did not bend to his will, that it was beyond his power to cow her with a heavy hand into sincere friendship —all this the *Geheimrat* was unable to understand. He determined to avenge his failure to force Britain into the Alliance.

Once already he had compelled the British to be accommodating, even to show prompt complaisance, shortly before the deflation of the Quadruple Alliance scheme. In February 1893 Abdul Hamid had granted the German 'Anatolian Company,' under the treaty of Kaulla, the concession for a railway to Bagdad. Sir Arthur Nicolson, then Chargé d'Affaires in the British Embassy in Constantinople, had done his best 'to block the concession through British intervention.' But the *Geheimrat* had made short work of the attempt. The laconic message reached the Foreign Office that Germany would withhold her assent to the British administrative reforms in Egypt unless her just claim in Constantinople was at once recognized. Lord Rosebery had at once given way before this unconcealed threat.

Perhaps that was the right tone to adopt towards Englishmen. In any case, after his disappointment through the peaceful ending of the Siamese conflict, the *Geheimrat* no longer fought shy of energetic

67

language. A series of conflicts very quickly set in. The incident arising out of the landing of German guns in Walfisch Bay was soon disposed of. Germany had sent them to quell the rising in South-west Africa; Britain made difficulties. Britain sought to prevent the German recruitment of coolies of whom the German colonists in New Guinea stood in need. Germany wanted to consolidate her hold of Samoa. Under an old agreement British, Germans and Americans exercised a condominium over the islands. Germany sought British support, but Britain made no move. Germany then coldly announced in London that she could not promise her support in future for any British interests. Germany could not always be seconding Britain's efforts. The British were trying to connect Pretoria by rail with Lorenzo Marques in order to secure a direct outlet in Delagoa Bay; the Germans and Americans blocked the scheme. A year later the Germans imitated the Walfisch Bay move: they sent gunboats to Delagoa Bay when the British proposed to land guns and troops there and forward them through Portuguese territory in order to quell a rising in the interior.

One solitary ray of light broke through the new clouds which had so quickly piled up after the failure to obtain the Quadruple Alliance. The British-German Colonial Agreement of October 15, 1893, assured Germany of a free hand in extending her territory in Cameroon into the interior of Africa. At the same time the British annexed the territory around Wade-lai, on the banks of the Nile. Germany's attitude remained, however, as frigid and ill-humoured as ever, grudging alike in word and deed. When Lord Rosebery hinted once more at the question of the assistance that the Germans might be able to offer him in the event, however unlikely, of Russians or French driving the British into hostilities, Germany warned Italy and especially Austria to dismiss any wild idea of friendly co-operation with Britain. She even began to show Britain that German co-operation was actually possible with France, that same defeated France of 1870 whom Britain so feared. In the spring of 1894 a treaty was concluded between French and Germans concerning Cameroon. Lake Tchad became the eastern frontier of Cameroon. Barely eight weeks later Britain set out to repay that stroke: she ceded to the Congo State the wide territory of Bahr-el-Ghazal— it was indeed, Egyptian territory and not British— in exchange for a very modest strip of land. This was to cut through Belgian Congo and connect northern Africa with the British colonies in the south, saving the British from the necessity of passing through German colonial possessions in building a north-south railway or telegraph lines. The strip of land was no more than twenty miles in breadth. But it got rid entirely of the difficulty of German East Africa.

Then there was a storm. All talk of a Quadruple Alliance was forgotten. The last vestige of friendly feeling, the whole unexpressed but yet discernible spirit of entente disappeared. Emperor William revealed his full indignation to the British Ambassador. Count Hatzfeldt, who had himself been the moving spirit behind the British-German rapprochement, bluntly declared to Lord Rosebery that in the future Germany would prefer to come to terms with Britain's opponents. The declaration was at once given practical effect: Germany joined France in protesting against the British acquisition of territory in the Congo. Britain had the further uncomfortable experience of finding the advice of the German Ambassador in Rome carry more weight than her own prestige with Crispi, the Italian Prime Minister. Crispi promised to make representations in London in order to secure 'the restoration of legality' in North Africa. Under this pressure Lord Rosebery felt it best to draw back.

Lord Rosebery in turn had been a little estranged from Germany by the events of the past year. His last conversations concerning assurances had brought in the end a very plain reply from Germany—that 'failing some British concession in return, no assurance could be offered.' On this he had changed his tone: he too embarked on threats. Britain would reconsider her policy towards Germany. Germany, however, did not seem to be impressed. France was now at her side, supporting her rights. Germany and France—which meant the Triple Alliance and France —were stronger than Lord Rosebery. So sure of themselves were Baron von Marschall and *Geheimrat* Holstein in their entrenched position, that they were careless even of giving open offence to France, who in all this question had come for the first time to their side. With France's support they had carried their point. That done, when France in turn asked German assistance they took the line that she must look after herself. They had associated themselves with her solely for the sake of the opportunity so afforded of applying methods of duress to Britain. France did look after herself. In August 1894 she concluded an agreement with the Congo State which gave her access from Congo to the Upper Nile and the Soudan. But these German masters of statecraft had forgotten France; all they saw was their success and Britain's humiliation. Lord Rosebery had been forced reluctantly to return the strip of Congo territory. That would give him to think, would enable him to consider whether British policy was well-advised. Always to be trying to get something out of other people, never to give anything, always to be merely offering bait to the others, to be making use of them for one's own interests, and then, as the German Foreign Ministry saw it, cheerfully to leave them in the lurch (as cheerfully as Germany had just done with France)— statecraft of that sort was immoral. Perhaps Britain, in abandoning the treaty over the strip of Congolese territory, had had for the first time in history to yield to external pressure. So be it: it should teach her a lesson. She had been given from *Geheimrat* Holstein's office a demonstration of the appropriateness of faith in force, of pressure, of methods of duress as the weapons of a policy that set no store either by patience or by psychological preparation of the way to its goal. Britain had overreached herself altogether: there was an end of friendship with her.

In nearly four years of working together, British and Germans had failed to speak a common language, to think in common terms. Neither side had understood the other; neither had been able to change its own outlook or do anything to adjust it. The Germans resented the reluctance of the British to enter into a formal alliance, to commit themselves to a written document. They failed to appreciate the reason why Britain could not make this one exception even if she entered into no other alliance whatever. They were ready to attribute to Britain every sort of shrewd practice for which they were themselves ready—a readiness characteristic of Prince Bismarck's time and now once more exemplified in their treatment of France. It was not made any better by the aggressiveness almost always to be found in their language. They looked with suspicion on the friends they hoped to make, distrusted them as enemies at bottom, credited them with readiness to make the same smart use of any opportunity for which they themselves were ready. They had no appreciation of the method of gentle gradations by which Lord Rosebery's tact had, in spite of everything, transformed the cold indifference of the two nations towards one another into a relationship which amounted already in reality to an entente. Undoubtedly the situation in the early 'nineties, and considerations of the balance of power, would have brought Britain to the side of the Triple Alliance in any emergency, treaty or no treaty. Britain's own advantage, as Lord Salisbury realized, lay in a 'psychological rapprochement.' The error of German statesmanship lay in its pursuit merely of catchwords, its disbelief in the genuineness of psychological, even of emotional factors, and its dismissal of their actual expression in promise or performance as worthless, hypocritical word-spinning. What they wanted of the British as allies was that they should take on these German characteristics. The British statesmen not merely committed the same mistake in the reverse direction: they were for 'psychological rapprochement' and therewith, as a matter of course, an un-hesitating championship of the new friend in matters affecting the European balance of interests; but there were other things that touched Germany's life or her future, and this the British forgot or failed to realize. For centuries they had been accustomed to sending out great adventurers and starting pioneer under-takings in every quarter of the globe, gaining new continents for the Empire, and they were filled with astonishment if ever they came across a ship flying anything but the familiar flag, or if some foreign com-pany sought to implant itself anywhere. Any balance of interests between the Powers in Europe had no relevance to the purposes of British colonial egoism. The connexion between the two was no longer to be denied, but this they would on no account admit, although it was just these questions of assurances and balance that filled their thoughts when they contem-plated sending a fleet to Constantinople or Egypt or Siam.

Perhaps the British statesmen had no responsibility at all for the immediate causes of friction in the dis-tant colonies. Never had Britain's merchant adven-turers, her commodores and companies acted in any other way but independently, damning the conse-quences and ready at any instant to show their teeth. Never had they asked London's permission: always they had acquired kingdoms for England on their own initiative. Their bull-necked acquisitiveness, their passion for conquest no matter whom they brushed aside, exasperated German opinion. The British statesmen did what they could to smooth away the incidents that were continually recurring on the edges

73

of the world. But it never occurred to them at all that there were also German merchant adventurers, German commodores and companies, equally eager to explore uncharted worlds. They saw only their own offer to the Germans, actually made good, in friendly agreement—the guarantee of equilibrium and security in Europe. The Germans saw only the other side—that Britain took all there was to be had in the wide world, and never gave away anything if she was first on the spot.

Time was bound to soften the rather rough edges of German statesmanship. There could hardly fail to come a type of statesman who did not confuse persuasiveness with stark force, other people's hesitations and reservations with traps and trickery, projects and proposals with pressure, diplomacy with the German's all too downright plain-spokenness. If, in the meantime, the British statesmen were to realize that it was not in the nature of things that one of two friends should for all time be strong and poor and the other strong and rich, if they would realize that equilibrium was not purely a matter of protection from aggression, but had its application also to everything which went to make up the vital interests of one party as of the other—then the way might after all be open one day to an Entente, perhaps even to more than that.

For the time, however, the friends parted.

Chapter III

GERMANY SETTING HER HOME
IN ORDER

AT THE time of General von Caprivi's succession to
the Chancellorship, Germany's internal situation was
none too satisfactory. The Reich was still not so
firmly consolidated, in spite of Prince Bismarck's
twenty years of labour for the State, that there were
no particularist tendencies in South and South-west
to be availed of, if occasion offered, for a separatist
agitation. Count Philipp Eulenburg, then Prussian
Minister in Munich, had noted that 'particularist
agitation continues in Bavaria among high and low,'
and that in Württemberg 'the idea of citizenship of
the German Empire has loosened its hold.' The situation in the Kingdom of Prussia, of which the Chancellor for the time being was Prime Minister, was
anything but a model for the other federal States.

The first thing—so General von Caprivi told the
Austro-Hungarian Ambassador, Count Szögyény,
about the middle of his term of office—was to make a
clean sweep of the Bismarckian heritage. Until that
was done his own work would fail of full effect. For
that it might be necessary to await the moment 'when
Bismarck passes away. But I am much younger, and
am thus in a good position for getting the better of my
predecessor in that matter.'

The burden taken over by Chancellor von Caprivi

75

from Prince Bismarck was a tremendous one even apart from the tangled maze of foreign policy. The Socialist law of 1878 was still in force, a burden and a disturbing influence in public life. The three class franchise still ruled for the Prussian state parliament. The taxation laws were entirely obsolete. The independence of the schools was not assured. All this was remarkable enough in Prussia; but even her army was in decline, and out of all proportion with the external marks of power that the Empire and Prussia had enjoyed since the days of Versailles.

In Reichstag and Abgeordnetenhaus—the Federal and Prussian Parliaments—the parties were coolly waiting, most of them unfriendly, to see how the new Chancellor shaped. His first concern on taking over the Chancellorship was the grave danger in which the country stood, with its widespread frontiers, between East and West, now that he had abandoned the friendship with the East, in which he had had no trust; his first efforts had, therefore, to be devoted to the strengthening of the armed defences of the Triple Alliance. He aimed in his foreign policy at friendship with Britain, seeking at the same time to consolidate the members of the Triple Alliance into a thoroughly sound and homogeneous body. If the Triple Alliance were faced with war, its member Powers ought to have at their common service not only their armed forces but their whole economic system. The Chancellor advocated commercial treaties on favourable terms with Austria-Hungary and Italy; later Roumania and, if they chose, other States could adhere to them. The fresh impetus given to trade would add to the power and the energy of the allies. Life would be made

76

easier for the poorer classes in Germany. Industry would profit by a rapid and marked improvement in trade. An immense improvement in trade did in fact come in Germany almost immediately after the conclusion of the commercial treaties, imports and exports rising to undreamed-of levels. The Reichstag had at once ratified the treaties at the first reading. But the Chancellor had to pay for his success with heavy sacrifices: the Prussian Conservatives were hard hit by an unwelcome influx of grain which ended the great landowners' control of prices, and from then on they were steadily hostile to the Chancellor.

He had abrogated the Socialist law. This he had been impelled to do by his own independence of thought and liberal outlook; and this again had alienated the Conservatives from him. But, in spite of the disappearance of the draconic old law, the Chancellor realized that the coming years would be bound to be years of trouble with the workers, a new and still restlessly fermenting world that had been born into this present age. He might be able himself to cope with them; or the social legislation which the young Kaiser had in view might really keep them quiet. But in any case he must not stand alone if matters should come sharply to a head, as they might do, with the workers and their spokesmen. If he should have to take a stand against the Social Democrats, he would be able to count under almost any circumstances on the support of the Conservatives. Only in other fields would they avenge his commercial policy. But the Chancellor needed more support than that amounted to. For a general support for his

77

policy he turned to those great forces, strong in their unity and their clear-sighted and confident leadership, whose pressure Prince Bismarck himself had often enough felt since the days of the *Kulturkampf*—the forces of the powerful German Centre party. And in turning to them he nearly met destruction.

Not everyone realized the extent of his success in his first two years' work; or, if it was realized, there was little inclination to admit it. He had put through his commercial treaties; he had improved relations with Britain. But everyone knew that he had also made an end of friendly relations with Russia. The Kaiser had raised him to the rank of Count. That merely proved that the Kaiser was satisfied with the Chancellor, that General von Caprivi was evidently doing everything the young and self-willed ruler wanted, agreeing to everything he proposed and never standing in his way.

But if the Chancellor seemed to be quietly pursuing his course, Emperor William II was all the more in the limelight, all the more prominently in evidence everywhere, attracting universal attention. The Kaiser was still a Prince Incalculable. He was a constitutional ruler; but in the visitors' book of the city of Munich he wrote this absolutist apophthegm:

Regis voluntas suprema lex.

He telegraphed *en clair* every opinion he had to express, every purpose he entertained in matters of state, the moment it occurred to him, to Count Philipp Eulenburg, although the Count implored him to exercise caution, since many officials were all too ready to babble, forgetting their duty of official secrecy. But the Kaiser had nothing to conceal. Always he had the best of intentions for Germany; and he was very youthful in his belief that everyone in Germany credited him with them. He was totally unaware that when his tutor, Hinzpeter, was not writing him letters full of inextinguishable devotion, he was talking all the time of Emperor William's 'megalomania,' so much so that Ambassadors reported the phrase to their own Courts; and totally unaware, too, that his sayings were being retailed to all the world, freely embroidered, in strict confidence by his entourage.

Professor Hinzpeter was not the only one who gossiped about the Kaiser's megalomania whenever he was not flattering him to his face. General Count Waldersee made sanctimonious entries in his diary expressing his concern at the Kaiser's mental trouble.

Even foreign dignitaries were infected by the pomp and circumstance in Emperor William's Court. The American Ambassador was often distressed at the fact that he alone was accorded no Court uniform by his State. The myth was spread by the Court entourage that the Kaiser himself, in a moment of exhilaration, sketched for the Ambassador a special uniform, with sword and feathered cap. At the very next Court, so ran the myth, the Ambassador exultantly appeared in it. The Court looked at Kaiser and Ambassador in silent admiration, fascinated by the All-highest flair for colour. So, in picturesque mockery, the invention was broadcast. It is true that Emperor William had a love of bright colours and imperial display. He was concerned with their effect on the people, knowing how shows count with them, how much they are impressed by them. But he was not engrossed in questions of finery to the point of regarding every moment

79

as wasted which was not devoted to the thinking out of new magnificences in the style of Louis XIV. He also thoroughly enjoyed military displays and naval manœuvres, but there was nothing infantile about all this except the representation of it spread abroad by his guests. The Kaiser's peculiarities and excesses were inventions of his own Court, all of whom were the very soul of devotion in his presence, and filled with the widely extolled spirit of German loyalty towards the Monarch—up to the moment of leaving the Palace. Then, in the very precincts, the most distinguished members of that Court set to work inventing enormities about the Kaiser, and retailed them in constantly grosser forms, until even society abroad was full of them.

The time came when all France was talking in that strain of the madman on the throne. Most of the Paris papers gave lengthy accounts of unmistakable symptoms of the Kaiser's malady: 'He spent his time in England thinking out new fashions—grey frock coat with broad, stuffed shoulders, grey hat, high-heeled boots. The Kaiser loves jewellery; he wore seven rings on each hand, and also bracelets and chains with pendants and actually golden garters set with brilliants.' On one and the same day, according to the Paris papers, the company on board the *Hohenzollern* had the opportunity of saluting the Kaiser in the uniform of a German, a British, and an Italian admiral. William II had salutes fired in his own honour. Not a minute passed but he revoked a thrice-given order.

No gossiping courtier divined his real thoughts; no one in all the country learned them. Day by day he proved a Prince Incalculable.

Copenhagen Summer 1905
The King of Denmark, the Crownprince
the German Emperor, the ~~Queen~~ Crownprincess and
Princess Waldemar of Denmark

Copenhagen Summer 1905
The King of Denmark, the Crownprince
the German Emperor, the Russian czar
Princess Waldemar of Denmark

Yet he gave public expression to his views in every place to which his duties as ruler called him, expressed them with a definiteness unknown in any past Emperor and King. He made his speeches from the throne, gave his addresses at manœuvres. He spoke before Provincial Diets and at the swearing-in of recruits. If he christened a ship or unveiled a memorial there was another speech to be made. By May 1892 he had made his twenty-sixth long speech since Count Caprivi's entry into office. And every speech was a momentous outpouring. The Kaiser had a particularly sharp, resounding delivery, and there was something in the timbre of his voice which had the same irritating effect on his hearers as the carelessness of ordinary forms in many of his actions. When he began to speak it was never quite certain where he would end. He used to settle the contents of his speeches, on quite broad lines, with von Lucanus, his *Kabinettschef* or chief private secretary, while out for a walk or a drive. For some time he tried to set his speeches down on paper after these discussions with the *Kabinettschef*. But he found that the written version never corresponded with the agreed plan, and also that he continually halted in reading aloud. So he got used to speaking without notes. But, under the influence of the platform and the assembly, he would be led away in the end by his real gift of eloquence, and carried far beyond the conclusion he had intended. Then the phrase born of a momentary impulse would set tongues wagging all over Germany and the world. In the two years since Prince Bismarck's retirement the impulses had been almost as frequent as the speeches.

Gradually the public formed for itself a picture of the Kaiser, based on his public appearances and the things he said or others said about him. It was a great mistake of the Kaiser's to fail to bear in mind how impossible it was for the public to correct its superficial impression of him by any insight into his essential character; to fail carefully to consider the effect which each word and gesture would be bound to have on his audience; to have no thought for the lack of comprehension and the lack of imagination of the mass of the people. The world knew nothing of the events which had led to the fall of Prince Bismarck. It was equally unaware that the entry in the Munich visitors' book was an innocent gesture made without any thought of what it might lead to. The Prince Regent had refused to sign, as head of the house, before the Kaiser, until in the end the Kaiser caught at the *mot* as a way of indicating that he bowed to the will of the lord of the land, and wrote down the unlucky phrase. The Civil Cabinet and Court officials all knew the truth as to the origin of the joking sentence; yet it was allowed to be broadcast to all the world as though written in earnest. Count Szögyény, the Austrian Ambassador, criticized as stupid the omission briefly to publish the truth as to the incident. But the myth of the Kaiser's peculiarities had spread its roots so far and wide in society and among the mass of the people, it had become so inseparably part of the popular impression of him, even when his impetuosity was dormant, that no official of the Court or the Civil Cabinet had the courage to contradict the story. The world was completely unaware that in spite of his natural hastiness Emperor William was almost always right in his judgments of things; or that before acting he always gave matters one more final careful thought. Only Chancellor von Caprivi was at ease in his mind; he alone knew that the Kaiser was always amenable to advice when he had audience with him alone, when all other personal influence was excluded and the facts were allowed to speak for themselves—guides to whom alone the Kaiser invariably submitted.

Neither the real Kaiser nor the real Chancellor was known to the people. Political and social gossip, popular judgments and rumours, their own characteristics and foibles—the Kaiser's strong propensity to vigorous and striking, even bizarre self-expression, the Chancellor's obstinate reserve, never explaining himself to anyone—all contributed to the obliteration of their true picture. And if no one else was doing so, there was one who kept his palette busy, painting vivid portraits of both in high tones and bold strokes, to give as lasting an impression of them as possible to Germany and the world as evil figures of the day— the resentful old Prince Bismarck in Friedrichsruh. It was certainly a novel spectacle, this campaign of a retired statesman against his inheritors.

There were moments when Princess Johanna, at dinner with trusted guests, would give full reign to her embitterment against William II, even in the presence of the servants. Then the giant of Friedrichsruh would reply in gloomy, melancholy tones from the other end of the table:

'Don't be too hard on him; I fear for him as for a son.'

But these milder impulses were forgotten when Prince Bismarck launched his attacks on the Emperor who had dismissed him, or his system or his advisers. The ex-Chancellor spoke in public almost as often as the monarch did. Students presenting him with a ceremonial cup in Kissingen, the Dresden *Liedertafel* serenading him in Sachsenwald, delegates from his constituency, delegates from Siegen listened reverently to his words while reporters took them down for the papers that would broadcast them over all Germany. The octogenarian Prince was a great fighter with voice and pen. Immense forces still raged within him, and he had no intention of allowing them to be curbed. He cared nothing if he knew the newspaper men whom he received to be enemies of Germany. He supplied the *Hamburger Nachrichten*, so closely associated with Friedrichsruh, with such a stream of views and news that it was soon common knowledge that the voice of the paper was only nominally that of its editor, and in reality that of Prince Bismarck. The Prince complained that the Kaiser went too often to see his English relatives. He considered the more intimate association with Britain to be an entirely mistaken policy. He condemned von Caprivi's commercial treaties. The *Hamburger Nachrichten* showed how the negotiations with Austria-Hungary could be better carried on—more in the way they had been in past years, when the negotiations had not been taken seriously at all, 'the various proposals of the Power in question being always received with great courtesy and in a tone of cordial agreement, but all the more definitely turned down in the end.' It was only a year since Prince Bismarck had himself sent Count Herbert, then Secretary of State, to London to try to procure the cession of

Heligoland by means of representations in various quarters. But the old Prince seemed completely to have forgotten that particular episode, since he attacked the new Chancellor for paying much too high a price for this very acquisition of Heligoland.

The peace of old age was still far from having descended on Prince Bismarck: in keen enjoyment of a coldly calculated revenge, he was writing his *Reflections and Recollections*, of which he directed the publication to be deferred so long that Emperor William was scarcely likely to be alive to read or reply to his attacks. He calculated that they would be bound to remain without a reply in any case. They could scarcely be published so long as Emperor William was still alive; and if they were, it would scarcely be possible for the German Emperor himself to reply to them. Thus, in any event, the first Chancellor would be the only one to speak. As to the Kaiser, he was ready to believe the worst of him. He believed that William II was at the back of a lampoon entitled 'The truth about Bismarck.' Actually the Kaiser had no knowledge even of the existence of that pamphlet. The Prince was afraid of his house being broken into, by order, and his papers stolen. He asked his legal adviser, *Justizrat* Ferdinand Philipp, what he ought to do in that event: could he defend his rights as a householder with a pistol in his hand? No one was contemplating any such outrage, certainly not the Kaiser. Legends and dark inventions of a disordered fancy took flight from Friedrichsruh. Visitors bore them away into all parts of the country. The Prince himself made frequent journeys away from home.

He spoke in Munich, and in the market place of
Jena. He spoke on foreign policy, on the failure to
renew the Socialist law. The whole tale of the 'new
course' was broadcast in every direction among the
mass of the people, accompanied by the unflattering
comments of the statesman who yesterday was Chancellor, and who remained in the eyes of the masses a
hero and saint and, above all, the best qualified of
judges. Needless to say, Chancellor von Caprivi was
incapacity personified. The Prince had described him
as the General who carried out every command of the
Kaiser's. His irritation with his successor turned to
hate when General Caprivi finally made a resolute
stand against him. In June 1892 Prince Bismarck was
to be in Vienna for the anniversary of his son's
wedding. Count Caprivi had made suggestions to
the Kaiser as to the attitude which the German
Ambassador in Vienna should adopt:

'In view of Prince Bismarck's action towards your
Majesty, the Ambassador cannot, of course, be
present on this occasion.'

'Yes, certainly the Ambassador must be very tactful and cautious. I cannot lay down for him how he
should behave towards Prince Bismarck. He must
know that himself!'

During the discussion of the matter, the idea of
the ex-Chancellor being received by Emperor Francis
Joseph had simply not occurred to Count Caprivi.
He sent instructions to Vienna: the Ambassador and
the members of the Embassy should show every
courtesy to the Prince, but should not attend the
celebrations. The Kaiser, however, felt certain that
the Prince would do his utmost to secure an audience

with Francis Joseph—a distinction out of which the followers of the fallen Chancellor would be equally certain to make all the capital they could. The Kaiser sat down and wrote to his ally. Prince Bismarck did seek an audience with Emperor Francis Joseph; and it was refused.

Then came almost a bomb explosion. Of all that Prince Bismarck had been unable to tell Emperor Francis Joseph, he now unburdened himself in the columns of the leading Vienna paper, a journal then of high repute in all Europe. He coined the phrase 'the wrecked wire to Russia.' He exposed, in doing so, his whole system in its hollowness and precariousness, its disregard of facts and of obligations, and the embarrassments and the dark future which were implicit in it. The Viennese editor, a journalist of keen and wide political vision, had carefully eliminated the worst passages from this princely confession, but its revealing spirit was not to be effaced.

It was then that the phrase 'Letter of Uriah' was coined, and rather audaciously launched against one of the greatest men in all history by Chancellor von Caprivi, himself a mere General, a mere reaper where the other had sown. The world forgot the course the great man had been following for years past; forgot how no pinprick had been too trivial for Friedrichsruh to apply, no difficulty too awkward for it to raise, no public attack too virulent for it to make against the system that had brought its downfall. The world forgot, too, the humiliation involved for Emperor William, the embarrassment and pain for Emperor Francis Joseph, himself the very model of good form, when Prince Bismarck, who had avoided the Berlin Palace on his journey, asked for an audience at the Vienna Hofburg. All that the world saw—and saw at once—was that with his phrase 'Letter of Uriah' Chancellor von Caprivi had put himself beyond the pale. All who had any sort of attachment to Prince Bismarck were now Caprivi's open enemies.

In the spring of 1892 an education bill introduced by Count Zedlitz, the Prussian Minister of Education, had been rejected by the Reichstag. The Chancellor had only been saved from falling by the Kaiser's refusal to accept his resignation. The Kaiser alone had kept him in office; he had had no support either from the nation or the political parties. From his estate in Friedrichsruh the Irreconcilable had directed his whole energy against his successor; he had continued to do so on his journeys. Count Caprivi was now once more in danger of falling at any moment, since there was no one supporting him; and then he would be so lost in the great shadow of Prince Bismarck that he would vanish from men's sight and memory.

No leader of a state was ever burdened in office with a fiercer feud or a pettier hate than Count Caprivi. His own silent endurance only gave increased prominence to the howling opposition around him, the shrieks against his every action.

His support of Count Zedlitz's bill was not really in accordance with his own liberal, modern way of thinking. The bill had aimed at giving the church new influence over the schools. The church was to be empowered to object to the employment as teachers of persons of whom it did not approve—persons who did not give religious instruction entirely in accordance with its wishes. The Chancellor's acceptance of the bill had gained him the support of the Centre party, which remained friendly towards him although the bill was defeated. But all the Liberals were against the bill. The agitation against it spread far beyond the moderate parties in the assembly; professors, artists, all the intellectuals in Germany came out with such vehemence against the principle of the bill that the Kaiser himself grew alarmed. On the rejection of the bill the Minister of Education resigned. The Chancellor, too, well aware of his none too assured position in the country, had asked leave to resign, but there was no necessity for that, although it was natural to him to propose to take on himself the consequences of the failure even if he was only indirectly responsible for it. When, however, the Kaiser refused to let him go, Caprivi made a real mistake: he separated the Chancellorship from the Prussian Premiership. He determined to confine himself to the Chancellor's office—and he thus lost his influence in Prussia. Up to then, when opposition had been offered in Prussia to his policy, he had been able to suppress it, being himself the foremost spokesman of Prussian policy; now, by his own action, he had provided the opportunity for opposition to obtain a foothold and develop. Count Botho Eulenburg, who succeeded him as Prussian Prime Minister, came to his new post as a Bismarckian in method. Prince Bismarck himself had had trouble with him on various occasions, not least on account of his propensity to intrigue. Caprivi continued on his way. The new Prime Minister set out on his own way, on the road to power.

It was less the ordering of Fate than the Chancellor's own firmly ingrained political opinions that drove him more and more into opposition to the still powerful Conservative party. Conservative as his own way of thinking was, he saw clearly the necessity of the building up, without regard for the special interests of particular groups, of a State which would at last be in accord with the demands of the time. The State as he took it over was backward, far outstripped by its western neighbours, and faced with whole collections of problems and critical issues. He had injured the Conservatives by his commercial treaties with Germany's allies; he aggrieved them still more by a new set of by-laws for rural communities, introduced by the Minister of the Interior, von Herfurth. In the east of Prussia the large landowners (*Rittergutsbesitzer*) and the rural authorities had hitherto carried on entirely separate existences alongside one another. This added to the difficulties of the State, since the landowners could not be called upon to take any share in the burdens of local administration. The Minister of the Interior proposed that no distinction should in future be made in administration and taxation between the big estates and the rural authorities. He carried his bill, but his victory itself brought him immediately to his fall. All who had agrarian privileges and vested interests to protect came together in the common realization that the time had come to put up a stand against a Government so arbitrary as to be ready not only to interfere with immemorial privileges but actually to put a stranglehold on them. At the beginning of 1893 the Chancellor found himself faced by the closed ranks of an exasperated Farmers' Union. Miquel, the able Minister of Finance, exerted himself to placate the Conser-

vative parties and win them over, but his efforts were
only of service to the Minister of Finance and not to
the Chancellor. Finally Miquel set about a reform of
the system of taxation. Up to then Prussia had not
made the acquaintance either of an income tax or of a
property tax. The taxpayer was under no obligation
to declare his income. The Minister of Finance imposed a legislative solution of all three problems,
based on the theory that the Reich should meet its
financial needs from indirect taxation, the Federal
States from direct taxation, and the local authorities
from the taxation of landed property and its yield.
In this way a gradual restoration of the national
finances might become possible; especially if compensation could later be found in other directions for
the heavy loss inflicted on the Reich by confining its
sources of revenue to indirect taxation. Miquel's
legislation, however, was strongly biased in favour of
the Conservatives. To ease the situation of the landowners, they were made a present of the taxes on
landed property and yield; they had only to bear their
local rates. Moreover, in assessing their income they
were authorized to include the present as a sum paid.
That put them in a privileged franchise situation.
The three-class franchise graded the voters according
to their tax payments, and the landowners were thus
brought comfortably within the first class of voters,
which they controlled either alone or with a few
others of their own rank. The new by-laws for rural
authorities which von Herfurth, the Minister of the
Interior, had introduced, had been intended to provide to some extent against this curious development,
if not entirely to prevent it. But the power of the

Rittergutsbesitzer and the big farmers made itself
felt: the assessment of their properties to local rates
remained in most places a dead-letter in spite of the
law. Their resentment against the Minister of the
Interior was none the less keen, and it extended
also to the Chancellor, while the Chancellor gained
nothing from their satisfaction with the Minister
of Finance.

It seemed a miracle that the Chancellor had lasted
so long. It was still stranger that he retained the
courage to heap up new problems in face of the hostility of the parties. His general judgment of problems
and parties was accurate. He knew that the Conservatives were bound to support him when he came to
the new army bill, even if they would have preferred
to do everything they could to undermine his position. He knew, too, that the Centre party, which he
had set out to win over by the ill-starred education
bill, would join the Social Democrats in opposing
the army bill. It was clear to him that, whatever
opposition might be offered, the army organization
had to be improved and radically reformed. Centre,
Liberals, and Social Democrats would refuse to pass
the estimates which were an all-essential part of the
bill. Emperor William himself raised objections to the
Chancellor's army reform plans. He was unwilling to
give up the three years' period of military service,
which the General proposed to reduce to two. The
Kaiser gave way, however. In reality, as soldiers in
their third year were regularly sent home as 'King's
leave men' for the harvest, two years' military service
had long been the rule. The great objection to this
was that it greatly reduced the strength of the army

in the late summer months. The new recruits only joined the colours late in the autumn, and their training was only completed in the spring; thus, if war were suddenly to break out, they would be quite useless and it would be necessary at once to call up reserves. It would, therefore, not be possible to begin a war with the military forces that the army should be able to put forth from its own strength; and, quite apart from that, mobilization was a confused and complicated business. Instead of demanding the three-year period of service, General Caprivi asked for increased effectives. He asked further that they should be called up not at the end but at the beginning of the autumn. The purpose he had in view was to increase the number of men with the colours at any moment and also to secure the means of training them in good time. The Kaiser had come round to agreement with this plan, but the Reichstag was far from agreeing to it. The Chancellor was a Liberal at heart and an upholder of the legislative forces at all times, so long as he could accept responsibility for them; but he refused to give way on his army bill. When it was rejected by the Reichstag he did not resign but dissolved Parliament. A few weeks later the new Parliament assembled and provided a majority for the bill. It was a strange and wonderful bedfellowship—Poles and anti-Semites—that yielded the majority; but there was no need for the Chancellor to worry about that. He had his bill safe and sound.

There was certainly another striking feature about the new Reichstag: the Social Democrats showed a marked increase in strength over their representation in the last one.

Kaiser and Chancellor stood shoulder to shoulder in the fight against the Social Democracy; but if their purpose was the same it was by no means easy at first to reconcile the plans suggested by their different temperaments and their divergent estimates, arising out of the difference in their age and experience, of what was possible. The Kaiser was youthful enough to envisage the labour question in terms of a romantic patriarchalism; he saw it as a question of state like any other, but one which it was the right and the duty of the constituted authority—the Monarch—to settle. To the Chancellor it was a question of opposing forces and a problem of social progress. The Kaiser rested all his hopes in the satisfaction of the needs of the workers—the determination of the duration of the day's work, the introduction of Sunday rest, the protection of women during pregnancy, the protection and advancement of juvenile workers; on all these matters it should be possible to secure progressive advance. He wanted the health of the workers watched over, and their safety in dangerous workplaces. Care should be had for the morals of the workers. Factory owners should not be free to lay down the conditions of labour arbitrarily. There should be collective agreements, inviolable whether by worker or employer. All these ideas were the outcome of the great scheme of protective labour legislation which had been the first of the Kaiser's concerns on his accession to power, a scheme in which all States were to participate. Other countries had been sceptical and unresponsive: Germany at least could set an example. The legislative proposals were introduced in the Reichstag immediately after Prince Bismarck's retirement; the bill to amend the factory laws was not only adopted, but the many further amendments were agreed to which were soon called for by the endless variety of industrial conditions and the manifold problems of labour protection associated with old age, with accidents and many other things. Emperor William considered that the humanitarian work which he had had in view had largely been accomplished, at all events in its broad first outlines, which indicated the direction of further progress. The opposition of the workers to the whole scheme of protective legislation and its underlying spirit, while they calmly took for granted the improvements and the amelioration of conditions that it brought, could not but astonish the Kaiser, especially as his plans of reform had been dictated by humanitarian motives of genuine nobility, and had proceeded from the quite sound idea that the workers would feel the more loyally attached to the national dynasty the more comfort they were assured under it. But workers and Social Democrats were no longer the two sharply distinguished entities or camps that the Kaiser imagined. Concessions, ameliorations, and healthy conditions of life were his largess to workers who were his loyal subjects and were to be kept, as his loyal subjects, in all possible well-being. Social Democrats were quite another thing for a ruler to deal with: a community which had worked its way into the social system and for ten or fifteen years past had constantly grown in strength and membership, a new and continually more provocative group, contemptuous of all tradition, declared rebels against the social system, out to destroy the ruler and the State.

He saw in them the enemy, purely political in its outlook, political in a way that endangered the existing
order. No phrase, no call to battle was too sharp for
the Kaiser when he set out to warn the new betrayers
and destroyers of the Reich:

'In my opinion,' he had shouted to a miners' deputa-
tion in Prince Bismarck's time, 'every Social Democrat
is simply an enemy of the Reich and the fatherland.'

The Kaiser seized every possible opportunity of
promoting labour legislation—with impassioned zeal.
Yet within two years of Prince Bismarck's retirement,
at the very time when he was actively furthering his
social work, he deliberately uttered against the Social
Democracy his phrase 'I place my trust in the army!'
At the swearing-in of recruits at Potsdam he declared
that they must fire on their own brothers if necessary
at the call of Kaiser and country. Scarcely two months
later, in the Brandenburg Provincial Diet, he told
all Germany's malcontents to shake the dust of the
country from their feet. His language was the language of open warfare, and in that spirit it was received. He realized that such language and such a
tone must attract an immense amount of attention all
over the world. But he held to his determination to
draw a clear line between the workers, for whom he
was full of concern, and the Social Democracy, which
he would allow no opportunity to do its work of destruction. He realized that all his opponents would
declare that, barely three years after Prince Bismarck's fall, he was treading in the very footsteps of
the old Chancellor. But there was this great difference: the Prince would have been for reforms by
means of machine guns in the squares as the first re-

1905.

The German Emperor wearing the uniform of a
Swedish Admiral ready to recieve King
Oscars visit on board H.J.M. Yacht.

source; the Kaiser had done everything possible to raise the social level of the workers and to remove the injustices from which they suffered. And machine guns were still as far as ever from his thoughts. For the workers he wanted to see a steady development in social legislation. He still believed that they acknowledged their debt to him for his social legislation. But as for the Social Democrats, he meant to compel them to keep the peace and to leave the State unharmed. His mistake was to fail to realize that no clear line could any longer be drawn between workers and Social Democrats, that they were virtually one and the same thing in the political field, or that the Social Democracy had become the political aspect, the political expression and synthesis of the workers' existence and claims.

The Social Democrats were not blind to the Kaiser's interest in the improvement of the lot of the workers; but they viewed it coolly and critically: these were belated and elementary concessions. They naturally offered no recognition in the Reichstag or in their papers of the lead which the young Monarch had voluntarily given to other States. No one made mention of the undoubtedly great value of the innovations which had been introduced, in an honest effort to make good the neglect and the actual injury of the past in almost all countries, and to improve the future condition of the people. What interested the Social Democrats in the Kaiser's action was, naturally, its relevance to their political programme. Alike among the rank and file and the Parliamentary leaders of the party, the exclusion from the concessions to the workers of any sort of concession to the Social

G

Democracy was felt as an offence. Thus the whole body of protective labour legislation amounted, in their view, virtually to nothing. There was nothing of cross purposes in this: Kaiser and Social Democrats were the most direct of opponents in principle and practice. Both sides knew that they were fighting a life and death battle with one another. Either there would be a working class divorced from Social Democracy—the Kaiser's open objective—or a Social Democracy controlling and leading the whole working class, the open aim of his antagonists. Chancellor von Caprivi was guided neither by the Kaiser's ethical values and readiness to enforce them nor by the will to power which was the dominant motive of the new movement. Here again he evidently viewed the problem in cool aloofness, desiring only to achieve what was achievable amid the uncontrollable march of events.

Count Caprivi was under no misapprehension as to the menace to the existing order implicit in Social Democracy. But he had no belief in the possibility of forcibly holding up a movement embracing millions of human beings. The aim and intention of its leaders, its writers and speakers, the intention of gaining control of the State, was the same which every social grade, every group and class had pursued in the past. The leaders' ultimate dream was of the rule of their comrades or at least their complete emancipation, the emancipation which the middle class had won through the great historic revolutions. The question was no longer whether the power of the workers and their Social Democracy, now that it had come into being, could be broken; the question was simply whether, with their enormous forces, they could be found their due place in the governance of the State, and whether they would agree to take their share in the work of government as members alongside other members. Count Botho Eulenburg, the Prussian Prime Minister, was for a short and sharp settlement of the new class conflict. With his approval, about the middle of 1893, the Minister of the Interior issued a decree aimed against Social Democratic propaganda and organization. It provided for sharper supervision of branches and meetings, and for the immediate employment of the gendarmerie to suppress disturbances when the police forces were inadequate for the purpose. The Prime Minister and the Minister of the Interior had high hopes of educative propaganda among the rural population, and of a campaign of moral enlightenment among the town workers on the part of all friends of the State—childish devices of statesmen who failed to appreciate the fundamental causes and the gigantic measure of elemental historic processes. Their devices were swept away.

But the whole question of the way in which to tackle this movement, grown now so formidable, was given an unexpected answer by the turn of events. Like incendiary torches there burst on the world a series of assassinations. Anarchists spread universal terror, launching murder and arson as signs of 'collective insurrections' among the horrified city populations. Independently and in isolation, they proclaimed, each by his own hand and deed, a gospel of revolution and annihilation of the existing order. Dynamite exploded in the Barcelona Theatre; Vaillant threw his bomb in the Paris Chamber of Deputies; bombs burst under unsuspecting bourgeois now in a Paris café, now in an oyster bar. A French police official was blown to fragments. Léauthier prepared his bombs for the Serbian Minister Georgevitch. He was not sure whether he would get the right man—'But,' he wrote shortly before the outrage was committed, 'I shall not be hitting an innocent man, so long as I bring down a bourgeois—any bourgeois.'

Suddenly the number of assassinations became legion. Not only society was seized with horror—horror invaded the very marrow of the Social Democracy. That movement had nothing to do with Anarchism. Its dream was of a new world, perhaps of a world under the domination of the workers. Nothingness, universal destruction, the madness of annihilation it utterly rejected. But the battle-cry of the assassins had in every case been one of hatred of the 'bourgeois'; and the Social Democrats were also out against the 'bourgeois.' Confusion might result, a very welcome confusion for defenders of the old order.

'These damned anarchists,' August Bebel, the Socialist leader, wrote to his exiled friend and fellow-Socialist Engels, 'are messing up everything for us. In France everything was going swimmingly—as well as man could wish. Now these fools have come and with their base idiocy done more harm than years can mend. A good part of these anarchists are complete imbeciles, and ought to be in a lunatic asylum. No one can blame the bourgeoisie if it goes its own way about protecting itself from such fools.'

August Bebel's private expression of his opinion of the anarchists did not prevent events from taking their course. In June 1894 a madman shot at Crispi, the Italian Prime Minister. A week later an idiot assassinated Carnot, the French Premier. Idiots or madmen, the brands or bombs that they threw were menacing the State and society. The Social Democrats might wash their hands of them, but the fact remained that the anarchists were hurling their missiles against the same antagonists against whom the Socialists were hurling their eloquence and their new doctrines and their countless claims. All the world was startled out of its every-day life of work and pleasure; the agitation and alarm were boundless. The French State adopted measures of protection. An Anarchist law was passed on July 28, 1894. It showed in its contents the whole strength of French jurisprudence. Anarchist actions were crimes of individual anarchists. The new law reproduced the provisions of the French criminal code applicable to murder and arson and homicide, in a sharpened form. It was made applicable to any future attempt to stir up rebellion against the organs of the State, against the army, the police, or any representative of the State. The law made no discrimination as to the sufficiency of the evidence in support of a conviction of anarchists. It was not enough to charge or incriminate an individual; a conviction was only possible by capture in the act or by the definite establishment of guilt without any loophole of doubt. The law deliberately made provision against the possibility of throwing suspicion on whole parties or collecting material for an attack on parties. Protection was sought solely through inflexible harshness in the punishment of crime actually committed or attempted.

Justice and security were achieved, but no new political arm. The French law was quickly followed by exceptional measures against anarchists in Italy.

The first symptoms of violent excitement in Germany were shown by the Press. The organs of the moderate parties put forward strong demands in commenting on the outrages. They called for war to the knife against the anarchists. They demanded new legislation against the Social Democracy, and the re-enactment of the old Socialist law. They advocated the transportation of anarchist incendiaries to distant islands. All sorts of bright ideas were offered to the police. They should work together internationally. Britain should at last give up her practice of always offering the right of asylum on political grounds to bandits and incendiaries. In Dresden and Hanover, Hamburg and Leipzig, the newspapers of the moderate parties cried out for exceptional action. The Clericals and Liberals dissented. Exceptional action against a political party was a resource that might be applied on occasion against themselves. The dangers did not loom large enough to prevent them from having thought for the preservation of their existing advantages. They were convinced, moreover, that a mortal threat against the Social Democracy would only consolidate its ranks. Many were the proposals put forward by newspapers and amateur statesmen. The franchise for the Reichstag ought to be altered. One fevered leaflet called on Emperor William to set up a dictatorship of the *Bundesrat*.

Chancellor von Caprivi remained unmoved. Count Botho Eulenburg, the Prussian Premier, saw that his day had come.

The Kaiser was greatly agitated. The moment seemed to him to be propitious for utilizing the excitement and the real alarm of the middle classes in proceeding against the subversive elements in the State. He considered the question of a stringent law for the defence of the realm such as France and Italy had just enacted. He sharply disapproved the moderate tone of the official Press, which had been advised by the Chancellor to be cautious and even sceptical in its references to the prospects of a fighting bill that had been introduced in the Reichstag. Von Kiderlen-Wächter, the *Vortragender Rat* in attendance, had to take down the Kaiser's views and transmit them to the Chancellor; the Kaiser expressed the desire that there should not only be 'outpost skirmishing in Prussia' against the Social Democracy but a general engagement in the Reich. Plans should be elaborated accordingly in the Ministry of State. The Kaiser was ready to agree either to a sharper application and extension of the criminal code or to the introduction of an exceptional law.

The more the Kaiser considered the problem, the more determined he grew to ward off the menace of the Social Democracy; he was prepared in the end to proceed from the defensive to attack. It did not interest him to find Prince Bismarck now actually agreeing with him to all appearance, so far as the Prince's views were expressed or suggested in his paper. After the disappointment of his hopes of his Vienna visit, and his public venting of his anger, Prince Bismarck had been able to realize that as a *frondeur* and a provocative critic he was entirely failing to recover any influence, and he was now showing more readiness

than hitherto to be conciliatory. His followers made
one effort after another to bridge over the differences
with the Kaiser. Finally Count Douglas, on behalf of
the Conservatives, sought an audience with the Kaiser
with the expressed intention of asking his assent to a
reconciliation with the Prince. There was no question
that Emperor William had become deeply exasperated
with the old Chancellor. After the bitter conflicts
during the Prince's last years of office there had come
the venomous hostility and deliberate, open obstruc-
tiveness which the Prince had shown to the Kaiser at
every opportunity. Prince Bismarck always chose
methods of attack to which it was impossible for
the Kaiser to reply: however he might welcome any
opportunity to speak, a Kaiser had to face such
things in silence. This Prince Bismarck knew, and
took advantage of it. If in the end the Kaiser was
goaded into a counterthrust, he found himself beating
the air. In the presence of his officers in the Lustgarten, feeling himself for once in the presence of
comrades, and comrades who had taken the oath of
allegiance to him, he might drop some hint of Prince
Bismarck's treasonable insubordination. It was quite
true that in Bismarck's last days of office, when he
had sought to mobilize foreign Cabinets in his behalf
or had poured forth his anger in the presence of
foreign Ambassadors, the Prince had done all sorts of
things that would have been regarded as very serious
in any other servant of the State. But the raking up
of all these past offences only sent the officers away
from parade annoyed, embarrassed, irritated with
the new Kaiser. The Kaiser was aware that Prince
Bismarck was an exceptional man, of extraordinary

eminence, no ordinary servant like the rest. But the very fact that the Prince was making use of his un-written privileges only in hate and the pettiest of enmity turned the Kaiser away from recognition of the unwritten to a deliberate and emphatic insist-ence on what was due to a Monarch.

'Reconciliation! My dear man,' he said to Count Douglas, 'I can patch up a quarrel with one of the Federal Princes or some other sovereign. But the fact remains that Prince Bismarck was my servant. From that standpoint I may forgive him if he has offended me. I am very ready to forgive the Prince if he wishes me to. Let him come when he likes. I shall always listen to his advice. But all that has nothing to do with a reconciliation.'

The phrase undoubtedly flew from mouth to mouth in many versions. Many people shook their heads. Anyone familiar with the incidents between Emperor William and Prince Bismarck could not but realize what the Kaiser must feel. But the only inci-dent of which the mass of the people had any know-ledge was that Prince Bismarck had built up the German Empire and that Emperor William had driven him away.

In the end the Kaiser recognized the necessity of an outward agreement. Everything was made difficult if the Prince went on firing incessantly from Fried-richsruh. Ultimately the signs multiplied that Prince Bismarck himself was anxious to come round. Count Moltke, Emperor William's aide-de-camp, suggested that it should be made easier for the old Chancellor to take the first step, and that he should seize the oppor-tunity to make it possible for the Prince to come to

terms. Prince Bismarck was ill. His doctor had
ordered him a bottle of old Steinberger Kabinett, and
there was none of this wine in the Prince's cellars.
Count Moltke mentioned the Prince's condition to
the Kaiser, and the Kaiser remembered that once in
similar circumstances a bottle of Steinberger Kabinett
from the Imperial cellars had saved the life of the old
Field Marshal Blumenthal. He sent the aide-de-camp
with the wine to Friedrichsruh. The Prince replied
almost as in the old days. The Kaiser invited him to
the Berlin Palace. There he asked after Emperor
William's children, and the Emperor after his forests.
The Prince was overjoyed. The conversation was
'only on general subjects.' The Berliners gave the
Prince an enthusiastic welcome. They gave even a
warmer welcome to the Kaiser when he rode alone
in the Tiergarten on the afternoon of the visit. The
Prince was driven back to the station in the Kaiser's
state carriage.

'*Il lui a donné,*' the Paris *Figaro* commented, '*un
enterrement de première classe.*'

Chancellor von Caprivi had left his card on the
Prince at the Palace—quietly, unostentatiously, and
correctly as he did everything. He was pleased to hear
of the sending of the bottle of Steinberger, of which
the Kaiser had told him only after the return of the
aide-de-camp, and equally pleased at Prince Bismarck's stay at the Palace. If the ex-Chancellor would
abstain from interfering in politics, or if he would
moderate his attacks, the new personal relations between him and the Kaiser were only to be welcomed.
The General also agreed to the Kaiser visiting the
Prince shortly afterwards at Friedrichsruh. The

Kaiser stayed for a meal; Prince and Kaiser sat and smoked, and the host showed great good humour. He spoke about home politics:

'Your Majesty's Ministers,' he said, 'need more rocket composition. They are not energetic enough for my taste. I am myself an old rocket.'

As the Kaiser saw it, there had been a forgiving and forgetting; as the onlookers saw it, a reconciliation. There was, in point of fact, no change whatever in the Kaiser's essential attitude. There had been difficult times with Prince Bismarck: it could no longer be helped; it no longer mattered. If the Prince welcomed his sharper language against the Social Democracy, it made no difference whatever to him. As for the Ministers, Emperor William considered his relations with them to be his own business.

Count Botho Eulenburg and Miquel, the Minister of Finance, seized at once on Emperor William's idea of disciplining the Social Democrats. It was not in any concern at the prospect that the Prussian Premier pointed out to the Kaiser that an exceptional law would be bound to lead very quickly to the necessity of dissolving the Reichstag, even to several dissolutions, until security and order were restored by a dictatorship and a *coup d'état*; his main motive in pointing out all this was rather to make sure of the Kaiser's agreement if he steered in this direction. He stood even closer to the Conservatives and the Conservative outlook on the world than Miquel, who had gained favour with the Conservatives through his taxation reform with all its repercussions, his occasional condemnation of the franchise, and his attitude towards various other problems of the time. There was a risk, moreover, that the Finance Minister might change his mind at the critical moment, as he had done in the case of Count Zedlitz's education bill. At first he had supported the bill, but in audience with the Kaiser he had opposed it, so that it fell. On the question, however, of action against the Social Democrats he seemed to have got rid entirely of his liberal impulses. He was back on the Conservative path, which might have distant lights beckoning attractively to him if he thought of his own career. The Minister of Finance expressed himself as at one with the Prime Minister. He expressed himself also to the Kaiser as in favour of a bold course. All Emperor William's advisers were for a bold stroke, all were eager for the fray, all urged him on.

Finally the Kaiser sent out his passionate appeal to the Reich from Königsberg. In Königsberg Palace he addressed the representatives of the Province of East Prussia:

'Well, gentlemen, it is on you that I now call. Up for the fight for religion and morals and order against the parties of revolution!'

Emperor William had been urged on on all sides. King Albert of Saxony and King William of Württemberg, his two guests during the manœuvres near Königsberg, had energetically advocated throwing down the glove; King Albert had again and again declared that he stood with a clear conscience for a dictatorship of the *Bundesrat*, for the forcible imposition of a new franchise; he had held out the prospect of winning over Bavaria without any difficulty to the idea of a *coup d'état*. But Emperor William had been much more cautious this time than might have been expected from all this agitation around him. He indicated broad lines of action which should have public support. His purpose was to urge all parties to come together. He informed the Chancellor of the attitude of the two Kings and their resolve to act in unison with their Emperor. But just as in his speech he had put forward no definite demands, advocated no definite measures, so in his message to the Chancellor he refrained from committing himself in any particular direction. He said that he 'would not shrink from proceeding to extreme measures,' that he demanded 'thoroughly energetic action,' but he gave no indication of the precise measures that he might have in view. His purpose was to rouse the Chancellor to action. The time had come when something really must be done. He would no longer allow the question of the Social Democracy to be pigeonholed, like that of the two little packets of powder which some crazy person, anarchist or criminal, had despatched to him and to the Chancellor from Orleans, a child's essay in assassination. He knew that the Prussian Prime Minister had various proposals under consideration. The Chancellor should also submit a definite plan.

The Chancellor was really deeply alarmed. The Königsberg speech and the Kaiser's telegram reached him far from the scene of events, far from the people who plainly were trying to influence the Kaiser,— while he was taking the cure at Karlsbad. He could see nothing at first to expect from the Kaiser's pronouncements but difficult complications. They made no actual demand for a *coup d'état*. But they called for radical measures, for a sharp campaign against revolutionism, of which, in the Chancellor's opinion, there was much less in reality than was assumed in the addresses during the Königsberg manœuvres, the Kaiser's speech, and his telegram. The Chancellor had ultimately given up the attempt to reply to the Kaiser's agitated contention that the anarchists, with their policy of assassination so resolutely carried out, and the Social Democrats, with their paper attacks on bourgeoisie and capitalism, and on the right of a State to take up arms in its own defence, and their cries for the overthrow of that state system, were virtually after the same thing in the long run, in their different ways, a new ordering of the State and the overthrow of the constituted authorities. But calm reflection in the peace of his spa enabled the Chancellor to see vast differences between the two. The Social Democrats were not the only opposition party in the world. The Opposition in England, for instance, powerful as it was, was accepted as a matter of course, as a part of the framework of the State, and had been vested in the end with a responsibility as opposition with which the Government would be quite unable to dispense. Every effort must be made to train the new and very inconvenient Social Democracy to confine its activities within Parliamentary limits, to serve as an opposition party in its admitted sphere. He had no knowledge at that time of the statement which Bebel, the Socialist leader, had made in the Reichstag, to the general astonishment, in reply to the question how he envisaged the State of the future—

'There will be no State in the future.'

It was impossible for the Chancellor to know whether the Social Democracy would not quietly take its own place in the old State. All that he knew

was that the door should not be bolted in the face of a
settlement on those lines. A few desperadoes, who
hurled dynamite about in wild-cat advocacy of political objectives none of which had been thought out,
or even in simple hatred of a society of which they
abjured membership, did not make the millions of the
Social Democracy into criminals. If the Princes and
their advisers of the moment at Königsberg thought of
actually spilling blood, the General would have nothing
to do with it. He would be the last to have anything
to do with it: he had always been taught that shooting
was only for the actual enemy on the field of battle.

He considered at Karlsbad whether he should resign, and actually wrote out his resignation, but did
not send it off. His Adjutant held up the submission
for a day, and then the Chancellor decided that before
actually sending it it would be better to clear up the
situation in Berlin. The situation was, indeed, quite
clear: Count Botho Eulenburg, in the Prussian Ministry, was pressing for the sharpest legislative measures,
even, if necessary, without the Reichstag—in other
words, with the application of whatever force might
be needed. He was thinking of the resuscitation of the
dead and buried Socialist law, of its drastic extension,
of a new and ambitious piece of legislation, which
should be brought into force whether Parliament
agreed or not. The Chancellor, on the other hand,
was thinking of protection from outrages on the lines
which had been followed against anarchists in France
and Italy. Crimes should be punished as crimes.
Gross political excesses should be restrained. But the
law for public safety should be passed by the Parliamentary methods prescribed by the Constitution. If

the Social Democracy was given reason to expect severe chastisement for any violence or excesses, and so effectively removed from the temptation to them, perhaps it would accustom itself of its own accord to more sensible labours. There was time enough for force if force was attempted.

But the Chancellor could see that he was alone in his point of view. It was plainly irreconcilable with that of the Prussian Prime Minister. And the Chancellor had thrown away his chances of winning over the Prussian Ministry of State to his own view on the day when the education bill had been defeated and he had given away the Prussian Premiership. Now that the Prussian Premier plainly had the Kaiser's approval of his plans, he seemed almost more powerful than the Chancellor. An alternative to the bill that had been drafted by Count Eulenburg had been worked out on the Chancellor's instructions in the Ministry of Justice by *Geheimrat* Nieberding. There had been two meetings of the Prussian Ministers in privy council, but no final decision had been arrived at. Strangely enough Miquel, the Minister of Finance, who at first had been all for sharp measures and a fighting policy, came over suddenly and quite unexpectedly to the Chancellor's side with a demand for a gentler attack on the enemies of the State. At the second meeting the Chancellor insisted that the views of the Ministers of the Federal States as to the nature of the new bill must be heard. The Prime Minister unexpectedly agreed to this. His tactics were to defer the decision. He was not quite sure of ultimate victory. Between the two sittings he had been negotiating with the Conservatives. The Conservatives had

Berlin november 19th 1906
The King of Denmark during the review
of the Alexander Grenadiers in front of the
Schloss at Berlin after his arrival.

Molde norway Summer 1900

The King of Denmark during the review

been negotiating with the Christian Socialist party. The Prime Minister felt sure of the support of the majority of the Conservatives for his plans, but their discussion with the Christian Socialists had ended in dissension. In the discussions between the parties it was also felt to be of importance to settle on the succession to Chancellor von Caprivi before proceeding to extremes. That question seemed of even greater importance to the Prussian Prime Minister, who regarded himself as the natural successor to Count Caprivi but had suffered the mortification of finding that his name was not mentioned. Into all these discussions there penetrated the protests raised by the alarmed Democrats and Social Democrats. Count Eulenburg began to hesitate as to the length to which he should carry his insistence on sharp measures. Then, to his astonishment equally with that of the whole country, there came the totally unexpected news that Chancellor von Caprivi had resigned.

The Chancellor felt tired of office. He still lived in isolation in spite of his eminence, which had at first tempted many to approach him in the vain hope of profiting thereby—'*un vieux garçon*,' as the Kaiser said to Szögyény, the Austrian Ambassador: a queer old bachelor who rarely came out of his shell and was scarcely ever to be seen in society. He had been alone with his grievances during the days of growing crisis when the Kaiser had held Court at Königsberg and received the Farmers' Union, bitter enemies of the Chancellor's whole policy, angry over the blows that their interests had suffered and, considering their rank, thoroughly seditious in their language. He had carried his vexation in silence to his remote bachelor

quarters when the Kaiser openly and deliberately
ignored him at a parade, at which only half-battalions
had been allowed by the Kaiser to march past to
receive their flags and not whole battalions as the
Chancellor had wished. He knew that the Prussian
Prime Minister was busily undermining his position
with the parties and that the police of the capital were
engaged in intrigues of their own against him, though
of all this those in his fullest confidence and his loyal
Adjutants could only bring him occasional details or
indications. He felt around him all that peculiar
atmosphere amid which a public authority like the
police exercised an unprecedented control over the
highest dignitaries in the land, spreading rumours
about their impending retirement, believing that it
could best preserve the unlimited power which it had
had in the old Bismarckian days by making life impossible for the new men and so bringing back the old
ones. But he took no notice of the hints: he silently
swallowed his disgust. He had met everywhere with
opposition to his plans; his convictions had come
everywhere into conflict with vested interests; and he
had begun to tire of the struggle. For a year past he
had been entirely taken up with the effort to achieve
progress in home affairs, and the control of his foreign policy had slipped out of his hands. The bridge
he had built over to Britain had been broken down
again by others. He would have to begin building
over again, with no assurance that the new work
would not be attacked and destroyed once more by
those strange forces in the German nation, at Court
above, away in Friedrichsruh, in his own office, in
the Prussian Ministries, among the parties, in all

sections of public opinion. General von Caprivi had tired of it all. Now he gave up. It was quite true—he had sent in his resignation.

Emperor William, however, refused to accept it. Filled as the Kaiser had been with the idea of a declaration of war against the Social Democracy, the Chancellor's opposition had given him pause. He went himself to the Chancellor's residence. The Chancellor brought him round entirely to his own view of the necessity for moderation. In this age it was no longer possible to combat ideas with armed force: they must be tamed with argument, with the appeal to reason, and gradually fitted into the social order. Emperor William declared himself no longer in agreement with the Prussian Minister's plans. He carried his assurances of his renewed confidence in the Chancellor to the length of asking him to transmit the rejected submission for resignation to Count Botho Eulenburg to note, with the explanation that the Kaiser saw no reason to part with his Chancellor either in the 'unbridgeable gulf' between Chancellor and Ministers or in any of the other circumstances adduced in the request for dismissal, which he had rejected.

Seldom in any historic incident have events followed so hot on one another's heels as from that moment to the end of General von Caprivi's Chancellorship. The Prussian Prime Minister read the rejected submission. The day after, while the Kaiser's guest at a hunt on Count Philipp Eulenburg's estate of Liebenberg, he himself tendered his resignation. The Kaiser wanted to retain him: there might still be a possibility of bringing the two opponents together in a common policy of proceeding on milder lines against the Social Democracy. He succeeded in getting the Prime Minister to make some advance towards a compromise: he would agree to consider remaining in office if, in spite of the 'unbridgeable gulf,' the Chancellor would simply state that he was willing to continue in collaboration with Count Botho Eulenburg. But an incident occurred on the day following Emperor William's efforts at composing the differences which brought the whole crisis to a sudden end: every detail of the conversation between the Kaiser and Count von Caprivi in the Chancellor's residence, of the position taken up by the Kaiser against the Prime Minister, of the whole confidential conversation between the Emperor and the General, was published in the *Kölnische Zeitung*.

Nothing that had gone before had so irritated the Kaiser against Count von Caprivi—not his bluntness, his almost sullen refusal to talk when he was occupied with his own thoughts, his pointed impoliteness, which he had even allowed the Kaiserin to feel at times; not the obstinacy with which he put forward only step by step, and with none of the energy which the Kaiser wanted to see, his demands in the Reichstag for further military progress over and above the great reform which he had effected. This astonishing incident of the revelations to the *Kölnische Zeitung* was, in the Kaiser's view, a grave breach of confidence. If the Chancellor could himself sit down and tell all the world at once what he had just been discussing in confidence with the Kaiser, and so snatch from the Kaiser's hand the decision as to the remaining in office or not of the Prussian Prime Minister, or

116

of anyone else, matters which it was for the Kaiser alone to decide, then no sort of collaboration with the Chancellor was possible.

He sent his *Kabinettschef*, von Lucanus, to Count Caprivi to ask whether the article in the *Kölnische Zeitung* had been suggested or written by the Chancellor. The Chancellor said that it had not been. He had had nothing whatever to do with the article. The *Kabinettschef* then asked the Chancellor, at the Kaiser's request, at all events to get the Kaiser out of the uncomfortable position he was in by 'taking the sting out of the points made against Eulenburg.'

It was quite true that General von Caprivi had had no cognizance of the appearance of the article. *Geheimrat* von Holstein, in his hidden office, had been occupied with other things besides foreign policy. He had been determined by his own intervention to clear away a situation which had for some time begun to have a threatening aspect for him. All his efforts to persuade Count Philipp Eulenburg to use his influence to keep Chancellor von Caprivi in office seemed this time to be failing of effect. The Kaiser's friend had the impression that the Kaiser was more inclined to part with the Chancellor than with the Prime Minister. At Liebenburg there were three Counts Eulenburg with the Kaiser. The *Geheimrat* had not been able to wait and see whether the three Counts Eulenburg would be stronger than the cool common sense which, after all, the Kaiser had ultimately shown at the Chancellor's residence in all the questions at issue. Count Botho Eulenburg—he was a man of the very type of Prince Bismarck. The *Geheimrat* saw himself faced with either the Count or even Prince Bismarck as the new Chancellor. He braced himself for a mortal thrust: he would end the public career of the Prussian Prime Minister—would deliver a thrust against him from which he would never recover. The Chancellor would remain as victor, and he himself would be able to work on in peace. Baron Holstein made his thrust; only he overlooked the fact that he would be striking at the Chancellor as well as the Premier. In handing over the article or the material for it to his friend the editor of the *Kölnische Zeitung*, he established the facts concerning the Prime Minister's policy, but he also established the fact of the Chancellor's breach of confidence.

The Chancellor had told the Kaiser the truth. He had had nothing to do with the article. But he declined to make any correction. The article correctly represented the facts, and the views underlying them. There they stood, and from them the irrevocable decision should be made—the decision on the personal issue and on the issue of policy. Either he would now go, or Count Botho Eulenburg must. The Kaiser, astonished at the rapid development which his desire for a settlement had brought, and annoyed at the impotence and insecurity of his position between his two closest advisers, now openly at war with one another, decided that he would dispense both with Chancellor von Caprivi and with the Prussian Prime Minister.

Nearly four years had passed since Prince Bismarck's retirement. Chancellor von Caprivi stepped down from the public platform—quietly and unostentatiously as always. Prince Bismarck's followers triumphed. There were none to regret the Chancellor's fall. But all who had a sense of justice were compelled to admit that the General's term of office had been filled with valuable and brilliant achievements; even if he seemed to be less sure in his handling of details. Amid every complication, in face of every problem, he had had in view only the thing to be achieved, never any question of party capital. And he had achieved it even against all the resources of party opposition. He had carried through the commercial treaties. He had sought and found new ways of approach to Britain. They might still have been cleared again if the Chancellor had remained, in spite of the industrious dumping of obstacles in which Secretary of State von Marschall and *Geheimrat* von Holstein had been indulging. The commercial treaty with Russia had mended even the 'wrecked wire.' He had given way to Count Zedlitz and his education bill, although the intention of the bill must have been in conflict with his own feelings: coolly and with keen insight he had recognized the Conservative strength of the German Centre party, its coming expansion, its importance and indispensability in the Germany of the future, and had deliberately set out to acquire and assure its support in spite of all its opposition to Prince Bismarck, who amid the crash of final disaster had made the same sudden discovery, only too late. Even in the Social Democracy he had recognized the massive, solid masonry which would one day uphold the very State which he found filled with the call to arms against its members as the enemies of society. The Chancellor had seen the outlines of the form which the Reich must gradually take between the Powers, and the forces which it must nourish within itself. He had looked out beyond the grievances of Conservatives or Liberals, landowners or Socialists, to envisage the real needs of the Reich. Towards those he steered his course with a boldness of conception and a keenness of vision denied to those who saw in him only a general of no importance. In his long letter on Prince Bismarck's dismissal, Emperor William called the Prince 'the greatest of Germans.' The phrase had, no doubt, escaped him in the heat of a time of excitement. A survey of the period reveals, however, General Count Caprivi as really the most outstanding personality that it had produced. No Imperial Chancellor attempted such a work of construction as he did.

The moment he had walked away, in his unpretentious dress, from the Chancellor's office, the world forgot his existence. It had shown all that arrogant depreciation of him as just an indifferent soldier (which he was very far from being), which seems always to be the privilege of contemporaries. It was left to history, with her contempt of contemporary judgments, to adjudge him a true statesman.

Chapter IV

THE PARTITION OF THE WORLD

PRINCE CHLODWIG VON HOHENLOHE followed Count Caprivi as Chancellor. When the crisis took the turn so utterly unexpected by the 'Consortium,' Count Philipp Eulenburg had suggested Hohenlohe as the man best fitted for the Chancellor's office. Prince Hohenlohe, a *grand seigneur* descended from a once reigning house, was a man of the old school, but one of wide vision, ahead of the times in which the Kaiser now set him up as leader.

'Hohenlohe is a Catholic,' Count Eulenburg had written in his report, 'but no Ultramontane, and Liberal rather than Conservative. Caprivi has no knowledge of the South Germans, Hohenlohe none of the North Germans.'

The new Chancellor was no stranger to business of state. He had been Prime Minister of Bavaria, and had been one of the builders of the German Empire; in the past he had been Ambassador in Paris, and Governor in Alsace-Lorraine. His reputation stood high in Germany and abroad. He had become a little old gentleman of seventy-five by the time the Kaiser called him to the Chancellorship. Shrewd and very kindly eyes lit up the weathered features of his well-shaped head; they beamed with genuine goodwill. He had something of the love of sparkle of the eighteenth century; he was fond of well-cut, witty

121

phrases, of ready aphorisms, which he would often express in French. When the Kaiser entertained in the hunting-box at Letzlingen, a goblet made out of a mighty stag's horn used to be passed round after dinner, a gift from Frederick William IV; every new arrival had to pronounce a verse in raising it before he drank. Prince Hohenlohe spoke like a cavalier of the days of Louis XV suddenly brought on the scene: his manners had much in common with that period—

'Vive la chasse et son loisir—
C'est le plaisir des rois
Et le roi des plaisirs.'

He was essentially a man of moderation, always preferring any possible compromise to the doubtful issue of methods of force or severity. He had had splendid success in Alsace even with the difficult, stubborn local patriotism of the Alemanni. He brought also to the Chancellor's office the clarity of outlook of his great age. He was full of indulgence for all things human, and regarded all things humanly. In political issues too, where he now had the initiative and guidance, he often brought to bear only the gentle, aloof irony of a pilgrim through a long life with its many burdens and its frequent disillusionments. He faced the problems of politics with philosophic good-humour.

'Various dates,' he said to the Kaiser, 'have been suggested to me for the elections, all of them in the spring. From my long experience I have come to the conclusion that the spring is not a good time for that sort of thing. In spring the sap rises and circulates in men, plants and animals, and people are very energetic and enterprising and in consequence very excitable, and talk a great deal and make a lot of noise. My suggestion is autumn. After the harvest people have had their fling, they have used up their energies and are much steadier in their judgment of political issues.'

Prince Hohenlohe was not the Chancellor for fighting or a *coup*.

He was entirely in agreement with the victory of Count Caprivi's milder draft over Count Botho Eulenburg's plans for a 'Subversives Bill.' He agreed too, that it was enough to apply the existing provisions of the criminal law, with increased severity, against revolutionaries. It was certainly no shock to him, with his Liberal outlook, to find not only the much-discussed 'Subversives Bill' thrown out in the Reichstag, but the efforts of the Conservatives to push at least a 'Little Socialist Bill' through the Prussian Diet defeated. He was not to be turned aside from his calm judgment, from his resolve to have nothing to do with a home policy of Bend or Break,—if only because he could see in it the danger of chaos in Germany owing to the encouragement afforded to her neighbours,—or from the mild policy dictated by his own good sense and his repugnance to the use of force, however the Generals might rage—the fire-eating Minister of War, von Gossler, or General Count Waldersee, who had returned to the scene.

As Commanding Officer of an army corps Count Waldersee would have found Hamburg decidedly monotonous if he had not happened on one occasion to drive over to Friedrichsruh, which was close by, and there discovered, in common with Prince Bismarck, that there was no longer any ill-feeling between the two. Once, at manœuvres at Rohnstock, Count Waldersee as Chief of Staff had had occasion to subject the Kaiser to sharp criticism for his conduct of his corps during the manœuvres. The General was always liable to suffer from over-cleverness, and had been concentrating on the manifest disappearance of the Kaiser's favour. If he flattered him the Kaiser would cut him short at times with a harsh word, and the all-too shrewd idea had occurred to him to try the opposite tactics as a means to a return to favour. At first Emperor William had listened in silence to the criticism, although he was indignant at the General's tactlessness in choosing the very moment when the Kaiser was surrounded by his guests, Emperor Francis Joseph and the Austrian Emperor's entourage. Afterwards he had admitted the justice of the criticism on points of military detail, but had then at once spoken in his capacity of supreme head of the army, and had told the Chief of Staff that he was discouraging his officers and reducing their fighting efficiency by setting them impossible tasks. Count Waldersee, dismayed by the incident, entered a careful but inaccurate account of it in his diary; the Kaiser, however, made him pay for so showing him up in the presence of his ally by removing him from the General Staff and appointing him to the Hamburg command.

Four years had passed since that psychological blunder of Count Waldersee's; now the General saw a way back to favour through urging his imperial master onwards to do battle against the Social Democracy. But whatever he might write to the Kaiser, whatever discussions he might have with the Conservatives, whatever he might try in order at last himself to have the ordering of Germany's fate as her Chancellor, neither the Kaiser nor Prince Hohenlohe was to be brought to the point of actually embarking on hostilities. Prince Hohenlohe had entries of his own to make in his diary:

'I am aware that plenty of politicians and highly-placed office-seekers are busy trying to discredit me with His Majesty. They want a change of Chancellor and imagine that with energetic action it is to be had . . . I am ready to go at any moment if His Majesty decides on those lines of action.'

But the Kaiser only seriously considered 'those lines of action' so long as the moment did not come for the definite decision to bring force to bear. He was certainly determined to block every avenue to revolution. In his impulsive way he frequently resorted in the presence of Generals, or, perhaps, of all too humble and obedient Ministers, to threats and extravagant language. Naturally he expected that his words would go no farther than his Generals or Ministers. But Generals or careerist Ministers took them as hints as to their road to success and quoted them with apostolic zeal, to serve His Majesty. When, however, the time came for the immediate and irrevocable decision, the Kaiser spoke in a changed tone. An amendment of the Constitution seemed to him only to be possible 'if the desire for it were indicated to him by Parliament and people.'

The Kaiser grumbled bitterly and often to the Chancellor about his indifference to the 'danger of revolution.' But when he had calmed down after one

of his outbursts against the Socialists, and had, perhaps, to deal with a proffered resignation from the
Prince, he would turn to those around him and say,
half humorously, half in earnest:

'It was essential that I should have an old gentleman as Chancellor, for he, of course, has to restrain
the young gentleman in his well-known impetuous-
ness.'

The old gentleman seemed important at the
moment not only for Germany's internal peace and
for solidarity in the Empire (the whole of the south
had faith in him in virtue of his good name and his
past career), but for her foreign relations, in which
his reputation, his experience of the world, and his
attractive personality and gift of conciliation were of
great value. As Ambassador he had made a great
impression on the French by his genuine worth, his
great courtesy, and his whole bearing. If Queen
Victoria spoke of him she called him simply 'my
cousin.' The Prince had estates in Russia. He was
not inordinately rich. He not only had to be assisted
out of the Kaiser's private purse in order to eke out
the official income of the Chancellor's post, but there
was no question that he had the best of reasons to
desire good relations between Germany and Russia
on account of his Russian property. In order to
secure himself in its possession he had let one of his
sons enter the Tsar's service. Here again, for himself
and for others, he had a human outlook on affairs
and their intricacies. Relations with Russia were not
good. Alexander III had just died. Even if he had not
had his Russian estate the Prince would have done
his utmost as a matter of conviction to improve rela-

tions with Russia. He was all for methods of conciliation. And his first concern was for the East.

Nothing could have been more entirely in accordance with the Kaiser's own views.

Less than a year had passed since the Cesarevitch
Nicholas had been on a visit to his relations in Coburg; the Kaiser had shown marked friendship towards him there. Queen Victoria had come to Coburg
to meet Empress Frederick, Grand Duke Vladimir,
the Grand Duchess, and Princess Alix of Hesse. The
Cesarevitch had come to Coburg to seek a bride, depressed and intimidated by his father's warning that
he was not openly to woo the Hessian princess unless
he was first absolutely assured of acceptance. The
consequence was that the Cesarevitch said not a word.

Emperor William brought his good offices into
play; not on his own initiative but at the desire of
Empress Frederick, and not entirely to the satisfaction of the old Queen. With noticeable tact he brought
the Cesarevitch and Princess Alix together. The
Princess's only trouble, and it was a grave one, was
her fear of having to change her faith if she became a
Russian. The Cesarevitch declared at once to the
Kaiser that his father and he himself were both
opposed to any renunciation of faith, or conversion.
Nothing of that sort would be asked of the Princess.
If she embraced the Orthodox rites she would be receiving something superimposed on her Protestant
faith, not something that must thrust it aside or take
its place. Empress Charlotte had observed the
Orthodox rites, but had always remained a Protestant
'dans son fort intérieur,' and had died a Protestant. In
the end the Russian suit was not dismissed. The

Kaiser took that as an assurance of cordial future relations, and, indeed, hoped in his heart that politically
it was a sign of good omen for the future. It might be
that the heritage of past grievances and suspicions
would be buried in the grave with Alexander III.
The Tsar was suffering from a grave and incurable
kidney disease. Russia's destinies would soon be
guided by Nicholas II. Emperor William had been
keen to win over the future Tsar. The Cesarevitch's
love for the Hessian princess was not merely a state
affair, a diplomatic fiction: he had from the first been
passionately her slave, almost hypnotized by her.
Overjoyed, he embraced the Kaiser.

'You have paved the way to my life's happiness. I
shall not forget it to the end of my life. All your life
you will be able to count confidently on me.'

The future Empress of Russia was no less carried
away by the emotions of the moment:

'I shall never forget that I owe my life's happiness
to you.'

Since then the Cesarevitch had become Tsar
Nicholas II of Russia. Whether the succession of one
Tsar to another was really going to bring a future of
better relations with Russia, Emperor William did not
yet venture to decide. His deepest feelings drew him
towards Britain. In Coburg Nicholas II had assured
him of his lifelong gratitude. Prince Hohenlohe, the
new Chancellor, viewed Russia with friendly feelings.
It ought soon to become clear what possibilities there
were of a rapprochement between Russia and Germany.

In spite of the mistrust of all things Russian from
which Emperor William could never free himself, in
spite of secret doubts with regard to Nicholas II which

Berlin November 19th 1906
Review before the King of Denmark
The 2d Lancers of the Guard.

assailed him even after the wooing at Coburg, he now turned in his foreign policy towards Russia. In doing so he had one single ultimate objective: Britain.

Disturbances which had broken out in Korea culminated in the Sino-Japanese war of 1895. Japan was the aggressor, although she herself had been responsible for bringing the unrest to a head through the assassination of the Empress of Korea; for the real reason of the war was the Japanese foothold on the mainland, and the influence so secured, after long-continued efforts, over the exploitation of the still unworked and even unsurveyed mineral wealth of China. China was beaten; but though the issue primarily concerned only the two Mongolian nations, half Europe was thrown into consternation by it. If Japan really established herself on the mainland in Asia, that would mean the barring of the way to Russian aspirations to Port Arthur, and to Russian penetration into Manchuria and deep into China. For Britain it might mean the loss of much of her Chinese trade. Germany saw the possibility of Japan, Russia, and perhaps other Powers once more securing territorial gains while she herself, as almost always hitherto, went empty away. When China appealed for the mediation of the European Powers, the signal was given for efforts for the restoration of peace between the two combatants, efforts inspired by all the sincerity, all the moral fervour, all the selflessness which the civilized nations had been displaying during that whole period of the partition of the world between them.

In the last decade of the nineteenth century explorers and armed forces, scientific expeditions and trading companies with purposes incompletely disclosed, moved unceasingly up and down Asia and Africa, searching the mainland and every island for opportunities of profitable investment. It was the age in which the souls of aboriginal tribes were won for civilization with fire and sword, with trade goods and alcohol; gold mines and diamond fields were endowed with the blessings of civilized control; territories were given away by donors to whom they did not belong, because the donors themselves had determined to take possession of other areas; the recipients of the discarded territory concurred in the fresh annexation although they in turn had no rights whatever over the territory annexed.

It was the age of 'compensations.' If any State took possession of something, another State was entitled then to take possession of something somewhere else. The only party not consulted in the matter was the party at whose expense the compensation was secured. So Christian nations of age-old culture and civilization plundered and stole, raided and murdered. The Christian witnesses of their plundering gave it their approval in return for licence themselves to plunder elsewhere. The right of the strong arm and the economic system of highway robbery had become the moral law of politics. Statesmen negotiated courteously, cordially, concerning the means of discreetly investing common theft with a new and universally recognized legality and respectability. No Power would allow another to get an Asiatic village or a strip of grazing land in Africa for nothing. The Japanese Minister in Korea had had the Korean Empress stabbed to death. Over that incident Japan went to war with China. Everyone knew that China was being outraged. Great was the agitation among the European Cabinets, all of them hostile to Japan's establishment on any spot on the mainland of Asia; if for no other reason, because it would at once bring an outcry for compensation.

Britain's first proposal was to go to the aid of the Chinese. A naval demonstration, and representations on the part of the Great Powers, would bring the Japanese to reason—in their arrogance they were refusing even to state their terms of peace to the Chinese. Britain went cautiously, however: the time might come when she would have need of the Japanese. The joint representations by the various Governments and the naval demonstration against Japan were soon whittled down to a simple warning, to be given jointly with Russia. The German statesmen suddenly showed a tact and caution not often to be observed: they were anxious to do nothing to give offence either to Japan or China. They refrained from associating themselves with the proposed action by the Powers, and it was abandoned. The Japanese soldiers marched on, and the Chinese appealed once more for help. Russia, France, and Britain advised the victors now to state their terms of peace. At first Germany allowed the three Powers to act alone; then, indeed, she decidedly embarked on a Far East policy of her own. Viscount Aoki, the Japanese Minister in Berlin, had given the Foreign Ministry an outline of what Japan intended to demand from the Chinese: the independence of Korea, the cession to Japan of Formosa and the Liaotung Peninsula, and a war indemnity. The moment had arrived for the consideration of compensations. That question seemed, indeed, so obviously to arise that it seemed best for the moment to dissuade the Japanese from their plans of conquest, so that there should be no demands for compensation from other quarters. Germany warned Japan accordingly. The Japanese replied courteously that they would proceed as they thought fit.

Russia, meanwhile, had grown impatient. Her first thought was to declare war against Japan. But Russia had no armed supplies in the Far East, and not even a naval base. The Russians were also doubtful as to their course because they had no knowledge of what Britain wanted. For once Britain wanted nothing. All the British merchants in China were of the decided opinion that the Japanese would not interfere with trade in China, but would promote it. It now became plain in Germany that the Japanese would not allow themselves to be baulked or robbed of all the fruits of their victory. The problem of compensation drew nearer and nearer.

Rear Admiral von Tirpitz, Senior Officer of the Far East Squadron, had reported to Emperor William that the Kiaochow Peninsula would be of value as the German base in the Far East of which Germany so stood in need. The Kaiser had thought first of Formosa, now Japan's objective. He shared the view which was universal at the time. If every nation was annexing territory in all directions, taking any lands coveted irrespective of the rights of ownership of their inhabitants, he was fully entitled to see to it that Germany should not always be the only one to be left out of consideration. Her commerce had grown too important, there was too much German property on the seas, for that to be allowed.

The Kaiser surveyed the broad lines of the question of annexations; the detailed negotiations with other Powers were in the hands of *Geheimrat* Holstein. Letters went to and fro between him and Count Hatzfeldt. Lord Kimberley, who had recently succeeded Lord Rosebery, had had a friendly discussion with Count Hatzfeldt a few months before in the effort to remove all misunderstandings between Britain and Germany. He was asked now to say whether Germany would receive any share if developments in the Far East were to render compensations necessary. Lord Kimberley replied very cordially: Germany would certainly not be left out of account. On this Baron Holstein troubled Count Hatzfeldt no further. He took no further interest in Britain. He knew that Prince Hohenlohe was for friendship with Russia. He knew of the Kaiser's great interest in the new Tsar. The Kaiser was plainly anxious for a new rapprochement with Russia. Kaiser and *Geheimrat* were working in the same direction. Both were annoyed with Britain. The Kaiser was after Russian friendship in order in the end to bring Britain to Germany's side through the threat of a possible close understanding which might embrace Germany, Russia, and even France. This much was plain, that his new attitude towards Russia, his efforts to bring Nicholas II under his influence, and to interest the Tsar in the Far East by an appeal to his imagination, to political considerations, to race instinct and even to religion, were accounted for by a broad political purpose of his own conceiving. Baron Holstein's principal aim was to be able, if he were successful in winning over Russia, to break up the Dual Alliance. His plan for winning over Britain was usually to adopt a sharp tone, or a sudden sledge-hammer gesture, as he had done in 1893 over Egypt. Friendship or an alliance with Britain was only to be secured, in his view, through deliberate and brutal menaces, through ruthless pressure. The Kaiser wanted to evoke at least the prospect of a Continental alliance which Britain might prefer to prevent by coming over of her own accord to Germany's side. He, too, was quite ready to let Britain be annoyed for awhile. Accordingly, Germany proceeded no further in her negotiations with Britain, but made to the Russians a proposal of joint action against Japan.

Russia did not agree at once. She naturally transmitted the German suggestion in the first place to Lord Kimberley. He was greatly astonished at Germany's independent action, but he had little inclination to take any energetic stand for British interests, which appeared to him to be in no way threatened. Russia, however, was troubled by the admitted intentions of the Japanese on Port Arthur. If Britain retired from the field, it would be better to act with Germany rather than with no other ally but France. The three Powers decided on joint action. They began a little hesitantly. It was uncomfortable for France to be marching alongside the victor of 1870. Baron von Marschall was rather puzzled at the Russians' dilatoriness. He saw all Asia in the melting pot: Port Arthur meant a new, Japanese Gibraltar.

The only person who took a decided course was Baron von Gutschmidt, the German Minister in

Tokio, who would allow none but himself to present the Note of the three Powers to Japan to the Foreign Minister, Marquis Hayashi. He came to Hayashi as Prince Bismarck had once gone to Prince Gortchakov —bearing a humiliating document that upheld the interests of other countries and was quite unnecessarily being transmitted on their behalf by Germany. On coming into the presence of the Japanese Foreign Minister, the German Minister considered it to be of the first importance to speak in harsh tones and model his style on that of a victorious general. In order to make it impossible for the Marquis to fail to understand him, he brought not only the document presented by the three Powers but the text of the secret instructions which he had received from Berlin. Marquis Hayashi was bewildered; the Minister was full of pride—

'My language,' he reported, 'made an unmistakable impression.'

The three Powers did not at once succeed in imposing their demand that Japan should dismiss the idea of any annexation on the mainland, and console herself for that renunciation with a money indemnity. Japan turned at once to the Tsar: she wanted at least to secure the southern extremity of the Liaotung Peninsula, if she could not have Port Arthur. The German Minister, however, was sure that the Japanese would take a demand coming from three Powers very seriously. Once more, entirely on his own initiative, securing the permission only of the Russians—the party most closely interested—he spoke out plainly to the Japanese. He requested a prompt reply. Japan must give way. Thereafter the

135

Japanese Empire regarded not Russia or France as its mortal enemy—Russia with her own Far East interests or France who naturally supported her ally—but Germany, who was totally unconcerned in the whole issue. In the end Japan yielded to the pressure of a Russian ultimatum. She concluded the peace of Shimonoseki: Formosa and its adjacent islands fell to her; a war indemnity was fixed; but of the mainland she secured nothing.

The question of compensations was now, of course, ripe for discussion. Germany had lent her aid to the Tsar. France had lent her aid to the Tsar. Russia had taken China's part. Germany had not only warned Japan to moderate her demands; she had let the Chinese know in confidence that it had been Germany who took the first initiative in getting the Powers to protest against Japan's action. Britain had done nothing to restrain the Japanese, nor had she advised the Chinese to give way; she had observed benevolent neutrality. Japan, it was quite true, had obtained not an inch of Chinese territory; but that was no reason why all the rest should receive nothing from China for all those services. The Powers proceeded to consider the matter.

For Germany, however, the question of compensations was by no means the most important question arising out of the Treaty of Shimonoseki and all that had gone before it.

The events in the Far East seemed to the Kaiser to provide a good opportunity for attaining his political purpose more easily by a roundabout way. Baron von Brandt, formerly German Minister in Peking, told him much about Chinese and Japanese, about the approaching union of all the Mongols for a war of extermination against the Europeans; and the Kaiser made a rather melodramatic use of all this. As always, he found an emphatic, clear-cut phrase, to send out into the world; it was aimed primarily at the Tsar:

'Peoples of Europe, guard your most sacred possessions!'

He drew an alarming picture of new mass migrations, of the influx of the yellow races, a highly-coloured but realistic picture of barbarians pressing onwards, against whom the Tsar would have to bear the brunt of the critical defence. With his message he stepped into the part of a new Protector and Lord of Christendom. Often he was well aware that he was making a theatrical impression. He believed that it was necessary to do so in order to stir up the masses, or even to influence particular individuals whose course he wanted to determine. Almost always his real purpose was a sound and sober one, and even amid the emotionalism that was a means of expression for him he scarcely ever lost his own sense of proportion. At the time when von Gutschmidt was striking a blow for his country as Minister in Tokio, the Kaiser assured the Tsar in writing that he would stand behind Russia in any enterprise which she might contemplate in Asia. He was quite pressing in his advocacy of Russian activity in the Far East—he wanted to turn Russia's attention away from the Balkans, from her western frontiers in Europe; he hoped to be recompensed by the Tsar in Asia for his complaisance; and he counted on his services to Russia steadily winning him her ruler's closer friendship, to the discomfiture and alarm of Britain.

137

He was full of the idea of an all embracing alliance of the continental European States. If that union should really come to pass, all would be lovely. Time after time Russia, France and Germany must come really to one another's assistance, even though the French made no secret of their reluctance. The three Powers had come into line for the first time over Shimonoseki.

'If your Majesty ever succeeds,' Count Schlieffen, Chief of Staff, had said to the Kaiser, 'in coming before the world on a common front with France and Russia, that is an enormous gain which we cannot but welcome. For it means that we are no longer in the line of fire, no longer the target aimed at.'

The way also to France led through Russia, if not by gentler means then under Russian pressure. The Kaiser was for positive, constructive work—a general Continental understanding, that would make it possible to live in peace on the Continent; or an alliance with Britain, even if Britain had to be frightened into it; or a Germany at peace with all the Continental Powers and at the same time in alliance with Britain. He was pursuing the same aims which *Geheimrat* Holstein was pursuing for negative purposes—proofs of friendship for Russia, whom Baron Holstein wanted to detach from France; pressure on Britain to induce her gradually to change her course, while the *Geheimrat* was deliberately hitting out at her time after time. All the impending developments seemed to fit well into this programme.

For immediately after the peace of Shimonoseki the Tsar was naturally overflowing with gratitude. He promised the Kaiser his support in any acquisition in the Far East which Germany might proceed to make. Germany might rest assured that there would be peace along the Russian frontier. The Tsar guaranteed Russia's pacific attitude to so friendly a neighbour. Britain would be compelled more and more to realize how serious for her in her growing isolation was the course of affairs on the Continent; especially as Emperor William did not forget repeatedly to remind the English of the way things were going.

Everything had gone awry between the two Empires since the frail seedling of amity sown during Caprivi's Chancellorship had been rooted up. Britain was busy rounding off her possessions in Southwest Africa. Friction came when the Boers finally brought their long-planned railway down to Delagoa Bay—their only outlet to the sea. That made their overseas trade independent of British ports. The opening of the line was made a great ceremonial occasion. Germany sent two warships to Delagoa Bay. The British certainly had grounds for annoyance, for the Transvaal was not an entirely independent State; the commerce of all States in its territory was regulated by international instruments, but its foreign affairs were conducted entirely under British supervision. The Boers, tough colonists of Dutch origin, with a considerable German admixture, gladly seized every opportunity of irritating Britain, who was greatly incommoded by their sturdy independence in regard to the internal affairs of their State. Once before, when Britain proposed to send her troops through Portuguese territory, Germany had sent torpedo boats to Delagoa Bay for the

protection of the fifteen thousand Germans in the
Transvaal; and subsequently President Kruger had
drunk to the German Emperor's health on the Kaiser's
birthday. The British in their annoyance made representations to the German Government. Germany
coldly pointed out the position of the Transvaal at
international law, her independence, and her trade
treaties with Germany. The warships now sent were
intended to be a demonstration that Germany would
not be deprived of her rights. The incident passed over;
but immediately afterwards there came fresh differences between Britain and Germany, when the Kaiser
set out on his annual visit to Cowes for the regatta.

Queen Victoria wanted her grandson to have a good
talk with Lord Salisbury. Salisbury, who made no
secret at other times of his dislike of William II, was
the very soul of cordiality when he came into the
presence of the Kaiser. He kept up an easy flow of
general conversation, and introduced each of the
Ministers to the Kaiser with some fresh witticism.
He was bubbling over with anecdotes.

'Lord Salisbury,' the Queen had told the Kaiser in
preparing him for the meeting, 'has a great liking for
epigrams, and his speeches in Parliament are full of
them.'

The Premier avoided talking politics, but came of
his own accord to the subject of Turkey—the 'sick
man' in Europe, whose collapse could no longer be
deferred. Conditions in Turkey were a scandal, continually producing fresh trouble between other countries. The best thing would be to make an end of it
all and partition Turkey. What had the Kaiser's impressions been when he was in Stamboul in 1889?

The Kaiser: I went first to Athens, then Stamboul. The comparison between the two is very interesting. Few signs of business activity in the streets of Athens, but crowds of newspaper readers and groups discussing politics. Stamboul filled with busy craftsmen and merchants, the shops humming with activity; the Turks gave the impression of an industrious people. One does not by any means get the impression of a 'sick man' from the workpeople of Stamboul.

Lord Salisbury: That is a very important fact; but all who belong to the upper ranks, especially the officials, the whole Administration, the governmental machine, the whole lot of the Bimbashi and even the Pashas, are totally corrupt. Justice, especially, is in a lamentable state.

The Kaiser: Undoubtedly that is true in certain respects. And in Stamboul there are a good many resplendent officials who have to be handled carefully. But the Koran is a very good code of laws for the Orientals, and, if properly applied, far preferable to a reformed code concocted by the Concert of Europe, which would be unsuitable to the East. After all, justice in Europe has its own imperfections, and they have not escaped the notice of the Turks.

Lord Salisbury: For all that, I think the time has come to make a clean sweep of Turkey and partition her into spheres of interest.

The Kaiser: That will not be so easy. The Turks have a great historic past, of which they are proud; especially of their immense military achievements. They are as proud of their victory at Mohacz and of the conquest of Stamboul as the British are of Agincourt and Malplaquet.

141

Lord Salisbury: So it may have been in the past. But the army of to-day no longer counts. It could not put up any resistance.

The Kaiser: It was once at the gates of Vienna. If the people were called to arms for the defence of their country, for the preservation of its existence, Europe would be amazed. Especially so if they had European leaders. I should strongly advise you not to underestimate Turkey's vitality. A partitioning will let loose infinite quarrels over the booty.

At that, Lord Salisbury dropped the subject. For the booty was just what he was thinking of. He had given Count Hatzfeldt, the German Ambassador, an indication of his plans before this conversation with the Kaiser. Russia was to be free to take possession of Constantinople. Austria-Hungary might have Salonica. France was to have Morocco, Italy perhaps Tripoli. What Germany was to receive had not been mentioned. Now Salisbury was faced with the Kaiser's dissent. His hints had been coldly rejected in Berlin; he had hoped to overcome that rebuff by means of the face-to-face talk with the Kaiser. But the Kaiser had not agreed; he failed to appreciate where British interests lay; he was, in any case, holding aloof, was declining to enter into the matter. Lord Salisbury, disappointed, changed the subject.

To restore the British Premier's good humour, William II began now to tell him one anecdote after another. Lord Salisbury's immense frame so shook with laughter that he broke his armchair. Emperor William's entourage sprang up to save his lordship from falling.

142

'I am glad,' Queen Victoria afterwards said to her grandson, 'that you had so amusing a talk with Lord Salisbury. Not everyone is able to make him laugh like that.'

The Queen wanted Emperor William to have another discussion of the issue with Lord Salisbury. Next day, after dinner at Osborne, she sent into the Park to find the Premier. But Lord Salisbury was nowhere to be found, although it was a rule that every guest of the Queen's should say exactly where he was going if he left the Palace.

Lord Salisbury confessed afterwards to his friends that he 'had simply run away.'

He had gone to London. The Kaiser, astonished, had waited in vain for quite a while. Lord Salisbury's enjoyment of the Kaiser's anecdotes had not mitigated his annoyance at the refusal of William II to hear of a partition of Turkey.

In his insistence on the maintenance of the integrity of Turkey, the Kaiser was returning to a pro-Russian policy. Russia was occupied at the moment with the question of her railway across Siberia, with Port Arthur, with trouble over Manchuria; suddenly she had lost interest in Constantinople, in the Dardanelles, in all the Balkan question, until she could set her affairs in order in the Far East. It was quite unnecessary for Emperor Francis Joseph to enter a caveat against Russia's ever approaching Constantinople; for the time the Tsar was entirely taken up with the Far East question, and agreed, or at all events affected to agree, to everything that Francis Joseph wanted. Francis Joseph was on a visit to the Tsar in St. Petersburg. He did not, if the truth were told, gain the happiest of impressions from his Russian visit, but the two rulers actually agreed that they would embark on no enterprise in the Balkans without mutual consultation and agreement; that they would discuss all Balkan problems and come step by step to agreement over them. Russia declared herself to have no interest in the Bosphorus, although Emperor William, in his zeal for Russia, was urging that Emperor Francis Joseph should not necessarily stand in the way of the Russians if they wanted Constantinople.

'We must put the Balkans under a glass shade,' Prince Lobanov declared, 'until we have settled other and more urgent matters.'

'I am not interested in the slightest in Constantinople,' the Tsar assured the German Emperor in Wiesbaden. 'My whole interest is centred on China—it is China that I am watching.'

That emphatic statement, it is true, did not prevent the Russian Emperor, in a Crown Council which he summoned shortly afterwards in St. Petersburg, from passionately advocating the carrying out of a *coup* against Constantinople. He was supported by Grand Duke Vladimir Alexandrovitch and Pobedonostzev, the head of the Synod, and it was only with great difficulty that Witte, the Minister of State, was able to get the plan shelved.

Germany's new friendship with Russia, and the steady worsening of her relations with Britain, were witnessed with some concern by the Triple Alliance Powers. The Viennese Cabinet was troubled at the estrangement with Britain. It was with discomfort that the Austro-Hungarian statesmen observed anything that might cloud their old friendship, never before interrupted by any coolness, with Great Britain. And Italy was well aware that at all times she was at the mercy of the British navy.

Apart from this, the relations between Austria-Hungary and Italy at the moment were scarcely those of allies revelling in one another's friendship. King Humbert had visited Emperor Francis Joseph in Vienna, and the Emperor had promised to go to Rome to return the visit. But King Humbert died, and the Emperor did not go to Rome. The Vatican had demanded that the Emperor's first visit should be to the Holy Father; only after that should he go to the Quirinal. King Victor Emmanuel felt deeply injured. He spoke unreservedly about it to Emperor William. The Austro-Hungarian Ambassador in Berlin, Count Szögyény, asked Emperor William to suggest ways in which Emperor Francis Joseph could make the visit in spite of the wrecking and unneighbourly attitude of the Vatican, and this Emperor William had done. But Emperor Francis Joseph refused to entertain the idea. The Austrian unfriendliness towards the Italian royal house and the Italian people did not pass away. It damaged the solidity of the Triple Alliance, which had been Emperor William's concern in making his suggestion, much more seriously than was thought in Vienna. It was, indeed, the first serious flaw that had developed in its structure.

About the same time Italy suffered grave reverses in Abyssinia. Her colonial forces were invested in Kassala by the Abyssinian troops. Emperor William suggested that Britain should send help. Britain, however, delayed. Lord Salisbury allowed the

Mediterranean Agreement to lapse. His method of assisting the besieged Italians was to despatch British troops to effect their liberation by occupying Assuan. The Italians in their utter military discomfiture declared that they would never march against Britain; but this dubious offer from a beaten nation did nothing to improve the relations either of the Triple Alliance or of Germany with Britain. Several times, amid the unpleasantnesses deliberately exchanged between the two sides, Emperor William dropped new hints of alliance with Britain. Lord Salisbury ignored the suggestion again and again—or, as the Kaiser put it, now as ever. The Kaiser went on with his Russian policy, his policy of a Continental Alliance. If any opportunity came of showing Britain that Germany was not entirely to be ignored or overborne, he made careful use of it.

This enterprise with an eastern policy aimed at conquering the west lasted nearly three years. For nearly three years the display of ill-will, defiance and aversion was continued in order ultimately to win over a Britain ready to treat a friend as a friend. Russia, Germany, France, Austria were all for the preservation of the Turkish Empire. When Crete rose against the Sultan, they united to prevent the cession of the island to the Greeks, who had British support. Crete became autonomous, but subject to the Turkey whom Britain wanted to partition. In Macedonia, where the peace was never secure from moving bands, Britain was for the sharpest measures; but nothing was done beyond the reforms agreed on by the Powers.

It was at this time that Emperor William said

146

plainly to Colonel Swaine, the British Military Attaché in Berlin, that 'Britain's whole attitude' was 'simply compelling' him 'to make common cause with Russia and France.' Shortly before this Baron von Marschall, the Secretary of State, had assured the British Ambassador that the issues still unsettled between the Continental States were likely to be 'settled without regard to British interests, and even with British interests availed of as objects of compensation.' The Kaiser had spoken to the Military Attaché in a tone of thorough exasperation; afterwards he had recommended British adhesion to the Triple Alliance. In speaking to the Ambassador, the Secretary of State had brought to bear only his brusqueness. Any dispassionate observer of the strange relations between Britain and Germany could have had no doubt that they could end only in one of two ways—war or an alliance.

There were moments when the actual outbreak of hostilities between the two Powers hung by a thread; moments in which the Kaiser, with his fundamental though undisclosed inclination towards Britain, was entirely at his wit's end. There were moments in which he yielded to suggestions from his responsible advisers, or refrained from vetoing steps which they intended to make, and at once regretted having done so. His Cabinet was constantly on the watch for an opportunity of wresting from Britain, in spite of her obstinate egoism, some tangible momentary advantage, a bit of colonial territory, a naval base; that was their one interest. His own aim was the alliance that would smooth away every difficulty. Two incidents made him doubt whether an understanding with Britain would ever be possible—the Jameson Raid on Johannesburg, and the great massacre of Armenians in Turkey.

The British irritation over the railway line to Lorenzo Marques, the British push to the ocean, just between German South-west Africa and the Portuguese territory, in order definitely to separate the two lands, and Dr. Jameson's raid—all were directly connected together; behind them all there stood the great genius of Cecil Rhodes. Long before, Rhodes had come to the Cape, a sick man, with no fortune whatever. He dug for diamonds, and worked his way up. Companies came into being of which he was the life and the body. In the end he became the most powerful man in Cape Colony. He was a *condottiere* of ardent initiative, of cool judgment of every practical issue, of unbending will—one of the men of great adventures of their own seeking who have stood forth in the end as founders of states and conquerors of sub-continents, a *condottiere* and statemaker of the type of Lord Hastings, of a type of which Britain has had many others, destined to be entered in later years in the tale of her heroes.

Grown to fabulous wealth and power, Rhodes pushed out into the immense plains which stretch behind the Portuguese territory, spreading northwest from the Transvaal into the interior of the continent. He took possession of the whole country, with no sort of authorization, entirely out of his own great resources—conquering vast new lands for Britain. Rhodesia, which he presented to the British Crown, was eight or ten times the size of the German Empire; together with Cape Colony it made up a very substantial fraction of the whole continent. Cecil Rhodes had yet further dreams, clear-cut and dynamic as all his dreams were: the conquest of Rhodesia was but the beginning of a progress that had started at the southern extremity of the continent and was only to end when Egypt had been reached. Then his full purpose would be achieved—the unification of the whole of the British possessions in eastern Africa, a single province from Cairo to the Cape. Unique in one respect was the creative work of this state-maker and tamer of a continent: his strategy knew no weapons. He fought with money, with railways and telegraph lines. The first line of communications for which he was working and scheming ran from the Cape to Cairo. The Transvaal stood in its path. The Boers and their country must become British sooner or later; they were the missing piece necessary if all the rest were to be bound into a British whole. He had no thought of bringing up guns against these Dutch settlers; his way was to encircle them. He had brought the British down to the Ocean between Germans and Boers. He had laid hands on Rhodesia, hemming the Boers in on the north. On their east was Portuguese territory, in which the British had great influence. The Transvaal was completely encompassed: the day would come when it must become British without a shot being fired or a soldier engaged.

Yet a shot suddenly was fired. Even kings by their own right and might have their viceroys. Dr. Jameson was Cecil Rhodes's representative in Rhodesia, Rhodes remaining at the fountain-head of his power, in Cape Town. The Transvaal was a gold country. A fifth or a quarter of all the gold on the earth's surface was extracted from its goldfields. The Boers prospected for gold, fifteen thousand Germans in Johannesburg were searching for it, and the number of British goldseekers coming into the Transvaal grew daily. Rhodes's grip on the Transvaal would be tightened, the capitulation of the Boers hastened, if the British immigrants into the country were granted the franchise. This, however, the Boers refused to allow. They prolonged the period of domicile required for naturalization to eleven years. Cecil Rhodes himself was ready to wait as long as that, for he had other resources against the Boers and was aware that they would be unable to hold out under his pressure. His objective was a new giant realm, a sort of new India; it would bring its gold with it. But the immigrant traders in Johannesburg, the British trading company installed with its charter in Rhodesia, and above all two Englishmen who formerly had been merchants in Hamburg, had no intention of waiting so long. They were not interested in Cecil Rhodes's dream of a giant realm, they were after gold. They incited Jameson to prepare a raid on Boer territory. These two business men were friends of Cecil Rhodes. They had worked with him in various enterprises. They did not communicate their plans to Rhodes, but Jameson saw no risk in allowing himself to be won over to schemes advocated by close friends of Cecil Rhodes. Rhodes had conquered Rhodesia for Britain; he had become a very great man. Quite apart from his own hunger for gold, which was not insatiable, Jameson determined now to conquer the Transvaal for his country. On his invading the Boer Republic the British settlers in Johannesburg would be bound to rise. He got together a troop of bandits ready for any adventure, together with mounted police and porters employed by the Chartered Company, and struck his blow. On the last day of 1895 he invaded the Transvaal.

At once a storm of protest broke out all over the world.

No one knew that the British Government had had no part whatever in the enterprise. Not a word had reached London either from Rhodes or from Jameson to convey the slightest hint of the intended raid. It was a painful surprise for the Cabinet, all the more since no one had any belief in its innocence. Immediately there was enormous excitement in Germany. Britain was trampling under foot a tiny, defenceless nation, half related to the Germans. She cared nothing for the fact that other nations had interests and rights in the Transvaal. There were fifteen thousand Germans living in Johannesburg, but bandits were shooting all over the town, and amid the chaos the Germans were defenceless. The agitation was shared alike by Kaiser and Cabinet and by the whole German nation. No one had any complaint to make of others' exaggeration of the case. Baron von Marschall and Baron Holstein not only saw a dark future; they made it dark. In all the long series of Britain's arbitrary and ruthless proceedings in the past there had been nothing that approached the evil arrogance of the Jameson raid. Count Hatzfeldt must ask for his passport if the British Cabinet approved what had happened in the Transvaal.

But Lord Salisbury did not approve of it. Moreover, he courteously reminded the German Ambassador

that there was in any case not much point in threatening Britain. The news reached Berlin that fighting
was going on between Jameson and the Boers. Count
Hatzfeldt had to deliver another Note to London:
Germany would permit no change 'in the international status of the South African Republic, which is
guaranteed by treaties.' Count Münster, the German
Ambassador in Paris, was instructed to make cautious
inquiries of the French Government as to France's
readiness to co-operate with Germany in opposition
to the incessant expansion of Britain's colonial power.
Orders, questions, notes, threats came hot on one
another's heels. The Kaiser, agitated and exasperated, morally shocked and politically bewildered, had
agreed to them all. He was, indeed, thoroughly unsettled and disillusioned; for some time it seemed to
him that his policy was entirely upset. His advisers,
moreover, pointed out to him that in a constitutional
State the Cabinet determines policy. Before he was
clear in his mind as to the whole affair, Baron von
Marschall recalled the second Note transmitted to
Count Hatzfeldt. It was no longer needed: the Boers
had thoroughly defeated Jameson and his followers
near Krugersdorf. Late at night the Ambassador in
London hurried to the Foreign Office. He received
the Note back, still sealed.

On the following morning, January 3, 1896, the
Kaiser went to see Prince Hohenlohe, the Chancellor.
There had been no definite arrangement for a discussion, but he felt the need to talk over all the excite-
ments of the moment. The morning passed amid
dramatic tension; for Baron von Marschall, the Secretary of State, had been greatly agitated from the

very moment when the news of the Raid reached him. He had written in his diary on December 31, 1895:

'Now we must act.'

On that same New Year's Eve he had driven over to the New Palace in Potsdam, to see Emperor William. He had suggested that a landing party should be ordered to proceed from the *Seeadler* through Lorenzo Marques to Pretoria, to protect the Germans. The Kaiser had agreed to this. Then news had come in streams from Transvaal, more and more serious in nature. On January 2 the Secretary of State repeated his adjuration to himself:

'Now the time has come for action.'

But the outbreak of hostilities had seriously upset his nerves. On December 31—quite apart from the instructions which he had sent to Count Hatzfeldt in London—he assured the British Ambassador, Sir Frank Lascelles, in the course of a talk 'on the Transvaal question,' that 'the day will come when the Continental Powers may come to an understanding at Britain's expense, and cut straps out of British leather.' Twenty-four hours later he was incautious enough to speak in similarly ill-weighed terms to Herbette, the French Ambassador, conveying the suggestion of a Continental understanding against Britain.

His eagerness to act had not died down when the Kaiser met the Chancellor. The atmosphere and the course of the discussion were determined by the Secretary of State. He spoke excitedly and voluminously. He was 'the only one pursuing positive ideas of action.' The question was raised of a protectorate over the Boer Republic, which stood in such need of it. But the idea was dropped again at once.

The conversation turned once more to the landing
party from the *Seeadler*; but the Admirals were reluctant. The Kaiser pointed to the necessity of ordering
a detachment of marines to stand by. It might be
necessary to send them out to replace the crews sent
inland from the *Seeadler*; otherwise the ship would be
temporarily put out of action. That question was also
dropped. In the midst of his own proposals, the Secretary of State went out of the room in search of
Geheimrat von Holstein and *Geheimrat* Kayser, the
head of the Colonial section of the Ministry; the two
were waiting in readiness, in case they were called on
for anything, in an adjoining room. Immediately
afterwards the Secretary of State returned with the
draft of a telegram.

He laid the draft telegram before the Kaiser. It
was addressed to the President of the South African
Republic, and congratulated him on having warded
off Jameson's assault and on the resolution with
which 'the independence of the country had been
defended from attacks from without.' The intention
underlying the telegram was unmistakable. Ostensibly it was addressed to President Kruger. Actually
it was hurled against Britain.

The Kaiser put the paper aside. He refused to sign
it. Baron Marschall once more demanded his signature, almost peremptorily. With the Kaiser there had
come the Secretary of State for the Navy, Admiral
Hollman. He took the Kaiser's side. He agreed with
the Kaiser in describing the document as 'incredible.'
A discussion followed; Kaiser and Admiral held to
their opinion. Prince Hohenlohe joined in the discussion. The Secretary of State, Baron Marschall, had

already convinced him of the need for the telegram.
It was needed mainly, the Chancellor and Secretary
of State argued, not for its effect on the Boers and on
Britain, but to satisfy public opinion in Germany.
Prince Hohenlohe adopted a graver tone than was
usual with him. He spoke as Chancellor of the Empire. He was there, he said, to represent the wishes of
the nation, as represented in the Reichstag, to the constitutional Ruler. He 'demanded' of the Ruler that he
'should perform his constitutional duty to his people,
in accordance with the carefully considered proposals
determined on by his advisers, for which the Chancellor, not the Kaiser, bore the full responsibility.'

There was only one way out for the Kaiser—to dismiss the Chancellor, and with him the Secretary of
State. He would then have stood entirely alone in the
difficult situation; not only that, but no one would
have believed that his reason for the double dismissal had been simply his determination not to sign
the telegram. Apart from that, the telegram was declared to be demanded by public opinion. It was not
likely that the Chancellor and Secretary of State had
acted without consulting *Geheimrat* von Holstein.
He could not dismiss the whole Foreign Ministry;
or if he did, he would be thought to be mad. If
another Chancellor came, the same process would
begin over again. He would have to set up absolute
rule before he could prevent the despatch of a telegram which he regarded as a mistaken one. He
signed, and threw down the pen:

'I have been badly advised. . . . Long after you are
dead, my dear Uncle, I shall have to pay for it with a
war against Britain.'

155

The Prince was little impressed by the Kaiser's remark. Nor was Baron von Marschall disturbed:

'It will pass, your Majesty.'

'You have made an end,' the Kaiser replied, 'of my visits to Cowes.'

The telegram was sent off. The storm of indignation in Germany on behalf of the Boers had its counterpart in England in a storm of indignation over this intervention from without in her domestic affairs. All Britain was aflame with a sense of outrage, no longer troubling whether the British Cabinet had any responsibility for the events in the Transvaal or not. That was one question; Germany's arrogance was quite another one. Baron von Marschall's declaration to Sir Valentine Chirol that the sending of the telegram had been an act of state, and had not represented the Monarch's feelings, made matters worse instead of better. It was a confidential intimation to Britain that every man in Germany, the whole German nation felt itself morally entitled to intervene. German sailors were beaten in London. British newspapers shouted for war. Not only in Britain but in Germany sensible people shook their heads over the unlucky telegram. In Britain, in Germany, in all the world it was plain to every clear-headed person that Emperor William ought to have thought twice over such a piece of folly.

The Kaiser had no knowledge of the details or the true background of the raid on the South African Republic. But he disapproved the sensational gesture which he had had to make out of alleged consideration for German public opinion. To soften the effect of the telegram he wrote a few days later to Queen

Victoria—a letter of explanation combining dutiful-
ness, peaceableness, and romanticism with the stiff,
bizarre style characteristic of him. But the incident
had left an unpleasant after-taste, and not only on
account of the attitude into which his advisers had
forced him. He determined to get rid of Baron von
Marschall at the first opportunity. His successor
should be Bernhard von Bülow, the German Ambassador in Rome, whom Count Philipp Eulenburg
never ceased recommending as the ablest of the
younger German statesmen.

But a more serious matter for the Kaiser was
Britain's attitude. Even though he credited the British Government with having really had no part in the
raid, there was no disguising the fact that Britain
went ahead step by step in the world, while nothing
was conceded to Germany. Whether Britain went
openly to work adding to her possessions or irre-
sponsible persons saved her the trouble, the effect
was the same: she grew richer and more powerful
every day. She always affected to be acting with the
utmost correctness. After the Jameson raid she cut
down the privileges of the Chartered Company of
South Africa; she brought the participants in the
adventure to justice, and punished them. All this was
perhaps genuine; or it might be merely for show. Even
Count Hatzfeldt was unable definitely to say as to that.

Ready as he was to make use of every opportunity,
the Kaiser never sacrificed even in politics his sense
of decency, loyalty to an ally, and straightforwardness.
There broke into his experiences with the Britain
whose friendship he wanted to win, the news of the
massacre of the Armenians of Turkey.

There had already been repeated instances of Turkish atrocities against the Christian Armenians in the past two years. But the events precipitated by the attack by Armenian students on the Ottoman Bank in Constantinople and the bomb-throwing from the bank, were of inconceivable horror. The Sultan ordered a massacre of the Christians, and it went on for three days. Earlier massacres had already deeply affected opinion in Britain. Time after time, after the murders of Armenians in July 1894 in the district of Samsun, Sir Arthur Nicolson, the British Chargé d'Affaires, had been instructed to protest against the 'unspeakable, inconceivable atrocities,' as Lord Rosebery had stigmatized them, with all the emphasis demanded by the indignation of the British public. Sir Arthur had already shown the courage to speak out in the most uncompromising language. After the mishandling of two Armenian professors by the Turkish courts he had carried his protest to the Grand Vizier, Said Pasha. The Grand Vizier had once more complained of the attitude of British public opinion, which 'might almost be called fanatical.' Sir Arthur telegraphed to Lord Rosebery:

'I replied that there certainly is in England a fanaticism for justice, and that I personally share it.'

In the end the two tortured professors were liberated. After the murders in Samsun the Sultan agreed to the holding of an enquiry by the British. It did not deter the Grand Seignior from replying to the attack on the Ottoman Bank by specially decreeing unprecedentedly murderous reprisals.

For three days police and Kurdish soldiers went up and down Stamboul killing. They went about it without another word. The Sultan's decree had referred only to non-Uniat Armenians. Its executors distinguished Uniat from non-Uniat at a glance. Like all Turks, they had an instinctive knowledge of the difference. The Uniat went about his work undisturbed. The non-Uniat was silently tapped on the shoulder by the police. He was then simply slaughtered with a single blow on his bent head, as fish are slaughtered. The dead bodies were thrown down by the wayside. Every two hours carts were driven through the city, to pick up the victims. Then came new murders and new collecting carts. Between fifty and eighty thousand Armenians fell in those three days.

Nowhere did indignation blaze up more furiously than in England. In every town, in every newspaper, in countless public meetings there was a wild and sincere outcry against a band of monsters. Amid it all the Kaiser recollected the plans which Lord Salisbury had discussed with him, just a year before, for the partition of Turkey into spheres of interest. The Kaiser abhorred the Turkish atrocities like any Englishman, like any other decent-minded person. But he was disturbed by the close connexion between massacre and intervention and Lord Salisbury's plans. The British people looked at the whole thing from a Christian standpoint; Lord Salisbury, beyond doubt, regarded it from the standpoints of Christianity and world policy. The Kaiser suggested that the Dardanelles forts should be dismantled, as a means of putting pressure on Turkey. That would help Lord Salisbury's plans. The Turks would be weakened, and opinion in Britain would be mollified.

Russia, too, would gain considerably; the way would be opened for her into the Mediterranean. Britain would be able to feel easier in Egypt.

Lord Salisbury agreed. British intentions against Turkey would be assisted rather than hampered. Objections came, however, from Russia. The Tsar was all for the opening of the Dardanelles, so far as Russia was concerned; but he demanded that the passage through the Straits should be prohibited for all other Powers. The Kaiser's suggestion thus came to nothing. The fires of unpolitical indignation continued to glow in Britain: eighty thousand dead, slaughtered like cattle by a 'murderous maniac.'

Ultimately Queen Victoria turned to her daughter, Empress Frederick, sending her several letters to suggest that she should use her influence with her son for joint action between Germany and Britain in regard to the Armenian atrocities. Emperor William had extracts from the Queen's letters sent to the German Ambassador in Constantinople, with instructions for a general report on the situation to be sent to him. The Ambassador reported that he had obtained incontestable evidence that the Armenians were being aided by large remittances from Britain. The massacre had been the result of bomb-throwing from the Ottoman Bank against defenceless Turkish women and children. The Armenians were the guilty party. They had, as it happened, been left in the lurch by Britain at the critical moment. Any step on Germany's part would amount to an entirely uncalled-for interference in Turkish affairs. The Ambassador advised that no action should be taken.

Later, when he returned to Berlin on leave, the

Kiel Week 1900

H.M.S. "Moltke" trainingship manning
Yards.

Kiel Week 1900

H.M.S. "(Majestic)". Torpedo-capturing evening.
Juda.

Ambassador gave further details. When the murders began, Armenians took refuge in the German Embassy. They bombarded the Ambassador with incessant questions:

'When are the Red-coats coming?'

'Haven't the Red-coats come yet?'

At first the Ambassador did not understand; then he realized that they were asking about British troops. He told them they were dreaming; but they held to their story:

'We were told from London to start a rebellion. We were then to ask British help against the Sultan. Then the British Mediterranean Fleet would arrive from Malta, send ashore a landing party at Stamboul, and depose the Sultan.'

All of them pulled money out of their pockets, shining new British sovereigns. They had had the money from 'an authority.' The Ambassador tried to bring them to reason:

'There are no Red-coats here!'

Nor had he heard anything to suggest that the British had any intention of coming. If, he said to the Kaiser, that was really how things stood, he was quite unable to understand why the British fleet had not turned up. The Turks could not have resisted with any possible prospect of success.

It was a fact that Lord Salisbury intended to send the fleet from Malta to Stamboul. He asked the Commander-in-Chief whether he could take the responsibility of passing through the Dardanelles and proceeding to Stamboul. The Admiral was prepared to do this, though he anticipated the loss of some ships. But he asked a question in turn: Could Lord

Salisbury guarantee that, if the Sultan appealed to the French for aid, the French fleet would not appear before the Dardanelles? That would make it impossible to return. Lord Salisbury was unable to give that guarantee, and the Mediterranean Fleet remained at Malta.

At the gates of Constantinople, half an hour's journey from the city, was the Armenian seminary of Rumely Hiszar. It was the headquarters of the many seminaries, spread all over Asia Minor, which were maintained out of the resources of rich Armenians and rich and pious English and Americans. Sons of distinguished Armenians, and poorer ones readily assisted, studied in these seminaries under English teachers. They were taught in English and learned English ways. The Armenian students left their seminaries for Oxford or Cambridge. They lived for years in England, and became saturated with British ways of thinking. Wherever they went in that pious country, filled with true Christian charity, they were received with the same ardent, romantic enthusiasm which had been felt by every Englishman when Byron went to Greece. The students formed Armenian conventicles; they founded literary associations; and they began, always surrounded and encouraged by British sympathy and compassion, to think of the liberation of the Armenian nation. From their fathers they had ample resources. They formed an Armenian Committee. Finally they advocated a rising against the Sultan. The same thing was constantly happening in the Turkish Empire: an oppressed race rose up against the Turks; the rising was suppressed; then came the intervention of the Powers.

The Armenians in London were unresting. Their gold flowed home in extravagant measure for distribution to the poorer students. Every day their British and American teachers told the students that Britain could not conceivably abandon them. First there came minor disturbances in Constantinople. For a while the police were very tolerant. They would put the rowdy students on board a vessel at night and send them back to their Anatolian homes. There came no rising, and no intervention, although, at all events in Asia Minor, the disorders steadily grew in importance and the patience of the police as steadily evaporated. Even the massacres of the past year had not brought really effective intervention from the Powers. Finally the students prepared to strike a blow in Constantinople, and the bombs thrown from the Ottoman Bank laid low women and children.

Then the Sultan struck. He knew that British gold had been found in the students' pockets. Nazim Pasha, the Minister of Police, reported of almost all the students whom he had arrested that their pockets had been full of sovereigns. In court they declared that they were expecting 'the British.' Abdul Hamid was nervous as to his personal safety. But he had no fear of the British; he was too well aware of the jealousies and divisions of the Powers. He did not investigate the extent to which the British Cabinet had been at work, or whether the rising had merely been encouraged by the sentimental Christianity of a few British dreamers. But so long as he was the lord of the realm he would not tolerate risings against his authority. He had no knowledge whatever of Lord Salisbury's reaction to the pressure of public opinion, of his plan of sending the fleet to Stamboul, first in order to save Christians in danger, secondly to make a beginning at last with the preliminaries to a partition of Turkey; he knew nothing of the messages between Lord Salisbury and the Commander-in-Chief of the Mediterranean Fleet. But he saw the rebellion, the gold pieces, the report of the Minister of Police. He ordered summary justice, and next day the carts began their rounds, picking up the dead.

Emperor William was speechless. He had then only the Ambassador's report, but later Nazim Pasha himself gave him further details that bore out the story. Of the fundamental causes of it all the Ambassador told him nothing, just as Count Hatzfeldt had told him nothing of the circumstances that had prompted the Jameson raid. The Ambassadors never looked beyond their palaces. All that they knew was what went on in their drawing-rooms, and what they were told by the representatives of the Powers to whom they were accredited. All that the dismayed Kaiser was enabled to see was the strange courses followed by British policy. Beneath the courtesy of the letter which he sent to Queen Victoria there was a note of challenge. He was unable to see how it would ever be possible to trust a nation with such political devices and processes. Almost he gave Britain up as beyond understanding. He did set forth the main guiding lines of his own policy. In the struggle between Turks and Greeks he joined the other Powers in supporting the Sultan against Britain. He gave express directions to von Bülow, the new Secretary of State, that he would have nothing to do with any support of Crete. Still less would he dream of acceding to the suggestion of the King of the Belgians, that the Governor of the island should in future be a German. Dual Alliance and Triple Alliance joined ostentatiously in the blockade of Crete, Britain holding aloof. During his visit to Silesia in the autumn of 1896 the Kaiser suggested to the Tsar that Russia, France, and Germany should stand firmly shoulder to shoulder against the yellow race, and also against any attempt at economic domination from America. The idea seemed to the Tsar to have something in it. He promised to discuss it with the French.

All this represented the Kaiser's scheme of isolating Britain and so bringing her perforce into an alliance. It was directly in line with his policy, as was the reopening by Count Hatzfeldt in London at the end of 1896 of the question of a firm alliance between Germany and Britain. But after the news of the Armenian murders and of Britain's supposed policy in regard to the Armenians, it was impossible for the Kaiser any longer to conceal from himself that his own feelings towards Britain were passing through a crisis. He had grown used to subordinating his own feelings to necessities of state; he was determined to conduct affairs of state with a due sense of realities; but he could subordinate nothing to justice and the banning of injustice. No nation in the world was free to indulge in such a policy as Britain's appeared to be. He recalled the conversation with Lord Salisbury at Osborne. It had revealed to him the distant future as Lord Salisbury envisaged it—Mesopotamia and Arabia as the great British causeway between Africa and Asia. Before that could be achieved, Turkey must be destroyed. As the foundation stone of the causeway, eighty thousand Armenian deaths were not too much.

The Kaiser's Christianity was not of that sort. Even in affairs of state, even if the glory of his Empire were involved, his Christianity could never be two-faced. He found Britain's hypocrisy, her brutality monstrous. No one told him that neither Lord Salisbury nor any member of the British Cabinet had had any knowledge of the British subsidies, that no Minister had given a single sovereign for an Armenian rising, or offered the slightest encouragement to any Armenian to rebel, however strangely the events might fit in with their ultimate aims.

The Kaiser had had a new and horrifying glimpse of British methods. He suffered in spirit, for he was himself half an Englishman.

Perhaps after all Tsar Nicholas was a man of better morals.

Tsar Nicholas II was entirely taken up with the expansion of the Russian dominions in the Far East. He was so little interested for the moment in Constantinople or any part of the Balkans, that on the way back to St. Petersburg he declared to Emperor William that for the present he would pay no attention at all to Balkan affairs. He agreed to the 'Protectorate' arranged on most friendly terms with Emperor Francis Joseph, the two undertaking jointly to watch over the inviolacy of the *status quo* in the Balkan peninsula. He was even reconciled with Prince Ferdinand of Bulgaria, the Prince having made the little Bulgarian Crown Prince adopt the Orthodox faith. The Tsar was a pious and God-fearing man, the Protector of his great Church, and it was now possible for an old quarrel to be buried. Prince Ferdinand was acknowledged by Russia as the lawful ruler of his country; the Tsar also did everything to induce the other European Courts to recognize Prince Ferdinand. Meanwhile he unostentatiously secured a series of small advantages from the Chinese. He had assured the Kaiser of his inextinguishable gratitude for Germany's treatment of Japan. Rear-Admiral von Tirpitz suggested that a coaling station should be acquired either in Kiaochow or Shantung, and the German Government made a fresh attempt to carry the plan into execution. It approached China and pointed out the services that Germany had rendered to the Chinese in the war; it counted on Chinese complaisance in regard to an acquisition of territory which it intended to make with or without that complaisance. That polite enquiry had been addressed to China a year before. Now the Germans began serious negotiations with the Russians in regard to Kiaochow.

It became clear that no one but the Tsar looked at all benevolently on the Kaiser's plans. His Cabinet seemed to take the obligation to show gratitude for Germany's services less seriously. Russia had already, at France's instance, defeated the efforts of the German banks to participate in the loan to be raised to cover the Chinese war indemnity to Japan. The Russian Far East squadron was to winter in Kiaochow. The Russian ships were there already. Germany could just as well find some other place. Count Muraviev, the new Russian Foreign Secretary, was a man of pronounced arrogance, pride of family reinforcing his pride of country: one of his ancestors had subdued the Poles. He was also a man of extraordinary astuteness. He was not going for a moment to think of renouncing Shantung and its chief town, Kiaochow: Russia had special claims to this territory; Russian ships had put in at Kiaochow on former occasions. Count Muraviev based his claim against Germany above all on '*le droit du premier mouillage,*' the right arising from prior anchorage.

The German Foreign Ministry was put into a difficulty. It examined the grounds of the claim. Precedents were industriously turned up, to test the reality and applicability of the '*droit de premier mouillage.*' The Kaiser was astonished. He sent for Admiral von Hollmann.

'You are an old seafarer. Have you ever heard that anyone whose ship drops anchor anywhere acquires any right in doing so? Would you mind asking *Geheimrat* Perels!'

Admiral Hollmann described Count Muraviev's legal discovery as 'Bunkum.'

Geheimrat Perels, the most reliable of experts in matters of maritime law in the Kaiser's opinion and in that of many other people, looked suspiciously at the Admiral at first. But the Kaiser's envoy, who was anxious to obtain the *Geheimrat's* opinion without influencing him in any way, put his question quite impartially, in the clearest and most straightforward way.

'Pure idiocy!' declared the *Geheimrat.* He wrote a memorandum in very decided terms; the Kaiser transmitted it to the Tsar. In the whole world there was no such thing as a '*droit du premier mouillage.*'

Count Muraviev evidently liked hatching jokes as a contribution to world history. His chartered right, his impressive language, his whole claim had been pure invention. The next time he began to talk in Peterhof of his *'droit du premier mouillage,'* the Kaiser laughingly referred him to the memorandum. That was the last time Count Muraviev spoke of his discovery. Emperor William proceeded to negotiate concerning Kiaochow in Peterhof with the Tsar.

Before going away he summoned Admiral von Hollmann to another audience concerning that Far East port.

'Ice-free?' the Kaiser asked.

'Yes, quite.'

Rear Admiral von Tirpitz had made inquiries of the Senior officer of the Russian Far East squadron.

'I had to lie at anchor there a whole winter,' the Russian Admiral replied.

'And what is it like there?' asked Tirpitz.

'Frightful!' the Russian answered. 'An old Chinese military camp. A horrible place. No bars, no dancing. Not a Japanese girl to be had there. I complained to my Government.'

The Russian officers' disapproval of Shantung and Kiaochow did not convince the Kaiser of the undesirability of the place. He told the Tsar at Peterhof that he would give Kiaochow a trial at all events.

'I would rather have you there than the English,' said the Tsar; 'I am quite content.'

'How far does your sphere of influence extend?' asked the Kaiser.

'About half-way along the Peiho and to the farther environs of Peking.'

Emperor William asked whether the Tsar was ready for Germany 'to settle along the other side.'

The Tsar agreed entirely. Nicholas II was not forgetful of services rendered.

'How much satisfaction has your Majesty got?' asked the old Adjutant-General Mussin Pushkin, who had been attached to the Kaiser's suite. 'How are you getting on with the Tsar?'

'The Emperor and I agree on everything.'

The old Adjutant-General did not seem very enthusiastic.

'There is something,' he said, 'which I am in duty bound to point out to your Majesty. I am very glad to hear that all goes well between your Majesty and the Tsar. But I must warn your Majesty not to fall into the mistake of assuming that if the Tsar says he agrees with your Majesty he actually does. If the Tsar differs on any subject but does not want to say so, he has a habit of avoiding discussion by entering entirely into the standpoint of his interlocutor. Consequently I can only advise your Majesty, if the Tsar seems to be entirely of your own opinion, to drop the subject. For the Tsar will certainly not be of your opinion.'

The Kaiser was disgusted. There was a hesitancy, a timorousness about the Tsar: often he would drop into an embarrassed silence in conversation. The Kaiser had taken this for shyness. He had been hesitant and shy as Cesarevitch at Coburg. The only occasion on which he had let himself go had been in his one sentence of thanks. In Silesia he had quietly assured the Kaiser that Russia was entirely abandoning her dream of Constantinople. That whole question, of such consequence to Russia, so burning a question for centuries past, the Tsar had treated as so absolutely closed that Emperor William had been rather astonished. The question was whether his attitude was dictated by his uncertainty; whether he had to be drilled into certainty; whether he walled himself off by an assent in order to do what he chose in the end or in order to cover himself while he consulted his advisers; or whether he was just playing with people and issues and aspirations.

'Your Majesty would do well,' the Adjutant-General advised, 'to be sure always to be the last to leave the Tsar's apartment.'

'But,' the Kaiser cried, 'I cannot rule Germany from Peterhof!'

The Tsar's entourage were very unrestrained in their confidences to Emperor William, and left a curiously uncomfortable impression on their guest. One of the Russian dignitaries told him how he had himself been mystified as to the character of the Tsar, and had actually told him so.

'*N'oubliez pas*,' Nicholas had replied, '*que je suis slave.*'

At times there was something in the look of Tsar Nicholas which was not to be explained by the dark, almost sensuous mysticism which he shared with the German princess, and which had undoubtedly been one of the things that had attracted him to her. There was something unspoken and unconfessed in the silent glance which he would give his interlocutor, always to withdraw it sideways at once, never letting it rest. Suddenly the Kaiser saw again in spirit the marginal notes which the Tsar had put on a report from his Minister of War. The Minister had drawn up the report on behalf of the General Staff, and had

sketched in it a plan of attack on Japan. Everywhere
on it there were notes in the Tsar's writing:

'Strike there and there.'

'Annihilate, annihilate, annihilate!'

'Take the whole lot prisoner.'

'Depose the Mikado.'

They were childish notes, but not only childish.
Emperor William also recalled the account given to
him by one who had accompanied Nicholas as
Cesarevitch to Japan, of an incident on the way. The
heir to the Russian throne had been visiting a
Japanese temple with Prince George of Greece. His
fear and reverence of the Deity were kept for Orthodox surroundings. The Princes merely made fun of
the gods in the temple. In front of the temple was an
enclosure in which ducks regarded as sacred by the
Japanese swam in a pond. It amused the Cesarevitch
and Prince George to shoot and throw stones at the
ducks. Suddenly a Japanese sprang up from behind
the temple. With his curved Japanese sword he
silently struck the Cesarevitch slantingly over the
head. The wound healed slowly and with difficulty.
After that, whenever there was mention of Japan his
gaze became fixed and his eyes glowed.

The Kaiser returned to Germany oppressed rather
than relieved. Even Tsar Nicholas was not entirely
to be trusted.

The negotiations with the Russians over Kiaochow
were continued from Berlin. The reply from the Tsar
to Emperor William's question put in Peterhof, when
it arrived in official garb, stated that Emperor
Nicholas was unable to renounce Kiaochow until he
could find a substitute for it elsewhere. But if Ger-

man ships wanted to winter in Kiaochow the Tsar agreed to that.

The German Foreign Ministry now informed the Russian Secretary of State, Count Muraviev, that Germany intended to approach China with regard to the entry of German ships into the port of Kiaochow. The Russian Admiral would be informed before their arrival. On this, however, Count Muraviev raised objections. Germany, he said, had agreed to come to an arrangement with Russia before despatching the ships. Meanwhile the German Minister in Peking reported that Li Hung-chang had actually leased the port to the Russians for fifteen years. Negotiations continued, obscurely and amid deep mutual suspicion. Then came the murder of two German Catholic missionaries in the south of Shantung. Rapid and decided action followed. Prince Hohenlohe determined there and then to have a quick settlement of the whole question, and went to work with energy. The Foreign Ministry doubted the wisdom of replying to the murder of the priests by the seizure of Kiaochow, whether the Russians liked it or no; but its apprehensions were swept away before the old Chancellor's resolution. The Foreign Ministry had informed the Kaiser that there were no ships available for an expedition to Kiaochow. He went to see Prince Hohenlohe in Letzlingen, in order to arrive at a definite decision in regard to the port. The Chancellor at once fell in with the Kaiser's ideas. He had already concluded his preliminaries for the coup in the Far East port. He had sent demands to Peking for punitive measures to be taken in regard to the murder of the priests, and he had little expectation of

Chinese compliance. He concurred in the despatch
of Prince Henry with a German squadron to the Far
East. He was entirely in agreement with the Kaiser
on every detail. The Kaiser, in any case, was clearly
no longer to be deterred from carrying out his purpose. The officials in the Foreign Ministry were
against it; and the Kaiser's entourage also spoke appre-
hensively of the great risks involved. The Prince was
unmoved—

'I care nothing about that: the Kaiser is entirely in
the right.'

In the forest of Letzlingen the decision was made
to despatch the German squadron under Prince
Henry to Tsingtao. At the end of the year the
squadron sailed.

Whenever the Tsars had spoken of the conquest
of the Straits, the motive which they had adduced
to the masses in Russia, and to the world at large,
for this plan of political expansion had been the
pious desire to nail the sacred double eagle on the
doors of St. Sophia. Amid the storms of indignation
that were still raging in Britain a year after the
Kaiser's telegram to President Kruger, an article published in the *Saturday Review* attracted much attention and had a lasting influence. It called for war with
Germany and gave a list of all the centres of world
trade in which German business men were competing
with the English. Into all these centres, according to
the *Saturday Review*, into the Transvaal, the Cape,
Central Africa, the Far East, the British flag had
'followed the Bible.' Russia set out to be the defender
of the Faith among the Osmanli, Britain on all sorts of
occasions. Prince Henry's reference, in his speech

before sailing, to the Kaiser's evangel, which he intended to preach before the world, was an indiscretion. The Kaiser's phrase in reply, heightened in colour as so often by his love of the oratorical and the picturesque—'If any should think of interfering with our just rights, have at them with the mailed fist!'—was uncalled for and ill-considered. But not one among the other Powers who sent their missionaries to every corner of the earth, to convert the poor heathen from error to faith and from their native savagery to the provision of raw materials, had any moral right to point a finger at the Kaiser and the Prince except on grounds of form. Nor did they: they observed a discreet silence. And while Germany at last got her one and only coaling station at the ends of Asia, they all, without any uncalled-for eloquence, entered thoroughly into the task of sharing the fruits of the sanguinary victory which Japan had won. The price was paid by China, who had enjoyed their friendship and support. Russia occupied Port Arthur, for which Japan had fought. She also annexed Dalny. Kiaochow remained German. France took Kwang-chow. Nor could Britain forgo participation in the general campaign for compensations for a settlement of differences between a Mongol nation and other yellow peoples. She went after Wei-hai-wei. Every page of this section of the world's history is filled with marching missionaries, marching soldiers, guns fired in Christian charity, conquest, domination, an orgy of violence and violation. General Baratieri marched for the Kingdom of Italy to the disaster of Adowa. France grudged the Italians their success before they gained it, and pushed also into the interior

of Abyssinia, from the coastal villages of Dobosk and
Shubuti. General Kitchener penetrated into the
Sudan and occupied Dongola and Berber. Captain
Marchand marched into the Sudan from another
point in France's interest, in order to forestall the
English. The English forestalled the French in
occupying the mouths of the Niger. Already they
were in Ashanti. Meanwhile France had made Madagascar a French colony, and had paved the way for
her suzerainty in Tunisia. But Britain outpaced all:
she had conquered Rhodesia, a continent within the
continent.

Yet Britain was not content. Germany could quite
safely be refused anything. She was merely troublesome and unmannerly. Only Germany imagined that
she was a world power because *Geheimrat* Holstein
sent threatening Notes from time to time to London
about the Bagdad Railway, or 'lectured' Britain. But
there was another Power whom Britain did fear—
France was marching forward. She had made Siam
her own sphere. She had annexed Madagascar and
Tunis, within a startlingly short time. She was demanding the evacuation of Egypt. She was forcing
the pace in the Sudan. She had come to terms with
Germany about Togoland. She was negotiating with
Germany about the Zambesi delta. She was more
influential on the Bosphorus than Britain had ever
been. A British Admiral had been unable to carry out
the plans of the British Cabinet for fear of the French
navy.

Yet Germany might become dangerous one day, if
the Continental Alliance for which the Kaiser seemed
to be working ever materialized. And France would

then be more dangerous than ever. Germany was the stepchild among the colonial Powers. She had arrived too late. The German Empire was not yet thirty years old. It might be possible to win Germany over to friendship with Britain if she were met in a real spirit of accommodation. France had too much already to rest content with modest offers.

Germany had sought an alliance with Britain five, even six times. And now the German Kaiser had made common cause twice with Russia and France— at Shimonoscki and on the Cretan question.

Old Gladstone, the friend of France, no longer stood in the way. Joseph Chamberlain, the new Secretary of State for the Colonies, now offered Germany an alliance.

Chapter V

TWO ROAD BUILDERS

JOSEPH CHAMBERLAIN, Secretary of State for the Colonies, had grown weary of the friction and trouble in British relations with all the world. Great Britain was entirely isolated among the Powers, and dependent wholly on her own strength and resources; everywhere for a long time past she had been pursued by envy and intrigue where any others were in a position to compete with her for influence and dominion. Unwelcome neighbours established themselves on the borders of her own territories. Rich areas in distant places which she had long regarded as her own private preserves, or at least those of her traders, were proving not so amenable to her guidance and control of their policy and trade as to leave her still sole mistress of their fate. Aims which she had set before herself in far corners of the earth suddenly became also the aims of other Powers. On various occasions—in the Sino-Japanese war, in Turkish questions, in the Cretan rising—the Powers had actually succeeded in forming a common front in face of which Britain had had to forgo her plans and aspirations. It was not difficult to perceive that Emperor William, who was always full of expressions of friendship towards Russia and of readiness to meet her wishes, was deliberately working for the gradual formation of a Continental coalition in Europe. If that were to come

178

into being, Britain would be robbed of her power, perhaps brought into a difficult and perilous situation. All through the last few years Britain and Germany had lived together on terms which could not be called excessively friendly. They had given plenty of annoyance to one another. But their differences had been a small matter, in spite of the acute situations produced by Dr. Jameson's raid on the Boers and the Kaiser's telegram to President Kruger, in comparison with the Russian menace to British plans of expansion in the Far East; and still more so in comparison with the unending series of grave clashes with the French since the beginning of the 'nineties. Egypt had been one of the principal anxieties during this period of British colonial history. The French had again and again demanded her evacuation. They had been well aware that General Kitchener had set out for the Sudan in order to safeguard the southern borders of Egypt as well as the territory already occupied; and yet they had themselves marched on the same objective. There was no telling what conflicts all this would inevitably produce ere long. If the French succeeded in the Sudan the whole Egyptian question would be opened up anew.

'Those French,' the Colonial Secretary had said again and again recently in conversation, 'are impossible people. They have their understanding with Russia. The best safeguard against that is an alliance with Germany. Those people'—the French—'are doing just the same to us as Spain did. We have had enough of that. With an alliance with Germany we can dictate peace to all the world!'

Joseph Chamberlain was young, clear-headed,

energetic. He was a big commercial man in politics.
He knew that the best way to make sure of one's own
advantage is to put good things in the way of the
partner with whom one intends to work. There was
nothing doing in the world unless the world was at
peace. In alliance with Germany, Britain could enforce peace. Then the two could proceed to business
to mutual advantage. He thought along quite simple,
broad lines. He meant to have the courage to proceed
along them and enter them in the book of the world's
destiny. Lord Salisbury, however, listened with
scepticism to his Colonial Minister's projects. He was
an old man. His statesmanship had always aimed at
producing tangible business results for Britain; but
in his statesmanship, in his control of politics and
diplomacy, while the first axiom was the greatness of
Britain the main thing was the command of technique and craftsmanship; that was for him the whole
art of statesmanship, and he had never accorded
front rank to the business man. He stood for a statesmanship of pure diplomacy; Chamberlain stood for a
counting-house deal between States. Lord Salisbury,
himself a man of cautious calculation, always brought
psychological factors into his reckoning, with whomever he was dealing. Chamberlain set above all else
the lure and the logical force of figures. Lord Salisbury was a man of long and wide experience. From
the days of Prince Bismarck's Russian policy to the
conversation with the Kaiser on the partition of
Turkey, he had experienced nothing but disillusionments. The young Chamberlain was only beginning
his first attempts at constructive achievement. Lord
Salisbury had no enthusiasm whatever for Chamber-

lain's picture of the future of Britain and Germany in partnership. He had no faith in its realization. For the moment, however, he allowed the Colonial Secretary to go ahead.

Joseph Chamberlain spoke out his whole mind. Difficulties, he considered, should not be made for the Russians in the Far East. They ought to keep Port Arthur, and Talienwan ought to remain under their influence. Britain should recognize the whole of Manchuria as a Russian sphere of influence. But with those wide new territories Russia should remain content for the present. If Germany would enter into an open alliance with Britain, no changes would be possible in the Far East or elsewhere in the world without the consent of both of them. He pointed out to Germany that the differences which Britain had with France and Russia were not unbridgeable in the long run. He did not do as the German statesmen had invariably done in announcing their wishes in the past, and offer threats as to what would happen if they failed to come to terms; but he admitted and laid stress on the fact that in emerging from her 'splendid isolation,' which had been rendered obsolete and valueless by the frequent combinations of late between the Powers, Britain had only the choice between Germany and Germany's two neighbours. Germany stood nearer to her, if only on account of the many interests which they had in common.

Germany had been endeavouring for many years to secure an alliance with Britain. The Kaiser had on various occasions worked for a great Continental coalition, but his main purpose in those efforts had been to win Britain entirely over to Germany. As

181

recently as the end of 1897 and beginning of 1898, Count Hatzfeldt, the Ambassador in London, had had many conversations in London in accordance with instructions from Berlin. Britain was to contribute to a rapprochement by helping Germany to acquire Kiaochow if the Russians made difficulties. In accordance with instructions from Secretary of State von Bülow, the Ambassador dropped all sorts of hints. The Russians had suggested an alliance against Britain. Germany was ready to support Britain if she decided to protest against the annexation of Hawaii, where the Americans had established themselves. Britain took these assurances of German friendship very coldly, and when Count Hatzfeldt gave expression to the desire in Germany for an opportunity of British-German collaboration at least 'somewhere in the world,' there came not the slightest hint from Britain as to where or on what matter any opportunity might exist.

Now suddenly the very purpose of German foreign policy, and especially of the Kaiser's, was attained. Surprising, however, as was the offer from the British Colonial Minister, the attitude of the German Cabinet was no less so.

Secretary of State von Bülow suddenly discovered that there was, after all, little to be gained for Germany from an alliance with Britain. Chamberlain had given an express assurance that Britain had no thought of making war on Russia. But the German Secretary of State was thoroughly convinced that Britain had secret intentions of doing so. She had numbers of armoured ships. Those would be of no service to Germany if she were at war with Russia and her ally France. That Britain could hold France in check with her navy alone along the French Atlantic and Mediterranean coasts and by threatening her colonies, that Italy was bound to gird up her loins and march with Britain at the word of command, that Britain had again and again fought with great armies of her own on the Continent from the days of Joan of Arc onwards, at Blenheim, at Oudenarde, at Malplaquet, at Waterloo—and that the man in the street in Germany was exercised over all this and discussed it as always in terms of well-worn stock phrases which in reality were entirely irrelevant— all this Bülow knew well, and dismissed it. He refused to enter into 'the gamble of a treaty,' and declined the alliance so long sought with Britain at the very moment when it seemed to have been attained. *Geheimrat* Baron Holstein held the same view of Chamberlain's offer; he only formulated his reasons for rejecting the alliance with more mathematical precision, as was his way. Apart from that, he knew better than Joseph Chamberlain what was now in Germany's best interest.

He trusted Britain no further than he could see her. Baron Holstein was well primed in every trick of statecraft. His statecraft had never been anything but a system of smart tricks and brutal pressure; he had never had thought for anything but Germany's own immediate tangible advantage, or what he regarded as that. The advantage of any other party had never had the smallest place in his thoughts. Consequently he saw from the first in Chamberlain's offer nothing but an attempt to apply the same methods to some purely British purpose. An alliance with Britain suddenly became valueless except in two events—

(1) 'If Russia attacks us';

(2) 'If Britain is less overbearing.'

Secretary of State and *Geheimrat* agreed that the first reply offered to Britain should take the form of good advice. The suggestion was offered that she would do better to renew the agreement with Austria-Hungary and Italy, which had been allowed to lapse amid the sorenesses and cooled relations of the time. Chamberlain's hint, that, if Germany refused, Britain intended to turn to Russia and France, was met by the Secretary of State with the doubtless very clever reply that Germany could only welcome a British rapprochement and understanding with Russia, since that union would render the French alliance unnecessary to Russia. It did not occur either to the Secretary of State or to the *Geheimrat* that in the event of a war between Germany and the new alliance suggested by Chamberlain—Britain and Russia—the French, without the slightest question, would set their armies on the march to recover the provinces lost in 1870. Baron Holstein regarded both the offer of alliance made by Chamberlain and his hint of a possible Russo-British understanding as pure humbug, with no substance and no serious basis.

The Kaiser took the question more seriously than either of them, although von Bülow had only told him of the offer and had made no mention of the accompanying reference to the possibility of a Russo-British alliance. The Kaiser was keenly anxious to see Britain and Germany united in a firm bond, but he was also keenly suspicious of British methods, which he believed himself gradually to have seen through.

His only motive at any time for approach to Russia had been one of piety: friendship with Russia had been the deathbed counsel of Emperor William I. But Russia's immense forces, stored up in every part of her dominions, spoke in her favour: they would make Germany unconquerable if the two Powers were to bind themselves together against all the world. It was also in Russia's favour that Germany had ultimately acquired Kiaochow through Russian complaisance: at all events, the Russians had not stood in the way of the acquisition. Emperor William had also given the Tsar definite assurances that Germany would place no obstacles in Russia's path in the Far East. He had himself encouraged Nicholas II in his Far East policy. On the other hand, he was well aware of the aversion of the Russian people, the Russian army, Russian society against everything German. The unexpected assurances of friendship from England made the Kaiser suspicious; but he regarded the Tsar as little better than incurably deceitful. His experiences in Peterhof had helped, indeed, to confirm his impressions. Yet the Tsar was bound, after all, to be guided by monarchical principles. The Kaiser had, perhaps, more in common with his fellow-ruler than with Mr. Chamberlain or even Lord Salisbury. But if his feelings offered no steady guidance, Emperor William said to himself in the end that he had not been following an entirely Anglophil policy for some time past in order to abandon it on account of his growing suspicions at the very moment when Britain made a genuine approach to Germany. All he needed was to be on the alert. He gave his decision to the Secretary of State—the Colonial

Secretary's offer must be given a favourable reception. The thing that the Secretary of State had kept back from him, he found out for himself and pointed out: if Germany refused the offer, Britain would be bound to move towards the Dual Alliance.

But the Kaiser wanted to be guided not merely by feelings but by certainties in the matter of the British offer. In Homburg Count Metternich seconded the advice sent by Secretary of State von Bülow:

'That's what it is, your Majesty—Chamberlain wants our bayonets.'

'But against whom?' asked the Kaiser. Count Metternich gave an explanation which directly contradicted Chamberlain's statements. It was based on evidence put before him in Berlin:

'Against Russia, your Majesty!'

'But,' the Kaiser objected, 'we are utterly at peace with Russia. We cannot simply fall upon her!'

'No, I know that,' admitted Count Metternich.

'An offer of alliance from Britain is a very serious matter,' the Kaiser continued. 'If Chamberlain has let it be seen that it is envisaged with its point against Russia, give him the sketch of our tradition.'

The Kaiser had in mind a document which had always been held in reverent memory as a sort of testament by himself and his predecessors. It spoke of the comradeship in arms of Russia and Prussia in 1813, of the great war of liberation that the two countries had fought. The Russian Emperors had held the sketch in equal honour.

'Morally,' the Kaiser added, 'we are associated with Russia by all sorts of ties, and I cannot sever them all for no reason whatever!'

The Kaiser then proceeded to consider the British Constitution and the restricted powers of the British Cabinets. An agreement entered into by one Cabinet might be repudiated by its successors.

'Chamberlain must, therefore, show that he has the Ministry and Parliament behind him.'

Count Metternich was instructed to telegraph this view of the Kaiser's to Berlin. The reply came from Berlin that the British Colonial Secretary had already secured the agreement of the British Ministers. He would also secure Parliamentary approval.

'That is not enough for me,' insisted the Kaiser— 'the alliance must be announced by the Government and ratified in Parliament.'

For a while, however, the Kaiser heard no more of the matter. After some time he was given this as Lord Salisbury's alleged standpoint:

'What our good friend Chamberlain says is not to be taken too seriously!'

Suspicion arose once more in Emperor William's mind. At times he was unable to escape from the impression that Britain's only purpose was to create a diversion, in order to carry through a new coup somewhere in the world and meanwhile keep Germany in a good humour. His thoughts turned once more to Russia. He had not heard much that was encouraging about the Tsar in Peterhof. But he saw once more in front of him the young and helpless and wholly unhappy Cesarevitch, to whom he had done a great personal service in his love affair, one which had affected the Tsar's whole life. He determined to put faith in him. Bülow wanted him to take the Tsar fully into his confidence on the British

proposal. Speaking as the responsible controller of
Germany's foreign policy, Bülow demanded that the
offer should unhesitatingly be exploited with Russia,
as under the influence of the British proposal the
Tsar might agree to give double as much as Britain.
He was constantly coming with suggestions and draft
messages for the Kaiser to transmit to the Tsar, and
this time again he suggested the terms of a letter from
Emperor William to Nicholas II, putting the question. It was a matter of outstanding importance. He
sat down at a table with the Kaiser, and the two went
to work on the letter, which was despatched on
May 30, 1898, and contained the following passage:

'You will readily appreciate the tendency of this
alliance: I am informed that the idea is to join up
with the Triple Alliance and bring in Japan and
America, with both of whom preliminary negotiations have already begun. You may calculate for yourself the advantages which acceptance or refusal may
have for us! Now, as my old and trusted friend,
please tell me what you can offer and are ready to do
if I refuse.'

The courier set off for St. Petersburg with the
letter. The Kaiser wanted to secure for Germany
either collaboration with Russia or friendship with
Britain: his own preference was for a British alliance.
His anxieties would be allayed if Russia really
stretched out her hand to him. If Russia did not re-
spond to his advance he would have to accept the
British proposals, in spite of his constantly growing
doubts and suspicions. Bülow, on the other hand,
had no particular desire for any agreement with Russia. He wanted Germany to preserve her freedom;

but if she must enter an alliance, he would rather that it were with Russia. No one could say what answer the Tsar would give. But Bülow the statesman was certain that a good trump card ought to be played if one held it; and that it was the acme of smartness to play off each side against all the others, so gradually rendering everyone except oneself suspect and suspecting them on that account. In any case, whether the Tsar declined or not, Secretary von Bülow and Baron Holstein meant to go on working to lead the problem with which Chamberlain had confronted them to the solution which seemed to them the most advantageous for Germany.

Chamberlain had in view a complete understanding with Germany, an assurance on the grand scale of the power of two capable, industrious, energetic peoples against the whole world. It would follow as a matter of course that each of the two allies should help the other, increasing his possessions and wealth and standing wherever it was in any way possible. Secretary of State von Bülow and *Geheimrat* von Holstein looked at the matter in a different way: the British proposal was a first-class opportunity. So long as Britain had hopes of getting the alliance she was after, there would certainly be colonies, compensations, pickings to be got from her. Chamberlain, that shrewdly calculating business man in politics, seemed to them, in fact, a 'naïve beginner,' an estimate which Count Hatzfeldt shared.

In the middle of May 1898 the Colonial Secretary came out on the public platform and announced from Birmingham to all the world that Britain's advantage lay in good relations with America and above all in an alliance with Germany. Both von Bülow and Holstein read into that statement the emergence of the favourable opportunity for arriving at an agreement with Britain in regard to colonial acquisitions in Africa.

For some time past Portugal's two African possessions, Angola and Mozambique, had been far from prosperous. She was ready to cede them to Britain in return for a substantial loan. Once already Germany had put obstacles in the way of Britain's freedom of action by sending warships to Delagoa Bay, and so laying stress on her interest in the fate of these territories. Lord Salisbury had accordingly considered it advisable to discuss the question of the Portuguese loan with Count Hatzfeldt. At once the voice of Berlin had been heard. Germany, it declared, could not permit Britain to secure influence with the Portuguese by lending them money. She must come to terms with Germany over the future ownership of Portuguese Africa. Thereafter Germany would have no interest in Delagoa Bay. That bay was the Transvaal's outlet to the sea; but the enthusiasm for the small, oppressed nation of the Boers, which two years before had peremptorily required Emperor William's telegram to President Kruger, had evaporated in the offices of the German Ministry of State: land was land wherever one got it.

Now, however, that Britain was after so big a thing as an alliance, it was possible at once to ask more. During the Spanish-American war of that year over the possession of the Philippines, von Bülow had sent a German squadron under Admiral Diederichs to that

island group. The Americans had been unable to conceive what German warships could be after in a conflict that affected only themselves and their antagonist.
They watched the German proceedings with suspicion. The expedition came to nothing: the Secretary of State had made confidential inquiries in
London whether it would not be felt to be preferable
that the Philippines should be neutralized rather than
allow the Americans to have them, but the idea had
been politely dismissed. Von Bülow had not noticed,
or had forgotten, how in Birmingham Chamberlain
had expressly laid emphasis on the necessity of good
relations between Britain and America. In any case,
the German vessels sailed away from the Philippines
with nothing achieved.

The Secretary of State considered whether, if the
Philippines were lost to the Spaniards, the remains of
their colonies at all events—the Marianne and Caro-
line Islands—should be bought from them. He paid
little heed to the American irritation over Germany's
apparent slight pushfulness. But if the hope of
acquisitions in the Philippines had turned to dust,
the Secretary of State intended at all events to make
up for the set-back now that he was negotiating with
this Britain that so wanted his friendship. He put
forward in London a whole bundle of things that
Germany wanted: Togo and Zanzibar, Samoa and
Walfisch Bay.

Lord Salisbury had not Chamberlain's love of a
big deal; only a few weeks before he had declared to
Count Hatzfeldt:

'You are asking too much for your friendship.'

Now he was almost amused. He wondered that

Germany did not lay claim 'to all Africa.' He rejected the whole bundle of suggestions.

But for the present Chamberlain was looking beyond these questions of detail. He had the British offer of alliance re-transmitted, this time to the Kaiser through the British Ambassador in Berlin. He put the proposal in even plainer terms: the alliance was to be the expression of the mutual liability to military assistance if either of the allies were attacked by two states. Emperor William saw in this a proposal of the utmost importance. He requested that it should be examined closely and seriously if Britain should repeat it officially. Secretary of State von Bülow differed. He disapproved entirely of the idea of an alliance with Britain. If Russia learned of it, relations with her would be entirely spoiled. For that matter, he saw no great advantage even in an alliance with Russia. It was gradually becoming clear to the Secretary of State how high and powerful a position this new Imperial Germany had attained, now that the Tsar allowed his policy to be determined by German advice, now that the Tsar was unable to attain his desires in the Far East without Germany's help, now that France was compelled at Shimonoseki to act jointly with her hated enemy Germany, and now, finally, that Britain, so often wooed by Germany and until recently wooed in vain, was herself knocking at Germany's door.

Germany's power, as the Secretary of State saw it, lay in Germany's independence. He meant to preserve his freedom in regard to his ultimate choice between these friends. In *Geheimrat* von Holstein's opinion, Germany alone was entitled to this free

Admiral von Müller, Chief of H. I. M. Naval Office, The German Emperor, Captain von Ingenohl, Commander Engelhardt, Chief Executive Officer, on board the "Hamburg" observing a rowing match.

choice: if Britain imagined that she ought to be equally free to choose, this, of course, was an entire delusion of poor Chamberlain's; he was a man obviously at sea among the rude facts of the world. The Secretary of State resolved to carry out the Kaiser's command, and to examine the new British proposal with the closeness and seriousness that the case demanded and that it was his own nature to apply. He advised the Kaiser with the utmost urgency to show no readiness to meet the British, and to do nothing that might amount to a commitment. Germany was the Power that would give either Russia or Britain predominance. Nothing should be done to gamble away that power. If the Kaiser was shortly going to England, on a visit to Queen Victoria, the British should be allowed to see that the fate of the world hung in truth upon Emperor William II. The Secretary of State said all this in plain terms to the Kaiser: his 'noble master' had become *arbiter mundi*.

All these broad, statesmanlike thoughts, these profound considerations pointing to the inadvisability of a British-German alliance, even the rejection of the aspirations put before Lord Salisbury, did not deter the Secretary of State and Baron Holstein from continuing their negotiations concerning the future partition of the Portuguese Colonies in Africa. At last Britain gave way. The Portuguese loan was to be shared between Britain and Germany. The customs in South Angola and North Mozambique were to be pledged to Germany, in South Mozambique and North Angola to Britain. The two Powers were to share the ownership of these territories if, as was to be anticipated, Portugal desired one day to sell her African possessions outright. Britain and Germany undertook to take common action against any intervention from other States in the affairs of the two colonies and against any attack on them.

Chamberlain regarded the agreement as a sort of payment on account, which should now be followed by the conclusion of the alliance. Von Bülow had suggested that first of all the earlier treaties with Austria-Hungary and Italy should be renewed; in reply to this Chamberlain had informed Berlin that it was Germany above all and now Germany alone with whom Britain desired close co-operation. Von Bülow, however, was silent. Baron Holstein considered that Germany's eastern frontiers would be menaced if Germany attached herself to Britain; and he saw an end of all opportunities for German colonial acquisitions if she declared for Russia. Accordingly Germany should declare neither for Russia nor for Britain. The Secretary of State considered it, however, to be advisable not to rob the British statesman of the hope of the alliance into which he, Bülow, was determined in no case to enter. He had secured the treaty concerning Angola and Mozambique. This was surely the way to go on; Britain could be lured into yet further colonial concessions.

Emperor William learned only at long intervals of the course of events, and then only half of the story. Critical turns in affairs were not, in the view of the Secretary of State, of such importance as to need communicating to the Kaiser. He added, moreover, to his proposals to Britain things of which there had been no discussion whatever. In June 1898 Tsar

Nicholas sent a reply to Emperor William's written inquiry concerning Russo-German collaboration. The Kaiser read, to his astonishment, that Britain had made precisely the same offer of alliance to the Tsar as to him. Naturally, the Tsar had declined the offer.

It was, as a matter of fact, not true that any offer of alliance had been made by Britain to Russia. Lord Salisbury had merely instructed Sir N. O'Connor, the British Ambassador in St. Petersburg, in quite plain terms to discuss with the Russians the means of settling affairs in China to mutual advantage. The Ambassador had begun by discussing with Count Muraviev in a general way the possibilities of improving Anglo-Russian relations. The Russian Foreign Minister had at once made the proposal of an *entente* between the two Empires, and had asked Sir N. O'Connor to suggest to Lord Salisbury to draft its terms. But the Ambassador had himself dismissed this idea at once as visionary, and had not wasted a single word about the proposal in reporting to Lord Salisbury; he had simply stated that he proposed, if occasion offered, to follow up the conclusion of an agreement concerning China with a discussion with Russia concerning Turkish questions. The British Premier, in transmitting his instructions to Sir N. O'Connor, made so plain the limitations beyond which he did not want to go, that the Ambassador preferred, for his own protection, to transmit them to Count Muraviev in writing, precisely as defined by Lord Salisbury. After that it would not matter in the slightest if Count Muraviev proceeded to put his inventive powers or his artistry in heightening the

195

colours of a report once more to the test, or if some
other Minister gave Nicholas II wrong information.
But the impression made by the whole affair on the
Kaiser was dismaying. Here was Britain once more
pursuing a double-faced, treacherous policy. The
Kaiser saw once more the Armenians who had been
slain in order to free them.

For the first time, perhaps, it was not merely in
accordance with his general plan that the Kaiser tried
to bring Russia, and with her France, into a common
front with Germany against Britain. In the South
Sudan, General Kitchener had defeated the troops
of the Mahdi at Omdurman. He had marched on at
once to Fashoda, where Captain Marchand had
arrived in the meantime with his French forces.
Marchand had set up the French flag and taken possession of the territory which he had reached. A grave
conflict between France and Britain seemed inevitable. Britain demanded that the French should re-
tire, pulling down their flag at Fashoda. In the end
France accepted that humiliation, but war had been
on the verge of breaking out.

Emperor William did not conceal his opinion that
the withdrawal was a blow to French prestige. He
wrote about it to the Tsar: perhaps Russia, France,
and Germany could now unite. Britain must grow less
exacting or more serious in her proposals to Germany.
Just then the Kaiser was inclined to visit on Britain
the two-faced policy of which he believed himself to
have evidence once more. Joint action so inspired
would perhaps, at all events, bring France at last a
little closer to the enemy of yesterday. There were
many open advocates in France of oblivion for 1870

and a reconciliation with her neighbour. But the Kaiser soon saw that this time his ideas were mistaken. The Tsar took no notice of his suggestion. Britain preferred to inflict no further humiliation on France, at all events in public. The danger of war passed away.

The situation was obscure for Germany. The Kaiser had got no further with his neighbours. And his love for Britain was suffering.

The Kaiser went on a cruise. He intended to visit the tomb of Christ in Jerusalem, and before that to go to see Sultan Abdul Hamid. In his annoyance with Britain, the Kaiser felt a special fitness in this visit to Turkey and the Turkish provinces which Lord Salisbury had proposed to him three years before to partition. The Sultan welcomed him not only with splendid and sumptuous ceremony but with real cordiality. In spite of Abdul Hamid's careful phrasing, the Kaiser had in the course of a few conversations a clear picture of the whole network of diplomatic toils that the Powers were weaving round the Grand Seignior. Abdul Hamid was aware of the caution with which he had to sail between Britain, Russia and France, and knew how unwelcome to them was Emperor William's friendship towards the Turks. He cultivated the Kaiser's sympathies, but also sounded his guest through the interpreter Munir Pasha—who did not always understand the Kaiser's French answers as quickly as Abdul Hamid himself—for all sorts of news and confidential information. This he would be able to pass on to the Great Powers, to London, St. Petersburg, and Paris, and by that friendly service he would smooth away some of their irritation at his entertainment of his guest, from whom, in the very act of pumping him, the Sultan was seeking protection against the Powers. But the Kaiser knew all about the very convenient system under which every foreign Embassy had its own well-paid chamberlain at the Sultan's Court, who supplied the material for all the despatches from Yildiz and also took charge of all information which it was desired to bring to the Sultan's ears.

Needless to say, the Ambassadors of Britain, France and Russia had done everything in their power to prevent Emperor William's visit from being a thing of pure joy to Abdul Hamid. The Kaiser had brought with him one of the new German army rifles as a present for the Sultan. Three Turkish chamberlains ran to the Padishah with the horrible news that Emperor William meant to shoot him. So childish an invention of the diplomats would have been unintelligible to anyone unaware of Abdul Hamid's mortal fear of assassination. The splendid banquet at which the weapon was to be presented was postponed day after day. New chamberlains came to take over the rifle, in order that the Sultan might make himself familiar with it before the Kaiser explained its construction to him. At last the Turkish chamberlain admitted to the German Embassy what was really the matter. Emperor William sent him back with the assurance that the laws of hospitality were as sacred to him as to the Ottomans: he quite understood the eagerness of the Ambassadors to prevent the presentation of the weapon by hook or by crook; no doubt they were in dread lest Emperor William's only object in bringing the Sultan the best rifle in the world was to induce him to equip his army with it and render it invincible.

Next day the banquet was held. The Grand Seignior did not seem to be entirely convinced, for he hid himself so far behind an iron fire-screen, surrounded by his grandees and generals, that when the Kaiser came in he was unable at first to see him. Then Abdul blinked suspiciously at his guest, and when the aide-de-camp handed the rifle to the Kaiser the Sultan disappeared entirely behind his screen, only coming out from it when his guest had discharged the chamber of the rifle. Then he breathed again, took the weapon with a smile of relief, and laid it jokingly on each of his grandees, who salaamed and paled in turn. The whole proceedings had a strong tinge of oriental childishness. There was less childishness in the Sultan's subsequent high good humour. He had an intimation sent to the German Ambassador, the former Secretary of State von Marschall, that he wanted a secret code in which to be able to communicate thenceforth personally with Emperor William. Needless to say, this request of the Sultan's got no farther than the Embassy on the Bosphorus. It did not reach Emperor William's ears.

A much more important result of the Sultan's good humour was that it led him to speak of the Bagdad Railway. This project, for a line to connect Constantinople with Bagdad and to continue on to Kuweit, on the Persian Gulf, had already a long history. In 1870 von Pressel had completed a short line of railway, extending from Haidar Pasha on the Bosphorus to Ismid in Asia Minor. Ten years later this was acquired by British capitalists. About the same time—1880—an international company laid down a network of railways connecting Constantinople with Europe. The representative of German interests in the company, von Kühlmann, formerly counsel to the Bavarian Eastern Railway, soon joined the Anatolian Railway Company financed by the Deutsche Bank and the Dresdner Bank, which was working on the plan, so often discussed already, of the Bagdad Railway. The first projects had been drawn up by two Englishmen, Chesney and Cameron, and had been studied by Disraeli, but had led only to the small line to Ismid. Towards the end of the 'eighties Sir William White, the far-seeing British Ambassador, recognized not only the economic but the great political importance of the project. He urged the Anatolian Railway Company to buy the tiny line from the British, and induced the British to agree to the sale. The Anatolian Railway Company resolved at once to extend the line via Eski-Shehir to Angora, and the Sultan gave permission for a branch from Eski-Shehir southwards to Konia to be built. Sir William White lent his assistance to all these plans and projects. On the day of the purchase of the Ismid section he declared:

'To-day Britain has won a strong ally in the East.'

The Ambassador was thinking of joint resistance by Germany and Britain to Russian pressure in the East from Persia and the Caucasus. At that time Britain was ready for any increase in Turkey's strength. When Gladstone came to the helm British friendship for Turkey turned into its opposite. There

was no more participation in the strengthening of
Turkey, and the whole complexion of the Bagdad
Railway project changed for Britain: military objections were brought forward, and dangers were seen
that extended so far as to the Persian Gulf and to the
gates of India. Britain had forgone the friendship of
Turkey, on whose favour the concession for the
railway depended. The days of Sir William White's
support of Germany were also gone. In the 'nineties
Britain was living generally in a state of irritation
with Germany. She gave no further help: it depended
on Turkey alone whether and how the work begun
should be carried forward.

For some time past Germany had shown nothing
but friendship to the Sultan. She had not concurred
in the cession of Crete. She had declared the Armen-
ian question to be an internal affair of the Ottoman
Empire's. In the many discussions between the
Powers concerning reforms to be imposed on
Turkey, Germany had consistently held back.
Finally the German Emperor had come to Turkey to
renew his professions of friendship for the Sultan.
When he continued his journey to Jerusalem and
Damascus, he wanted to visit the tomb of Saladin.
He wanted to give a public and solemn assurance of
his friendship for all Islam. During his visit to the
Sultan he took pains to exhibit to the Sultan all the
genial charm which he had so readily at command
when he desired, or when he was not robbed of the
opportunity to display it. And Abdul Hamid made no
secret of the fact that charmed he was.

He gave, indeed, tangible proof of it: Emperor
William went on to Jerusalem with the definite

agreement that Germany should build the whole immense line of railway to Bagdad and on to Kuweit.

Neither on his journey to the East (on which he had been accompanied by von Bülow) nor after his return did the Kaiser have any further news of British proposals, or of Chamberlain's plans of alliance. The British Government had sent no 'official' proposal, such as the Kaiser had desired, to Berlin. It was not clear whether Chamberlain had changed his mind, or whether news of the Kaiser's confidential question to the Tsar had filtered through, through the latter's relations at the Court of Copenhagen or otherwise. Not until the end of the year did plain evidence come that the British Colonial Secretary had not given up his plans. In a great speech in Wakefield he made once more a public plea for an alliance with Germany, as a step in Britain's interest and making for her security. The speech sketched a whole programme. Chamberlain spoke of bringing America into the alliance. It was to be a great union of the Anglo-Saxon and Teuton races.

Bülow and Holstein put their own construction on the great idea. At once they set up a clamorous agitation for the Samoan islands. The situation in Samoa, which had been under discussion for a year past, seemed to the German Cabinet suddenly to have grown so urgent that no tone was sharp enough to adopt in order to help to cool the Colonial Minister's enthusiasm for his plans of alliance.

Germany, Britain, and America had originally agreed to recognize and support a Government which had been temporarily set up in the disturbed islands. The disturbances had not been kept under, troops had been landed by the British and Americans, the German Consul had protested, and in the tumult a German planter had been killed.

Bülow complained that the treaty had been broken, and asked British consent to the despatch of a Commission to Samoa. He proposed to the Kaiser that the German Ambassador should be recalled from London if Britain withheld her consent. The Ambassador was himself to use the threat of his recall as a means of pressure. The Colonial Secretary informed the Ambassador that Lord Salisbury agreed to the despatch of the Samoa Commission. But Count Hatzfeldt, usually so cautious and hesitating and so strongly inclined to compromise, sent to Berlin with the news of the result of the pressure which he had actually applied the rather strange advice to 'do no more now than wait and see whether Britain will set due value on our friendship.' The Secretary of State did everything to heighten the Kaiser's exasperation. He made no mention of Chamberlain's conciliatory intervention. In the end the Kaiser complained to Queen Victoria that Britain was confusing Germany with Portugal or Patagonia. He added that he would not go again to England so long as Lord Salisbury was in politics.

Nobody was more astonished at this letter than Lord Salisbury himself. He wrote a memorandum on the matter for the Queen. Attention must of course be paid to the claims for compensation which Germany was entitled to put forward in regard to the disturbances in Samoa. He suggested the King of Sweden as arbitrator. Without doubt all the misunderstandings between the Kaiser and himself would be cleared up at once as soon as it was possible for him to speak again to the Kaiser in England.

The Colonial Secretary intervened again. He knew already that in the language of the German Cabinet 'compensations' meant the acquisition of territory. Chamberlain was impatient: he wanted to get forward with his big plans. Accordingly he offered 'compensations.' He had to take account of the views of the very independent Australian States, and for this reason the establishment of the Germans in the South Seas was more inconvenient to him than almost any other form of compensation, even one which was of more value than the rights which Germany had in the South Sea Islands under her agreement with Britain and America. Chamberlain offered her the delta of the Volta in equatorial Africa if she would give up Samoa. The possession of the delta would add considerably to the value of the German colony of Togoland. But Admiral von Tirpitz had views to express. In his opinion the Volta delta was by no means equivalent in importance to Samoa. Not only was it intended to make Samoa a naval base of the greatest importance; Germany needed above all an island on which she could set up the central station for her world cable system. The Admiral's opinion was not shaken by a memorandum from the National Post Office in which Samoa was described as unsuitable for that purpose. Germany declined the Volta delta, and insisted on Samoa.

Chamberlain withdrew in annoyance from the negotiations. The German Ambassador had let it be seen that only this unlucky Samoa question stood in the way of the attainment of the desired alliance. Meanwhile the Colonial Secretary had quite troubles enough for the moment: the Boer war had broken out. Emperor William was now to intervene himself in all this wrangling over Samoa. He came to terms over it in a single hour with Cecil Rhodes.

Cecil Rhodes came to Emperor William with the famous *Meditations* of Marcus Aurelius, which he brought the Monarch by way of compliment and recommended as an introduction to affairs. But that was not his whole purpose in coming. He was in pursuit of business with Germany for Britain, and offered business in return. He had still been unable to realize his dream of constructing a railway and telegraph line from the Cape to Cairo. Once more he had tried to obtain from the King of the Belgians facilities for carrying the line through the Congo. But King Leopold had had trouble once already over that, and had refused to consider it.

It was proposed that Rhodes should be authorized by Germany to carry the railway and telegraph line through German East Africa, on condition that at the same time he laid down a line connecting the German coast with the British main line, and that for the whole of the construction on German colonial territory he made use of German rails and rolling stock, and German steel masts for the telegraph line, and that he employed German labour. The Secretary of State hoped at the same time to win Rhodes's support for the German desires in regard to Samoa, if the Kaiser succeeded in gaining his sympathies for Germany. Count Bülow regarded it as important that William II should receive Rhodes. A few points which the Kaiser wanted made clear before the audience developed quickly into a memorandum which the Secretary of State transmitted to the Kaiser with comprehensive map material. The Monarch, in surprise, threw back on the Foreign Ministry the negotiations over questions of detail; he would, moreover, only grant an audience if Rhodes sought one. The Secretary of State, however, objected. The Foreign Ministry was, unfortunately, unable to conduct the discussion with Cecil Rhodes. Rhodes spoke only English. Interpreters would thus have to be employed. The Secretary of State had no command of English, and both Cecil Rhodes and the Foreign Ministry refused to allow interpreters in a discussion that was to be kept strictly secret. There had been the same difficulty in Brussels. Since English had to be spoken, the Kaiser himself afforded the surest guarantee of exactitude of expression and of secrecy.

The Kaiser was not very elated at the task with which his advisers had entrusted him. If at the next discussion on colonial affairs in the Reichstag his agreements failed to secure approval, he would again be regarded as carrying out a personal policy. The Secretary of State was prepared, however, to accept the responsibility for that. The Kaiser therefore agreed to the audience.

'I had my anteroom in the Berlin Palace—the Rheinsberger room, so called after the collection of portraits of the young Frederick with his Rheinsberg friends—prepared for the audience, and awaited the South African dictator with the firm resolve to do no dishonour to the young Frederick as his successor.

'The door opened and Rhodes came in. Before me there stood a giant, of very substantial girth, and head and shoulders taller than I am. A square-cut face, out of which a pair of bright, shrewd eyes directed their steely gaze searchingly at me, the whole lit up by a jovial expression. For perhaps half-a-minute Emperor and dictator measured one another with searching glances, each with a map of Africa under his arm. Then the tension was relaxed by a strong handclasp between the two men. Conversation English.

'*Ego:* You have come about the Cape-to-Cairo line?

'*He:* Yes, that is to become my great life's work.

'*Ego:* You want to go through the hinterland of German East Africa?

'*He:* Yes! Since the King of the Belgians will not let me go through the Congo State !

'I spread my map out on the table. It was an English map, obtained specially by the Foreign Ministry from London. When Rhodes saw it, he exclaimed:

' "Throw away that rubbishy thing, it is not a bit of use! This map of mine here is better."

'He spread out a map on which his plans were sketched; it was the German one!

'He described his plans for the Cape-to-Cairo line, which was to connect Egypt with the Cape. This, he said, had got to be put through. Every European State which had colonies in Africa, in its neighbourhood, or situated along its route, would share in its benefits. He was therefore asking for permission to be allowed to carry the line along the section of its route which passes through the hinterland of German

East Africa. I then went through the conditions which my Government and the Colonial Administration had laid down as an equivalent return for the permission. All of them without exception were accepted and agreed to by Rhodes.

'Now I brought out the *pièce de résistance*, Samoa. When I told Rhodes of the matter and described its course, how the Foreign Office in London was not to be induced to come to a definite settlement, and yet the whole African transaction hung upon it, there was an explosion of wrath from Rhodes such as I have seldom witnessed. The British authorities and the Foreign Office in particular were presented with a choice collection of British *epitheta ornantia* that could not but refresh the spirit of any listener who had grounds for irritation with the British—all spoken from the depths of his soul. After he had thoroughly expressed his feelings he ended his monologue with the sentence:

' "You shall get Samoa, I will see to that."

' "You shall get," I replied, " your permission for telegraph and railway line."

'That ended the negotiations. Duration twenty-five minutes. A conversation followed on various topics.

'I asked how the visit in Brussels had gone. Rhodes said curtly:

' "The King is a great financial genius, but he is the devil in person!"

'As he left the King's chamber he found himself surrounded by an enthusiastic crowd of people financially interested in the Belgian Congo, and the Minister Lambremont said to him:

' "You were impressed with the far-seeing intelligence and with the aims of His Majesty our King, were you not?"

'Rhodes replied simply:

' "I have been talking to Satan!"

'Then, without further ceremony, he went away past the Belgians, who stood there open-mouthed, as if turned to stone. Comparing his negotiations in Brussels, he said, with those just concluded, he could not sufficiently express his thanks for the great readiness shown to come to terms and the practical and straightforward way in which the matter had been dealt with. He had been greatly impressed by Berlin and its huge industrial establishments, especially by the A.E.G., and by the active business life, which gave the impression of an excellent organization of the existence of which he had had no notion at all until then.

'A few years ago, he said, he had intended to come to Berlin from London, but had unfortunately been dissuaded from doing so by the Government and the Foreign Office. That, as he now saw, had been a great piece of stupidity. For if he had been able as early as that to bring about with me a settlement of the Cape-to-Cairo line he would have asked for my mediation with Ohm Krüger, in order to induce the Boers, like us, to give permission for the carrying of the railway line through their territory. Then there would have been no Jameson Raid and no Boer war following it, as the Boers would have lent a willing ear to the German advice and would have allowed the line to pass through, which would have disposed of a main cause of the war. That was probably what the "people in London" had been afraid of, and so they had talked him out of the idea of the visit to Berlin, doing him an ill turn. Then, too, he added, the so-called "Kruger telegram" would never have been sent. Anyhow there was no reason why I should turn grey over the rage it excited in London. From my standpoint I had been entirely right. He had not been at all annoyed with me over the telegram, as the Jameson Raid had been an enormous folly and I had not been in possession of the facts about it. The thing that mattered for Britain in Africa was not the ambition of get-rich-quick individuals but the carrying through of the Cape-to-Cairo line.

'Then he came to general problems of civilization. Every great Power in Europe had to find for itself virgin territory abroad, in order to open it up in the service of the introduction and spread of civilization. He looked at the map of the world every evening in search of new fields. Britain would 'look after' Africa. Germany's mission was to open up Asia Minor or Turkey. I ought to have a railway line laid down from Stamboul to Bagdad, and at the same time to have an irrigation plan drawn up for Mesopotamia, in order that cotton might be cultivated there. He had seen remains of the irrigation canals of Nebuchadnezzar.

' "Africa for the Britons, Asia Minor for the Germans!"

'I replied that plans for the railway were under discussion, but that we were afraid there was going to be opposition from London, where all Germany's civilizing efforts were constantly regarded with suspicion and envy and jealousy. He replied that Britain had destroyed the confidence of Islam and antagonized Turkey by her entirely wrong-headed policy in the treatment of the Mohammedan world; Germany had gone to work wisely and shrewdly and had made a friend of Turkey: that must now be turned to account for the opening up of Mesopotamia—

' "There we British have nothing to seek and no reason whatever for hindering you in your civilizing enterprise. If difficulties should be made for you in London, as over Samoa, just let me know, and I will soon put through what you want, as you will see in the case of Samoa."

'With that we parted from one another. Before leaving, Rhodes gave me a small copy of Marcus Aurelius, to which he habitually turned every day; the copy had many marked passages.

'Later I was able to signal to the navy the news that Samoa had become German. Rhodes had been as good as his word.'

Cecil Rhodes, when he left Berlin, was beaming with pleasure at the success he had achieved. The Kaiser's satisfaction was also great, and still greater was the admiration of Secretary of State von Bülow for his 'noble master.'

From the moment when Britain was plunged into troubles of the Boer war, Emperor William had done everything to show his impartiality—and to combine neutrality with chivalry. The Tsar had rejected the hand held out to him. In spite of the friendly tone of Nicholas II's reply to his letter, its evasions had their effect on Emperor William. The Russians were far from pleased with his journey to the East, and its great success in the permission secured for the building of the Bagdad Railway. They had suddenly found in Germany a rival on the Bosphorus and in Asia Minor, and reproached her with strengthening Russia's mortal enemy Turkey. Count Muraviev had nothing better to propose at this juncture than a new secret agreement on the Dardanelles question, drafted entirely in Russia's interest and full of fresh opportunities of entanglements for Germany. All this once more deepened the aversion from Russia which was always latent in the Kaiser's breast. He did not know that France and Russia had again renewed their Alliance in July 1899, almost immediately after the rejection of Russia's desires in regard to the Bosphorus, or that the renewal must have been under discussion actually during the negotiations for the proposed secret treaty with Germany. But, even without knowing this, he saw that virtually no prospect was offered by any approach to Russia. Now, through his own negotiations with Cecil Rhodes, he had achieved a great success. Rhodes had actually secured Samoa for Germany in London. The outbreak of the Boer war, and the brave defence, successful at first, put up by the Boers, had aroused the same enthusiasm among the impressionable masses in Germany which had been evinced in the days of Emperor William's telegram to President Kruger; and they shouted their enthusiasm and sympathy and their attitude on the issue to all the world, though they had not the slightest acquaintance with the origin and circumstances of the conflict. Britain had condemned the Jameson Raid, and had brought Dr. Jameson to justice. She had visited heavy penalties on the instigator and the participants in the Raid. That incident had been a victory for the Boers. Thereafter they had stood out against every attempt to procure for British enterprises even the amount of assistance that Emperor William had just agreed to, to the advantage of both sides. Their success had gone to their heads. They were determined to exploit it. It had become evident that they had protectors and patrons in the world, working even against the all-powerful Britain. Their strength seemed to lie in their weakness. They began putting difficulties in the way of the British at every opportunity. Where there were no difficulties they provided them themselves. They hampered and restricted the activities of the British residents at every turn, and they shut themselves off from the great Empire that lay all round them. They became in very truth the stone that blocked the communications for the British between their African territories.

At last the storm broke. It was in any case a brutal war of the big antagonist against the little one. The fact that the little one had been exasperating the big one to the very limit of endurance, that these stolid and hard-headed Netherland peasants, with their limited horizon, had preferred war to a reasonable business settlement, was visible at that distance to no one. It was with mixed feelings that the British statesmen resolved on war. They knew that once they had tamed these peasants they could endow them with the benefits of British progress; but this they themselves felt to be no adequate exculpation. However, nothing had been secured by the good way of peace, and the operation had to be performed.

The onlooking world, and the German public

above all, was voluble in its expression of loathing of the aggressor. The Kaiser tried to stem the current. He shared the feeling that a small people in far Africa must not make the question of its fate one of such importance as to spoil the relations between nations of many millions. He took a deliberate stand against German public opinion. He went on a visit to England. Queen Victoria and British public opinion greatly appreciated the intention underlying the Kaiser's attitude. In London Emperor William found himself held in higher esteem than ever. Lord Salisbury and Mr. Chamberlain, in concluding the treaty concerning Samoa in the middle of November 1899, had certainly given their consent partly because, with the Boer war on their hands, they had no need of any other quarrel. But Chamberlain saw that the whole atmosphere of British-German relations had somehow changed. Cecil Rhodes had spoken to him of Emperor William and his outlook. That had been the deciding factor in regard to the treaty concerning Samoa, and the granting of the treaty was to be the prologue to Chamberlain's discussions with the Kaiser.

Chamberlain spoke with the Kaiser himself on the alliance project. He spoke of Germany, Britain and America as making up the unit that had to be brought into being. The Colonial Secretary was well aware of the German desire for expansion in the world. He was fair-minded enough to admit at once that it was justified. He himself broached various suggestions. Germany had just acquired Samoa. Some settlement must be arrived at ere long in regard to conditions in Morocco. It was true that Sir Arthur Nicolson, the

British Minister in Tangier, was continually advising
a Moroccan policy confined virtually to the introduction of conditions worthy of humanity. He also clearly
favoured a measure of recognition of French rights
in Morocco. In any case the best advice that Sir
Arthur Nicolson felt he could offer to the Sultan,
whose own inclinations were for friendship with Britain, was that he should have particular care not to
offend French susceptibilities. Chamberlain, however, had other ideas in regard to the future of
Morocco. He wanted Britain to establish herself in
Tangier. Germany, he thought, should make sure of
the Atlantic coast. He had no intention of making any
difficulties for the Germans in Asia Minor. Let them
build the Bagdad Railway by all means; British
capital should be forthcoming to assist in the work.
The Kaiser was deeply impressed with all this,
though for a moment the suspicion came into his
head that Chamberlain was making this offer of
Morocco in order to drive him into conflict with the
French.

Mr. Balfour also spoke with the Kaiser. Lord
Londonderry, the Viceroy of India, arranged the
interview; it was felt that the freedom of ordinary
social intercourse might facilitate discussion and promote agreement. Mr. Balfour gave the Kaiser the
impression of a vivacious sceptic, a thinker with a
cheerful appreciation of practical advantages worth
pursuing, a philosopher and at the same time a
realist. His smile had a touch of superiority which
did not wound but radiated obliging courtesy. His
conversation sparkled with wit. Holding the lapels of
his always open frock coat, he displayed a pleasant

donnishness even before the Kaiser. He conversed on the philosophy of religion, on which he had written a brilliant book. He presented a copy of the book to the Kaiser. He also made a passing reference to the Bagdad Railway. It was clear that he was in agreement with Chamberlain; the Kaiser was merely receiving a fresh assurance from him. Amid the many subjects which Mr. Balfour touched on besides religion and philosophy, he had a few words to spare for the artillery. The thinker acutely pointed the difference between guns and howitzers; the interpreter of faiths knew exactly what long-barrelled guns were, and siege guns; he talked easily of large calibres and small. He spoke of all this with many a witticism and with real technical knowledge before coming at length to the problems of the dismounted cavalryman in action. The Kaiser was amused, but he gave the explanations Mr. Balfour wanted. The most astonishing thing in the conversation with Mr. Balfour seemed to the Kaiser to be the tact and adroitness with which he raised political questions. He spoke almost with the confidential openness, not emphasized but still perceptible, of the undoubted ally of the morrow.

The two Ministers could not but feel that Emperor William had given support to their plans. Chamberlain had brought forward details, Mr. Balfour had brought the atmosphere and confirmed the will to rapprochement. Chamberlain left the Kaiser with the assurance that every step should be further confidentially discussed with the German statesmen. Secretary of State von Bülow had come to London with the Kaiser; Chamberlain got into touch with him.

The German Secretary of State entered with the greatest alacrity into the Colonial Secretary's suggestions. Chamberlain repeated to him what he had said to the Kaiser. Count Bülow discovered with surprise that the Secretary for the Colonies saw even in the German plans of naval construction, which Bülow announced to him, no obstacle to an understanding with Germany. At all events, Chamberlain raised no objection to them. Finally Count Bülow had a suggestion of his own to offer for the consolidation of friendship between the two nations. Let the Colonial Secretary lay before the public the ideas which he had just put before him. The echo which they would call forth should show the extent to which they could be carried into execution. Chamberlain agreed at once. He named an early day on which he would lay everything before the British public in an important speech in Leicester. But Count Bülow was unwilling to do things by halves. He proposed to the Colonial Secretary that in his own speech on the new German Navy Bill in the Reichstag in the middle of December he should give a reply expressing his cordial agreement with Chamberlain. The Colonial Secretary parted from Bülow with great satisfaction over the agreement come to. A few days later in Leicester he made his appeal to the British people:

'But there is something more which, I think, any far-seeing English statesman must have long desired, and that is that we should not remain permanently isolated on the Continent of Europe, and I think the moment that aspiration was formed it must have appeared evident to everybody that the natural alliance is between ourselves and the great German Empire. We have had our differences with Germany, we have had our quarrels and contentions, we have had our misunderstandings. I do not conceal that the people of this country have been irritated, and justly irritated by circumstances which we are only too glad to forget, but at bottom, at the root of things, there has always been a force which has necessarily brought us together. What does unite nations? Interest and sentiment. What interest have we which is contrary to the interests of Germany ? . . .

'I cannot conceive any point which can arise in the immediate future which would bring ourselves and the Germans into antagonism of interests. On the contrary, I can foresee many things in the future which must be a cause of anxiety to the statesmen of Europe, but in which our interests are clearly the same as the interests of Germany, and in which the understanding of which I have spoken in the case of America might, if extended to Germany, do more, perhaps, than any combination of arms to preserve the peace of the world. . . .

'If the union between England and America is a powerful factor in the cause of peace, a new Triple Alliance between the Teutonic race and the two branches of the Anglo-Saxon race will be a still more potent influence in the future of the world. I have used the word alliance sometimes in the course of what I have said, but again I desire to make it clear that to me it seems to matter little whether you have an alliance which is committed to paper or whether you have an understanding which exists in the minds of the statesmen of the respective countries. An understanding perhaps is better than an alliance, which may stereotype arrangements which cannot be accepted as permanent in view of the changing circumstances from day to day.'

Chamberlain had done his part in preparing British public opinion, so far as a public speech could do so. A fortnight later, exactly as arranged, Secretary of State von Bülow rose in the German Reichstag. And he brusquely rejected the British approach. He made of Chamberlain a hopeless visionary. More reasonable, in the eyes of the German Secretary of State, was a policy that took advantage of the opportunities of the moment, considering that Britain was beyond doubt embarrassed by the Boer war. The one thing needful for Germany in the new era was her navy:

'In the new century Germany must be the hammer or the anvil!'

And Germany's radiant youth and strength were the guarantee that she was destined to be the hammer. Once more the Secretary of State yielded to the intoxication of his visions of power for Imperial Germany. He fully concurred with Count Hatzfeldt's advice from London to go quietly ahead and tie the British Colonial Secretary down to definite proposals, while Germany reserved her entire freedom. It was characteristic of that shrewdly calculating but often irresolute diplomat that he could proceed from a one-sided sense of justice to the crassest and most ruthless self-seeking, deserting high aims for purely momentary advantages. If Britain's hands were bound in her foreign policy, and Germany were free, Britain, he argued, would have to pay for the smallest

German concession with compensations at every step. Such ideas were the very essence of the Holstein spirit. The Ambassador joined the *Geheimrat* in his entire approval of the line taken by the Secretary of State. Sour words for Britain were, indeed, an old specific of the *Geheimrat's*.

Count Bülow not unnaturally felt that he owed the British Colonial Minister an explanation. British public opinion had shown no particular enthusiasm for Chamberlain's plan. Public opinion in Germany had turned sharply against it. Chamberlain and Bülow alike could scarcely have expected anything else. Chamberlain had nevertheless resolved on his speech because he felt that the time had come when a beginning ought at length to be made with a campaign to influence, convert and conquer public opinion. The German Secretary had found it convenient to forget what he had agreed in England to do: he had made no effort to convert public opinion but had run with it. Prince Hohenlohe had long been weary of the burden of office, and had informed the Kaiser of his desire to resign shortly. Count Bülow knew that he was the heir to the Chancellorship. A Chancellor with an Anglophil outlook would not have been accepted readily, if at all, by the German nation. Consequently no dismissal of this ridiculous British effort at a rapprochement could be too curt.

He explained confidentially to Chamberlain how his public attitude had been forced on him by public feeling. Phrases and declarations in the Reichstag were not the same thing as an exchange of ideas between two statesmen. He was sure that Chamberlain would understand this.

Count Hatzfeldt himself plainly differed from Bülow as to the duty of honouring a firm agreement. He had known Bülow's father, who had himself been at the head of the Foreign Ministry in Prince Bismarck's time. He had often been disturbed to find the old Secretary of State's statements wide of the facts. Now he was being constantly asked about the latest incident by those familiar with the events that had led up to it; and his replies were candid rather than discreet. He spoke slightingly of Bülow's father:

'But as to this man,' he went on, referring to Bernhard von Bülow, 'we shall find him making an appalling mess of things. He is a lazy liar.'

The Colonial Secretary had suffered a severe rebuff. Not only had his secret plans been reduced to ashes, but he had been exposed in his own country. He noted Count Bülow's confidential explanations.

'Never again,' he declared to his friends, 'shall I have anything to do with that fellow.'

The second British offer of alliance had been buried.

At the outset of his career Bernhard von Bülow had worked under Prince Bismarck. The Prince had soon been struck by his adroitness and adaptability. It was natural that Bülow should have chosen a career in which his father had risen to high rank. He had manifold connexions in society. He had gained the friendship of Count Philipp Eulenburg, who had felt him to be a kindred spirit in wit and intelligence. His rise had been a simple matter.

From the Foreign Ministry in Berlin he went as a very young Counsellor of Legation to the Embassy in

Vienna. There were various troubles there, such as
are liable to occur frequently in the life of a cavalier
not blessed with unfailing prudence. However, Bernhard von Bülow made a happy marriage. He went as
Counsellor of Embassy to St. Petersburg. There were
troubles there too; the Ambassador's wife refused to
receive the young diplomat's wife. *Geheimrat* von
Holstein now intervened from Berlin. The *Geheimrat*
set greater store by sinners than by the immaculate.
The Ambassador's salon, he ruled, must be thrown
open; General von Schweinitz's wife gave way. Baron
Holstein became more and more observant of the
young diplomat. He entered in his records the case
he had just dealt with, and thenceforward dug up and
stored up data of possible use in the event of later
trouble with the protégé of the moment. These
social incidents were forgotten; they were preserved
only in Baron Holstein's register. Bernhard von
Bülow became Minister in Bucarest. Here his real
education began.

Everything about him was ingratiating and captivating. He was a man of wide knowledge, and his
courtesy and amiability were no less outstanding. He
had a stately presence; was not exactly slim but not
really heavily built: his face had a polished, rosy soft-
ness, with not a single line to indicate any particular
characteristic. Everything in that face fitted in with
the single impression of pleasantness and geniality:
everyone who met him saw at once, even if this
statesman said nothing, which rarely happened, that
he was a man of never-failing readiness to oblige. He
took careful pains with his dress; his elegance was
unostentatious like his whole nature: he rather re-

called the *bons vivants* who came on the stage in the comedies of manners of his day; he had a touch, too, of the fashion plate. He was a man of large and lively gestures; his arms, his hands, even his shoulders chorused his speech. He was never to be seen out of doors without gloves and stick. His hats matched the rest in colour and form. He had not the composed, lordly elegance of the Englishman; his preference was for a richer, more decorative general impression. He liked a touch of emotion in life and clothing. He strove after a perfection of harmony that should pave his road to power, to fame, and to the hearts of all the world.

His conversation had a gentle, discursive character, warm, persuasive, bewitching. He stood always amid clouds of words and cascades of phrasing amid which even a steady head grew dizzy. As Minister in Bucarest he had made the discovery that cordial and cultivated dialogue was a different thing from the speeches which he seemed destined one day to make in the great forum of the Reichstag. His oratory was not then entirely perfected; he had not yet mastered the devices of climax, of paradox, of wit. He was sensible enough to realize that even Demosthenes was not a master at the very outset. More sober and easy-going, however, than the Greek, he did not begin by making a journey to the sea at Constanza in order to measure his tones against the thunder of the waves; he practised his speeches and coined his phrases while the shower splashed down in his bathroom in Bucarest. Day after day he did this; grotesque as the idea may seem, the Minister perfected his oratory actually to the tune of the water-tap.

223

In the unspoiled, stolid North German society of his time, not over-blessed with the refinements of art and intellect, culture and charm—a society that had sprung from the parsimonious soldier's court of Emperor William I, and one in which the modest enjoyments of the great reached their culmination in regimental banquets and country house parties, attendance at the provincial diet alternating for the rest with military parades—Bernhard von Bülow's distinction and his connoisseur's approach to life attracted attention at once. His conversation was not of horses, of agricultural shows, of the art of manuring. No strong language, no coarse phrase, such as had often been heard even in Prince Bismarck's exalted circle, ever escaped Bernhard von Bülow's lips. His conversation was of art and science. He seemed to have read everything, to have felt the rapture of all the poets. He lived among them. Through him they made their appeal anew to humanity. He had them at command as thoroughly as any actor reeling off his lines. The fine phrases of the poets trailed after him and obeyed his call, whether he was carrying on a confidential discussion or speaking in the Prussian Parliament or at some lively party. He rose in the morning with a verse on his lips. At night, when he drove home, he had a line from the treasure-house of German poetry as farewell offering to his host or parting friend. In this hard, plain, narrow North German society it was something new for a statesman to live with Goethe and with Dante, to join to mastery in solving the problems of practical daily life a relating of them all to the eternal heights. Bismarck had been a giant of

224

Norderney Summer 1900
Prince Bülow, German Chancellor and
Princess Bülow recieving the German Emperor

steel; Friedrichsruh had been no home for Goethe or Dante. Caprivi had been a modest, placid Prussian General. Hohenlohe had come from the south of Germany. He counted for nothing in the realm of art; in matters of social refinement the South had always been even more sadly to want than the North. But amid the society of the Prussian marches, east of the Elbe, Bernhard von Bülow, with his erudition and his distinguished manner, with his intelligence constantly on the alert and constantly in play, coruscating with apt quotations from his poets and philosophers, was a sheer miracle.

His affectionate familiarity with poets and philosophers had been the result of years of energy and application. Amid the light official tasks of Bucarest, so soon as the water tap was turned off he went to his worshipped classics. He studied them in the most serviceable editions, preferring the handiest format. He would repeat verses and dicta, page by page, until he had them completely by heart. In the end they were at call from memory in impeccable accuracy, the very moment that an appropriate occasion or the force of suggestion brought them to mind. But he was well aware that quotations alone and even well-managed periods did not give a speech all the needed effect on its hearers. He had studied the negligence of manner that impressed in the salon. When at length he was actually to stand up before the Reichstag as Secretary of State, he studied with his confidant in the Foreign Ministry, *Geheimrat* Hammann, every pose that was to accompany his speech. The *Geheimrat* recommended at one passage something like Mr. Balfour's attitude:

'Now open your coat, straighten your back, and catch hold of the two lapels.'

The Secretary of State had a try. The *Geheimrat* felt that the gesture was not yet quite satisfactory. He made it himself two or three times in front of the Secretary of State:

'Not like that; try as I am doing it now.'

Geheimrat Hammann complained to a friend of all this plaguery with the Secretary of State. However, in the end Bernhard von Bülow managed the gesture almost as well as Mr. Balfour.

'Watch,' old Prince Hatzfeldt said next day to his neighbour in the Reichstag—'here is the lapel business coming.'

A second later the Secretary of State made his gesture, boldly and broadly. It looked as spontaneous as his ideas did. The bathroom practice, the memorizing of classical quotations on an adventurous scale, the painstaking study of effective gestures made up in the end a technique which this statesman employed with virtuosity.

He was a virtuoso in the Reichstag, which for ten years gave its support and its approval to his statesmanship; a virtuoso in his many dealings with newspaper men, whom he honoured with a confidential and friendly intercourse in which there was no condescension, and a virtuoso in his relations with the Kaiser and the Court. So great at all times was his geniality, his eagerness to captivate, that the day came at last when no one could say what this amazing master of manners and manipulator of phrases had actually been telling him. Flattery and attentions followed breathlessly on one another's heels, in sentences which had no time to reach their end. His voice had the sonorous, pleasing hum of a 'cello as he began at once to weave his blandishments around the person whom he had done the honour to address:

'As you have just very properly remarked, my honoured friend! No, no—it is really a wonderful pleasure to me! We two, who have worked together such a lot! Well, as you said so well just now. . . .'

Meanwhile the honoured friend would have failed to get out a single word. But the artist gushed on. Whomever he met, he found simply delightful, and told him so. Things that other people had done mechanically and indifferently as a matter of the veriest every-day routine, he saw always as filled with depths of hidden significance, and trumpeted the fact, beaming:

'My dear friend! So early in the morning on the beach with that fat cigar! My word, what an achievement to be able to enjoy it and take in at the same time this grand morning air!'

He was the soul of good-nature. He had the child-likeness of big men. If anyone revealed to him that somebody was his bitter enemy, he at once invited the enemy to dinner. And the 'cello played, and the clouds of words floated in the air until the room grew dim. He was the first German statesman with charm, the first of modern type.

And his subservience was almost limitless. When he went to see the Kaiser, he bent almost forty-five degrees in his humble obeisance before the Monarch. Not a word that the Monarch spoke would he ever forget. To him Emperor William was not merely the 'noble master,' the 'illustrious sovereign'; he was genius itself. The Emperor always had the most brilliant ideas. No one saw into the heart of things as he did. From him alone came the solution, and it was always the best one.

'Now, there is indeed a new idea, to get us over this difficulty!'

'What a brilliant inspiration of your Majesty's!'

Often the Kaiser would stand and look sceptically at Count Bülow:

'Ah, well! Ah, well!'

So great was the admiration of the Secretary of State—and now the new Chancellor—for his master, that at times he was even seized with honourable qualms lest all his overflowing praises should unduly increase the Kaiser's good opinion of himself. But his amazement at the abilities of William II overcame him ever and again—at audiences, during walks, at Court festivities. He painted his adoration of the Kaiser in the boldest colours; in his expression of it he did not flinch from the fullest self-abasement. At a Court ball he found Prince Max Egon Fürstenberg stuck fast in a doorway through the pressure of the throng of guests, and unaware that the Kaiser, who was talking to someone else, had come so close to him as almost to touch him. At that moment Count Bülow clapped him on the shoulder:

'As you said so well just now, Prince—and that speech of yours yesterday, really, it was magnificent—once more quite extraordinarily magnificent!'

Prince Fürstenberg had not exchanged a single word with Count Bülow; he had only just come up against him. It was impossible for the Prince to get out of the way of the Kaiser, who was moving gradually back from him,—first because he had not seen the Kaiser, and secondly because the whole bulk of the Count's big frame stood in his way. The Count was loud in his admiration of the Prince's speech—until he gave a sudden start and broke off, with his hand to his mouth:

'Good God! There's His Majesty!'

His pleasure and alarm, needless to say, had so carried him off his feet, and had also led him to speak so loudly and excitedly, that the Kaiser could not fail to overhear—which was the Count's intention.

Count Bülow admired the Kaiser's decorous manner, his chivalry, his lightning perceptions, his readiness to assist in putting people into touch with one another, his willingness even to do a job. Often the Count had some desire which he wanted to bring to the knowledge, perhaps, of the Tsar. The Kaiser might draft a letter in English himself, or else the Count would have it laboriously drafted by one of his young Counsellors of Legation. Then he would sit in respectful silence while the Kaiser put the communication into English.

'What do you do with these drafts?' the Kaiser asked him on one occasion. 'Where do you keep them?'

The drafts were, needless to say, precious things:

'In a special cupboard in my office.'

It was a weakness of the Kaiser's to overvalue finished political papers. Respect for the Monarch prevented the Count from admitting that the special cupboard had no existence, and that the Count had simply thrown the manuscripts for the time into one drawer or another, where they lay mixed up with family letters and all sorts of things, crumpled and disordered and only half complete. All that mattered to the Count were the events and the decisions of the day. In these lived—for that short moment—the high mission and gifts of the Kaiser, so blessed in their consequences for the German nation; in these and these only the Kaiser's own fulfilment of himself had its existence—and its extinction.

'If there is one thing,' the Count would say sometimes, 'that I deeply regret and find painful to think of, it is the fact that I have so little time for making your Majesty's thoughts better known to the world. But some day I shall be free. Then I shall write a book about your Majesty.'

The Kaiser looked sceptically at him: 'My dear chap!'

'No, really, your Majesty, I shall, and a book such as has never yet been written.'

Emperor William II was already and had long been the centre and the whole content of the Count's duties and mission in life. Yet when, about the time of his taking office as Chancellor, the Ambassador Count Anton Monts asked Bülow how he envisaged his office, Count Bülow's answer was:

'I hope to tide the Empire over the interval be-between William I and the successor to William II. Then things will be all right again.'

In all things, with Bernhard von Bülow, the statesman won through in the end.

Bülow the statesman hated the small details of office routine. He rarely read through papers put before him, but he would often write marginal notes on them; and his staff had got so used to these that they knew of each one what its source was, the letter or document in which it was to be found. He was entirely dependent on *Geheimrat* von Holstein, owing to the Baron's intimate knowledge of every subject, his intimate knowledge of persons, and his familiarity with Count Bülow's own personal and private affairs. The Count never took a step until it had the *Geheimrat's* approval. With all its abundant wealth of word and phrase, Bülow's was but a poor head, flabby and uninspired in its thinking.

He had a slight acquaintance with Russia. He imagined that he knew Italy; when Ambassador in Rome he had reported how Crispi, the Prime Minister, had been entirely convinced by him of the necessity for the 'restoration of legality' in Africa. At that very moment Crispi was concluding a secret treaty with Britain. Bülow failed to realize Italy's dependence on Britain. Count Monts explained to him the hold Britain had over the Italian ports. Chancellor von Bülow was unable to follow the explanation, and quite unable to grasp what the Ambassador was after.

He had no liking for Austria-Hungary, and no knowledge of England, land or language or people. For him statesmanship had nothing to do with construction, or with the weighing and balancing of forces; statesmanship was the art of getting the better of other people, of playing off everyone against everyone else, of diddling and deceiving by means of concessions with no reality in them, till some advantage, no great matter what, had been won.

'When you have to do with Britain and the British,' the Kaiser had advised Bülow when he became Secretary of State, 'be absolutely frank and straightforward! When the Englishman finds someone standing out for his interests in the same open, matter-of-course, indeed ruthless, way as himself, he understands and respects him. Then one gets ahead. But carefully avoid shilly-shallying, or playing the 'cute diplomat, or finessing! The Englishman resents it and thinks you are not straight.'

The Kaiser, of course, did not realize all the refinements of diplomacy. Count Bülow let the information confided to him from Russia 'trickle through' to the British. He pressed the Kaiser to let the Russians know of the British offer of an alliance. To the Kaiser all these affairs were the subject of a spiritual struggle; to Bülow they brought the pleasure of 'finessing.' His statesmanship was a thing of brightness and neat phrases: the 'whale,' he said, could never endure the 'bear.' Systems of alliance must be elastic, extensible. It was the period of picturesqueness and metaphor in diplomacy: the diplomats covered their nakedness of ideas with fine feathers of empty phrasemaking. Much of it was taken over from the Bismarckian legacy, misconceived and unintelligently parroted. Many bright metaphors came from Baron Holstein: Count Bülow absorbed them avidly and retailed them in vivid mixtures. He knew nothing of European inter-connexions, still less of extra-European. He absorbed ideas as he absorbed quotations, always as alien things: he played with them and gave expression to them without comprehending them. Never had statesman supremer skill in covering with phrase and verse the appalling emptiness of his brain than Bernhard von Bülow. The world called him intelligent: in reality he was of very restricted intelligence. Never did he recognize a sign in the heavens, never a change in the horizon. He assumed every opponent and every partner to be lying, as he himself was. He did not know that his opponents had long ago discovered that he not only was not straight but was an embarrassed mass of stupidity and universal muddledness. He disliked work and rarely took trouble over anything. He did not listen even to the Kaiser. When the audience was over and he had had a thorough account from the Kaiser of some matter, Bülow would at once beg the aide-de-camp to tell him what the great Sovereign had just been saying. He had not grasped it, or had forgotten the gist of it. When the aide-de-camp had repeated everything to him, he would beg two hours later for another audience. He was not only a wool-gatherer, he was careless and indolent.

His restricted political vision was balanced by economic ignorance. 'What *are* preference shares?' he asked an Ambassador one day after he had become Chancellor. The Ambassador explained the term for a solid hour, and still he did not understand.

One great, amazing gift he certainly had—the gift of completely hiding all these inadequacies under a fine presence and masses of deftly spun words: but no leading statesman of the world ever had such poverty of intellect as the fourth of the German Chancellors. Emperor William felt the stimulus that seemed to proceed from all that brilliance. He felt the effect of all the flatteries, in which no greater master will ever be seen. All Germany saw in him a true leader, and in the end a statesman of the stamp of Prince Bismarck; Reichstag and Press alike succumbed to his spell. Such complicity was its own exoneration.

Germany's road to ruin was made yet more precipitous by the statesmanship of the 'finessing' Chancellor Count Bülow.

A few weeks after Count Bülow's speech in the Reichstag on the new Navy Bill, German steamships were held up by the British in South African waters. They were searched for weapons, and were confiscated. The German Cabinet at once sent a series of Notes of sharp protest. The British had certainly been in the wrong, and the incident was not unwelcome to the Chancellor as a reinforcement of his speech, which had been so meticulously attuned to the anti-British feeling in Germany. Feeling in Germany did, in fact, grow considerably hotter. Admiral von Tirpitz, Secretary of State for the Navy, followed the Chancellor's lead, taking advantage of the embittered temper of public opinion to gain support for the building up of the German navy. Up to now there had been no such thing as any German sea power worthy of the name. Even Italy and Russia were stronger on the seas than the German Empire. General von Caprivi, as Head of the Admiralty and of the navy organization, had been the first to devote serious attention to the subject, concerning himself mainly with torpedo warfare and the strategic tasks of the navy. Ten years had now passed since General von Caprivi's successor at the Admiralty, Vice-Admiral Count Monts, had demanded an increase in the fighting fleet: that was in 1890, when he had called for four big battleships. In so passing beyond the question of the defence of the German shores, he had been the first to point to the possibility of coming de-

234

cisions on the high seas. Emperor William had himself approached the problem of a strong German navy, and finally, in the autumn of 1895, had come to the decision to make every sacrifice in order to create it. At that time President Kruger's toast and the dispatch of German ships to Delagoa Bay had brought friction with Britain, and in the conversations which the British Ambassador, Sir Edward Malet, had with Emperor William and Baron von Marschall the friction had shown itself in a continually increasing sharpness of language. In the summer of 1897, Vice-Admiral von Tirpitz had been placed at the head of the German Admiralty. He had then gone out with the Far East Squadron, had done valuable surveying work, and had advised the occupation of Kiaochow. In the Straits Settlements he studied the British. He arrived at the conclusion that they were not only squeezing out the Germans wherever they could, but that in the Settlements they hated the Germans because of the undeniable progress which German business was making in the world. The Vice-Admiral also studied English history. He arrived at the conclusion that Britain could not set herself free from the traditions which for three centuries past had determined her attitude on the seas and toward the seas. He saw Holland's power broken by an English Admiral, who made no bones about any grounds of war if he was able to get from the Dutch anything that might be of use to the English. Admiral von Tirpitz took that struggle with the Dutch as symbolic: the day would come when Germany would count for just as much or just as little with the British. He would strain every nerve to prepare against that day. If the

235

British in the Straits Settlements hated the Germans, if the Vice-Admiral was able to note that hatred at every move, if he found it expressed in every British newspaper that he took up, his own hatred of Britain was no less. In his torpedo work under General von Caprivi he had shown himself to be an organizer. Now that he had become Secretary of State for the Navy, he intended to create a German Navy that should count. In the autumn of 1897 he introduced the first Navy Bill into the Reichstag; in 1898 the Reichstag resolved to complete seventeen battleships in six years. Admiral von Tirpitz considered that for the moment Germany's coast defence was sufficiently assured to enable preparations to be entered on for great decisions on the high seas. The problem was new and strange to the German public; he entered on a campaign of enlightenment with the energy of the Kaiser himself: the Kaiser invited Deputies to come to him to be shown from statistics and from comparisons with the navies of other nations how necessary it was to build German ships of war; Secretary of State von Tirpitz inspired the German Navy League, founded in 1898, and won over university professors, industrialists, writers to the idea of a big navy. The Vice-Admiral was of one mind with Count Bülow, though the Count would have liked to carry through even bigger measures: Tirpitz was working to secure a certain steady pace in building, and keeping count meanwhile of technical advances, while Count Bülow saw in the coming big navy a political weapon ready to hand. But their occasional differences of opinion amounted to little. Both had the same main purpose, and each supported the other in it; Bülow secretly feared the powerful personality of Secretary of State von Tirpitz, while the Secretary of State knew how much Count Bülow could do to further his plans—with Emperor William, in the Reichstag, and among the general public. For the sake of the way they were able to play into each other's hands, they kept at peace with one another. A fortnight after his discussion with the British Colonial Secretary, Count Bülow spoke in the Reichstag on the humiliating way in which Germany was looked down upon by her neighbours.

'These times must not recur! We do not intend again to be, in Friedrich List's phrase, serfs of humanity!'

In Danzig in September 1898 the Kaiser had launched his phrase:

'Our future lies on the water';

in October 1899 he said in Hamburg:

'A navy is a bitter necessity for us.'

In January 1900, on the strength of the popular indignation in Germany over the British detention of the German steamers, Secretary of State von Tirpitz demanded the passing of a new and drastic Navy Bill. Not seventeen new battleships were to be built in six years, but thirty-four in seventeen years. He spoke himself on his programme in the Reichstag in February 1900.

'We are of the opinion that the navy asked for in the Bill is so strong that it will preserve the freedom of the North Sea. Our naval battles of the future must be fought there.'

Tirpitz aimed at securing Germany from all danger of blockade. No Power should in the future be so strong as alone to dominate the seas. The Secretary of State for the Navy developed a 'risk theory.' He meant to have the German navy so powerful that even the mightiest sea power in the world would be engaging in a life-and-death struggle with no certain issue if she were to attack Germany anywhere on the seas. If that end were attained, no naval Power would ever attack. This was a challenge to Britain and her sea power, which up to now had known no challenge and no limitation. She was no longer to be allowed to do entirely as she chose; she was to be made to renounce the heritage that she had possessed until now. If Britain accepted the 'risk theory,' she would have abdicated her dominion of the trade routes of the world. She would then have been beaten without a battle. It was not the building of the navy but the openly enunciated 'risk theory' that was the actual announcement of the intention to make an end of British domination. The challenge in the 'risk theory' was a challenge to a competitive struggle.

Admiral von Tirpitz and the new Chancellor, Count Bülow, imagined, if no one else did, that they had disguised their actual plans so cleverly under a phrase and a diversion from the true issue that Britain would fail to see what was really up. They supposed that Britain would merely recognize in their plans Germany's inalienable right of self-protection, and would fail to see that the freedom of disposition of her own navy had been taken away. So Chancellor and Navy Secretary 'finessed'—both of them, be it understood, far more adroitly, far more cunningly and astutely than 'our poor Chamberlain.'

In his secret heart the Kaiser hoped still for the

alliance with Britain. If the day came when that was actually concluded, the two navies would be a single power. The British Colonial Secretary had been made acquainted with the naval plans during the negotiations in London. He had not for one moment felt them to be any impediment to his plans for an alliance. He had not spoken one word of objection to them. Within the alliance, to which the whole course of the negotiations led him confidently to look forward, these plans increased the value of the ally, made the ally the more welcome. If the alliance fell through in the end, then indeed the carrying into effect of the 'risk theory' would be a permanent cause of estrangement. Only the path to Russia, so it seemed to the Kaiser, would then remain open and Russia, in his opinion, was a much less reliable ally. But if Germany turned to Russia her demands would be stiffened—with her thirty-four battleships, her sixteen new armoured cruisers, her thirty-two new light cruisers, her sixteen torpedo-boat divisions, all her powerful new fleet.

Britain returned the confiscated vessels, and promised compensation. Lord Salisbury, however, remained of the opinion that Britain had been within her right in detaining the ships, and made no secret of his dislike of Germany: her Cabinet, he felt, had taken advantage of the incident to send sharp Notes to Britain at a moment when she was struggling with the difficulties of a war which up to then had not been exactly a successful one. In face of the continued efforts towards an alliance with Germany, her Cabinet's language seemed quite uncalled for. The aged Lord Salisbury, prone at all times to suspicion, had long since seen through Count Bülow: Germany, he saw, was acting as though she meant to agree to the alliance with Britain, but what she was really after was colonies and every other possible tangible gain, and no entangling alliance. Lord Salisbury gave open expression to all this, but Bülow attached no importance to the exposure of his real attitude. Only the Kaiser did everything to ward off the consequences of the new quarrel.

While the Kaiser was in London, Queen Victoria came again and again to the subject of the British defeats in South Africa. They hurt her pride, and she was distressed at the loss of many men who were well-known to her. She came back again and again to military questions, and finally asked her grandson's opinion of the British system of an army without a General Staff, and a campaign directed by instructions from the Ministry of War. Emperor William passed an intimation of the Queen's desire to Count Schlieffen, the German Chief of Staff, and passed his comments to the Queen. Whether Count Schlieffen's advice was made use of or not by Field Marshal Lord Roberts, the Queen thanked her grandson warmly. A few weeks later there reached the Kaiser a carefully veiled suggestion from Russia and France that a favourable moment had just come for a joint protest against the Boer War. Hints of action of this sort had been made to him by Count Osten-Sacken, the Russian Ambassador in Berlin. Now Russia and France definitely asked for Germany's view. The Secretary of State reported the proposal to the Kaiser, who was taking part in the manœuvres of a naval squadron off

Heligoland. William II believed that he saw in this a dark Russo-French scheme, hatched for the ill of Germany. The Secretary of State was rather in favour of joining in the move than not, but the Kaiser decided to decline to take any part in it. He was convinced that if Germany had given her consent the two Powers would at once have left her in the lurch and placed her under the suspicion, in English eyes, of having been the prime mover in the whole matter. He sent a telegram to Queen Victoria from Heligoland, telling her that he had received a proposal from the Dual Alliance Powers, Russia and France, to make difficulties for Britain in her South African War, and that he had given them a plain refusal. The Prince of Wales had no responsibility for British affairs of state, but the Kaiser informed him at the same time.

Secretary of State von Bülow noted the two telegrams with concern. His disapproval took the form of an expression of anxiety lest there should be any unfortunate result from the precipitate action of his all-highest lord. Russia would never be 'capable of such infamy' as merely to be hatching a plot in order to get the Kaiser blamed for it.

'Things of such importance,' the Secretary of State urged, 'need first to be thoroughly examined to discover the truth about them, and then to be dealt with in carefully elaborated Notes. Brief telegrams might under certain circumstances produce harmful results, especially in so rigidly constitutional a State as Britain. It is to be hoped that no evil results will ensue; but the Secretary of State is gravely concerned.'

The Prince of Wales in his reply expressed astonishment and incredulity in regard to Emperor

William's news. Queen Victoria sent first a telegram expressing warm thanks; a few days later she wrote to her grandson. Shortly after receiving the telegram from Heligoland she had been informed from an official quarter of 'a step of quite unheard-of malevolence' taken by the German Government in Paris and St. Petersburg, proposing 'a joint attack on Britain by the three Powers while she was in the throes of the Boer War.' The bringer of the news had added to it suspicions that reflected on the Kaiser. The Queen had listened patiently to all this, and when the bearer of the strange news had had his say she had handed him the Kaiser's telegram—to her visitor's great astonishment and confusion. The Kaiser had taken the exact measure of his opponents, and the telegram could not possibly have arrived more opportunely. She could only thank him for the friendly service which he had done her and her country.

The anxieties of the Secretary of State continued unabated until the Kaiser passed him the letter that he had received. On that Count Bülow stood awhile in an embarrassed silence; then he was filled with pleased surprise; finally he burst into expressions of unbounded admiration for the statesmanship of William II.

Since the Kaiser had already decided the matter, the Secretary of State had to send to St. Petersburg a reply declining the Russo-French proposal. He pointed out the necessity of avoiding every sort of complication. If Germany was to make common cause with the two Powers she must first have the assurance that the three nations guaranteed one another's possession of their territories. France would never agree

to this; 1870 had not yet been avenged. Count Bülow
let the British know that he had simply kept his freedom by putting forward demands which could never
be fulfilled; Russia would have to try some other means
if she wanted to play off Germany against Britain.

No doubt the Russian Cabinet guessed that there
had once more been friendly discussions in the past
year between Britain and Germany; perhaps they
were still going on. Its attempt at mediation in the
Boer War had failed. Soon after, when the Boers
themselves sought Berlin's mediation, it was almost
flatly refused. President Kruger came to Europe to
seek support for his country; Emperor William did
not receive him. Germany's turn towards Britain
seemed plainer than ever to the Russian observers.
Other means must be tried of relaxing the new ties.

China was aflame. Perhaps the way to Britain lay
through the Far East. The Boxer sect had risen in
China, and the masses were being goaded against the
European settlements. Warships of the Powers,
cruising in Far East waters, were shot at from the
Taku forts, near Peking. Their marines stormed the
forts; but the unrest grew. The rising spread through
the Yangtze basin; Peking was its main centre. The
European troops were too few in number and too ill-
equipped with munitions and stores to attempt a
march on Peking. In Tokio, however, the Foreign
Minister, Viscount Aoki, sent for the British, German,
Russian, French and American Ambassadors. Japan,
he said, was ready to send her own troops to Peking
to protect the Legations and foreigners. She was
ready to be the mandatory of the Powers in China.

He asked the Ambassadors to transmit this Japanese proposal to their Cabinets.

Britain agreed to the proposal. Russia and France declined; Germany evaded a direct reply. America's reply was also indecisive. But the unrest went on spreading. On June 18, 1900, the German Minister, Baron von Ketteler, left his Legation in spite of a warning not to go beyond its precincts. He pooh-poohed the idea of any danger:

'Nothing can happen to the German Minister.'

But the Chinese dragged him out of his rickshaw and murdered him.

Now the cry was insistent for military intervention by the Powers. The Chinese rebellion had hit Germany hardest of all. Not only had German settlers been murdered, but a gross affront had been offered to Germany's prestige. Joint intervention by the troops of a large number of the Powers was now resolved on. It was an enterprise full of pitfalls, and once more Japan, who was directly affected in everything that happened and every step taken in China, owing to China's proximity to her, undertook the initiative. Viscount Aoki sent for the German Chargé d'Affaires. He said that he had induced the 'Emperor' (as, like all Japanese, he called his ruler) to transmit to the German Cabinet the suggestion that a German Commander-in-Chief should be set over all the troops intended for China. The German Chargé d'Affaires, Count Wedel, thought this proposal a very delicate matter. He pointed out that it would arouse jealousy among the other Powers. He agreed, however, to inform Berlin by telegraph of what the Viscount had said to him.

Count Bülow replied at once that anything likely to produce disagreement among the Powers must be avoided. 'His Majesty's Generals,' moreover, who were 'accustomed to victory,' must not be exposed to any risk of failure. Count Wedel confined himself to communicating to the Japanese Foreign Minister the German apprehension of disagreement among the Powers; he said nothing about Generals accustomed to victory. For thirty years past Germany had been engaged in no war anywhere, and Generals victorious in manœuvres hardly came into the matter.

However, the Japanese Foreign Minister's proposal was carried into effect. The suggestion of 'a step that will please the German Emperor' had been transmitted by a confidant of *Geheimrat* von Holstein to an influential friend in London. Lord Salisbury was not enthusiastic, but neither was he adamant. First of all, however, Emperor William had come to a direct understanding with the Tsar. Russians, Germans and Japanese formed the bulk of the detachments for Peking. The choice for the leadership of the expedition lay between a Russian General—possibly the ambitious Minister of War, Kuropatkin—and a German. The Kaiser had asked Tsar Nicholas whether he would himself nominate a Commander-in-Chief or would agree to the appointment of General Count Waldersee. The Tsar was aware that the Chinese unrest must once more open up questions in the Far East. Germany might be helpful in their solution. It was advisable, moreover, to do something to detach Germany from Britain. He agreed to the appointment of Count Waldersee.

With the Tsar's consent secured, the Kaiser now

proposed to the other Sovereigns, including the
Emperor of Japan, that there should be a German
Commander-in-Chief of the expedition. Viscount
Aoki had himself been the first to suggest Count
Waldersee for the command to the German Chargé
d'Affaires, but Emperor William's telegram men-
tioned no name. Count Wedel, a little surprised
at an entirely unaccustomed deficiency in politeness
on the Kaiser's part, regarded the matter as settled.
Soon after, however, there came a reprimand from
Geheimrat von Holstein which filled Count Wedel
with doubts as to the quality of the administration
under the new Chancellor, Count Bülow, and the
Foreign Ministry. Holstein complained that the
Chargé d'Affaires had failed to inform him of the
arrival in Tokio of a telegram from Emperor William.
Either the *Geheimrat* must have kept Viscount Aoki's
suggestion from the Chancellor's knowledge, or
Count Bülow must have left the Kaiser in ignorance
of it. In any case the Kaiser clearly had no knowledge
of it. In addition to this, Count Bülow had evidently
made no mention of the Kaiser's telegram to the
Geheimrat. All that was plain to the Emperor of Japan
was Emperor William's lack of courtesy—while the
latter was completely unaware of the trouble.

General Count Waldersee became Field Marshal
commanding all the troops in China. On his departure Emperor William made to him an unfortunate
parting speech, describing the atrocities committed
by the Chinese rebel sectaries and demanding reprisals:

'As a thousand years ago the Huns under their
King Attila made for themselves a name which looms

gigantic to this day in tradition and story, so may the name of the Germans be impressed by you on China for a thousand years to come, in such wise that no Chinese shall ever again venture even to look askance at a German.'

The text of the Monarch's speeches was subject to revision by Count Bülow. Any phrase which the Kaiser was told went beyond the mark, he was always ready to strike out at once—if anyone in his entourage had the courage to make the necessary representations to him. On one occasion he had offended the Hansa cities by an unfortunate phrase. No one in the Civil Cabinet and no one in the Chancellor's office had ventured to bring the phrase once more to the Kaiser's notice, after he had spoken it but in time to prevent it from spreading over the world. At last a gentleman not belonging to the Court, bolder than the rest, ventured on the rashness of a representation to the Kaiser.

'Strike out the sentence,' the Kaiser said—'you are quite right.'

But Count Bülow had no reason to quarrel with any speech of the Kaiser's, for the simple reason that he agreed with all of them. All he could do was to express admiration and offer congratulations on their power and the genius and mastery they showed in form and content.

So, in parting with Count Waldersee, William II went on with his reference to the heavy scourge which the rebels in China must be made to feel, with the same severity which Attila's Huns once applied. Emperor William was right in ordering that there should be a heavy punishment. The Chinese had dealt

247

inhumanly with the Whites. And it was not only the Germans that he wanted to have protected in this way for all time. Once more there had risen before his eyes the 'Yellow Peril.' For all that, the phrase concerning the Huns did grave damage; it dug deep into the consciousness of Germany's contemporaries.

In carrying out his duties in the Far East, Field Marshal Count Waldersee made more use of his abilities as a diplomat than of his powers as Commander-in-Chief. The Kaiser's choice had fallen on him because he valued his great military ability and also realized his gift of suppleness in negotiation. Count Waldersee's own impression was that the Foreign Ministry had supported his selection for the command in order 'to prevent him from carrying on any further intrigues.' The Japanese troops obeyed him implicitly. The British he hated—cautiously. Whenever possible he left them out of his dispositions. With the French and Russians, almost entirely colonial officers and troops, he got on splendidly. Lieutenant-Colonel Marchand, who had a vivid memory, as had all his brother officers, of the hauling down of the Tricolour in the Sudan, described to Count Waldersee the exasperating humiliation of Fashoda. The Generalissimo captivated all with his comradely geniality—so much so that new thoughts of fraternization sprang up. In future, the Russian and French officers felt, they would prefer to work with the Germans against Britain. They were caught by the glamour and the visions born spontaneously of a moment of comradeship in arms.

There was no longer much in the way of laurels of victory that could fall to the German Generalissimo on the battlefields of China. The Boxer rising had already been virtually suppressed. There remained little to do beyond the setting up of tribunals and the safeguarding of the restored order. Japanese divisions had penetrated into Peking through an aqueduct known only to them; and immediately afterwards the Russians had stormed the city. The Capital had fallen before the Count arrived in China. Now the Russians wanted to withdraw all their soldiers from China. They were secretly in touch with the Viceroy, Li Hung-chang, and their aim was to induce him to abandon Manchuria to Russia. He was more likely to agree if they withdrew the forces which they now had stationed in the Capital and the Yangtze-Kiang area and all over the province of Chihli. The other Powers would then also have to consider the withdrawal of their troops. The Russians wanted Manchuria, and they wanted to have no foreign Power in the adjoining provinces of China—the area of the unrest—and least of all Britain. Britain, however, would not dream of abandoning the railways and works and her merchants' great trade in these provinces. Her troops remained in China. On occasion the British forces brought from India were even further strengthened, for one expedition or another, by troops from Weihaiwei. The Russians thus found themselves compelled once more to defer the final evacuation of their expeditionary force. Very soon it became clear to Count Waldersee that the Boxers and the Boxer rising had lost all interest, and that all that the Powers were thinking of in China was the acquisition of spheres of influence. He had carried through a successful expedition to Paotingfu, whither the xenophobe Chinese Empress had fled with her Court; then he had cleared the Teiho basin of the Boxers. His further military tasks included the imposition of the surrender of the murderers of von Ketteler and their trial, the chastisement of the abettors of the murder, and the punishment of the Empress and Prince Tuan, who between them had either launched the rising or tolerated and encouraged it. But for the Powers the area of hostilities in China had long dwindled to the problem of a new and profitable partition.

Through General Prince Engalitchev the Russians tried first to set the Generalissimo against Britain. Count Waldersee assigned to General Linevitch the important railway line from Shanghaikwan to Peking, the Russian commander undertaking to guarantee the transport of all forces for military purposes. Count Waldersee described this as a measure dictated by military necessity; but the Cabinet in London saw with vexation the handing over of the line of communication with Peking to the Russians. To deepen the new tension between Germany and Britain so produced, the Russian Cabinet returned once more to the proposal which it had made in midsummer for the neutralization of the whole of the Yangtze basin.

Germany's reply to the Russian proposal had been that the question of the Chinese fleet at the mouth of the Yangtze must be regarded, together with that of the protection of foreigners, as one for all the Powers. During the negotiations which began in London, Lord Salisbury had at first made no objection to the Russian proposal; but in August 1900 the Prince of

Wales had let Emperor William see that the British had no enthusiasm at all for the idea. Count Waldersee's reports confirmed the extent to which British enterprise had struck root in the Yangtze basin. The Kaiser had then described to his uncle the two possibilities in regard to Britain's attitude towards affairs in that area. Either Britain intended to claim a special position, and if so she must make it and maintain it for herself; there would remain for her the question of stemming the progress of Russian penetration—or else a policy of the open door for all could be instituted. One thing, in any case, Russia had secured: Germany's attitude towards developments in the Yangtze basin was becoming of the utmost importance to her general relations with Britain.

The Prince of Wales decided for a policy of the open door in the Yangtze basin. He would try to win over Lord Salisbury to that policy. The Kaiser promised to support Britain's view. After a great deal of discussion, in the course of which Lord Salisbury was at first in doubt for a considerable time as to the exact limits to be set to the future neutralized Chinese territory, a formal agreement was at last arrived at between Britain and Germany concerning China—the Yangtze Treaty. Under it the whole course of the Yangtze-Kiang and all China's seaports were to be kept free for all nations to trade without impediment. Russia was to have freedom of economic development in Manchuria. She was also to be free, if she wished, to take possession of one of the Amur ports. But neither Britain nor Germany nor any other nation should acquire any Chinese territory. Britain and Germany would support one another against any attempt to interfere with their existing rights in China.

Lord Salisbury had finally proposed that the agreement between the two Powers should apply to the whole of the Chinese territory 'in which they have influence.' But Secretary of State von Bülow only liked firm, precisely formulated commitments when their basis was some big advantage of his own seeking. In the treaty instrument he secured the insertion of the more general provision that the obligation of the two Powers to support one another applied only to that Chinese territory 'in so far as they are able to exercise influence.' It would thus be possible for Count Bülow to stretch and twist the whole treaty as he thought fit.

Despite this manœuvre, the British Cabinet had the satisfaction of seeing an agreement with Germany on the Chinese question actually concluded. The impression was excellent; perhaps good progress would now be made with the great question of the alliance. Even Mr. Chamberlain was ready for once to forget the injury that Count Bülow had done him.

In January 1901 came the death of the greatly lamented Queen Victoria. In her last sleep Emperor William had held her in his arms until she ceased to breathe.

Immediately after her death, when British feeling had warmed towards Germany, the people appreciating very greatly the Kaiser's sympathy and chivalry and his own really deep grief, Chamberlain made a third attempt to bring Germany into an alliance. If this attempt failed, he was determined never to make another.

Chamberlain's idea was a mighty system of allied forces. Amid all the labour of the negotiations with Germany, so rich in disappointments, he had paved the way two years before for an alliance between Britain and Japan. Marquis Ito, the Japanese Ambassador in London, returned to Tokio at the beginning of 1901 to replace Marquis Yamagata as head of the Government; and he took with him to Japan the outline of the terms of alliance. For months thereafter Britain and Japan, ostensibly in independence but not without perceptible signs of collaboration, sought to win over Germany at last. Japan knew what Britain wanted from Germany. What Japan wanted from Germany Britain would be bound to learn when she had concluded the alliance with Japan. Only Germany had no idea what the two wanted of her. Amid the great encirclement with offers of friendship and alliance from East and West, Secretary of State Count Bülow and *Geheimrat* von Holstein set to work thoroughly to smash up the ring of peace.

For all the self-control with which Chamberlain had dismissed and forgotten his experiences with Count Bülow, he remained sensitive and easily roused. Count Hatzfeldt, the Ambassador, had had experience of this a year before, when the Secretary for the Colonies complained of the tone adopted by the Germans in dealing with the incident of the detained German ships. Now, in his new soundings and suggestions, Chamberlain kept far more in the background than a year before. Count Hatzfeldt was confined to his bed, and the new conversations were carried on on his behalf with the Counsellor of Embassy, von Eckardstein—first by the Duke of

Devonshire and soon after by Lord Lansdowne, who had taken over the conduct of foreign affairs from Lord Salisbury, an overburdened Premier and now rather a tired one.

The Counsellor of Embassy was bound by close family ties to British society and British life, and in the negotiations of three years before he had shown his goodwill and his capacity to strike out an independent line of policy; Chamberlain and the Duke of Devonshire now, in the new confidential conversations with him, spoke candidly and quite unreservedly. Britain wanted an alliance with Germany. A beginning, moreover, ought to be made with the regulation of affairs in Morocco. Britain intended no longer to stand alone in the world. It was quite open to Germany, of course, to refuse; but the hour would then have arrived for Britain to join France and Russia.

'I particularly mistrust the present overtures from Chamberlain and Co.'—so ran the first reply from Holstein to Count Metternich, then in London in the Kaiser's entourage—'because the threatened understanding with Russia and France is such an utter fraud.'

The Kaiser was disturbed. He could feel the cordiality that surrounded him in England. Once more he favoured the alliance. Russia was as much of a nightmare to him as ever. She was the last resort if there was no chance of joining Britain. But for his part he exulted in the British offer. He telegraphed to the Secretary of State:

'So now they are coming, to all appearance, after all our waiting!'

Count Bülow shared von Holstein's view of the new proposals. He saw no trace of serious intent in them; he saw only duplicity. He warned the Kaiser. In vexation the Kaiser declared:

'I am not going to fall between two stools.'

Chancellor and *Geheimrat*, after this, pursued the work of understanding in their characteristic way. In the spring Britain considered that the moment had come for Germany and Britain to protest against a treaty drawn up between Russia and the Chinese Viceroy, Li Hung-chang, on Russia's rights of dominion in Manchuria; Count Bülow, however, left Britain in the lurch. Lord Lansdowne had asked that Germany should fulfil her obligations, relying on the general provision which the Chancellor had elaborated with so much astuteness for the Yangtze Treaty. The Chancellor had been caught in his own toils. He now began, however, coolly to give play to his gift of exegesis, in the Reichstag, and coolly made use of it to extricate himself from the agreement which he had made. This time the British Colonial Secretary suffered no disappointment; he had had one such experience already. Only his reserve and aloofness were intensified. For the present, however, Lord Lansdowne went on with the negotiations. He might have better luck.

Britain wanted an alliance with Germany. Chancellor and *Geheimrat* demanded Britain's adhesion to the Triple Alliance. The *Geheimrat* had no intention of leaving a 'back door' through which Britain could make good her escape if he raised a storm in Europe. Count Hatzfeldt advised that the alliance should first be concluded between Britain and Germany; the

Triple Alliance would then be brought in automatically. The danger seemed to him real and serious that Britain might turn to Russia and France. Count Metternich, who had been designated as successor in the Embassy to the invalid Count Hatzfeldt, sent a special report advocating compliance with the British desires. But Chancellor and *Geheimrat* adhered to their opinion.

Yet even these two must have been given pause by the strange news brought home by Embassy Counsellor Count Wedel, the German Chargé d'Affaires in Tokio, on his return home on leave. Before he left for Europe he had had another comprehensive discussion with Viscount Aoki. The Viscount was a friend of the Germans; he had married a German woman. He had a perfect command of the German language. He neither hated nor loved the Russians, but he saw more plainly than any other Japanese that Russia intended to lay claim to Korea. The moment Russia attempted to do that, there would be war with Japan. All Japan's preparations were made with an eye on that coming war. She was determined to face the war. She had no need of her great and well-equipped army, the fruit of heavy sacrifices, for the defence of her island shores. No one would attack the Japanese in their islands. But if Korea fell into Russian hands the continent at her side would be lost to Japan. She would not have so much as a bridge across to it. She would be blockaded: the expansion of her island power would be at an end; separated from the world by the vast Pacific, cut off from the neighbouring continent in which her future progress lay by a strong, broad wall, she would sink into oblivion. If

Drontheim July 1900
The German Emperor wearing the Uniform of a
Norwegian Admiral ready to recieve the
King of Norway. Captain Ingenohl Commanding
the "Hamburg" chartered as a Yacht to
replace the "Hohenzollern" undergoing repairs

that was to happen, she might as well disband the army which was the guarantee of her future on the continent; and decades of effort would have gone in vain.

'The army,' Viscount Aoki declared, 'would have become of no service; we might as well throw our guns into the ocean.'

It made little difference to Japan whether she were beaten in a war over Korea or abandoned Korea without a blow. Consequently she was determined on war —the only means of preventing Korea from becoming Russian. Viscount Aoki wanted to know what would be Germany's attitude in the event of a war between Russia and Japan. Friendship between Russia and Prussia had the support of an old tradition; and he was disturbed at the thought of that. The enquiry was a delicate one, and he would not entrust it to the Japanese Ambassador in Berlin. Perhaps Count Wedel would be able to set his mind at rest.

The Count reported to Berlin. Chancellor von Bülow sent his thanks for Viscount Aoki's confidence. Count Wedel should expressly declare to the Foreign Minister that in a war between Russia and Japan, Germany would remain neutral. The Japanese Foreign Minister now went further. Japan, he said, was so strong that she could deal with Russia unaided, giant though Russia seemed—to such unexampled efficiency had she brought her armaments and her army. Nevertheless, Japan needed an ally. France's attitude was doubtful. She was Russia's ally. With Britain, Japan would arrive at an agreement and a signed treaty: that she knew already. But no one could keep France quiet better than her strong neighbour

Germany. The Prime Minister, Marquis Yamagata, and he himself and all Japan, whose sons had gone in such numbers to Germany to study, were for an alliance with Germany. Just as Germany would be at France's rear if she took part in a war against Japan, so Japan stood at the rear of Russia if she should ever attack Germany. Japan wanted an alliance with Germany. She also wanted one with Britain. She wanted to see Germany and Britain and Japan placed in complete security by a great bond uniting all three.

Soon after this memorable conversation, Count Wedel left Tokio for Europe. Just before his departure there had been a change of Ministry in Japan. Marquis Yamagata had turned over the seals of office to Marquis Ito, who was back from the Embassy in London. Marquis Aoki also retired. But in Japan the course of affairs of state and the direction of policy are not governed as in most States. The leading Ministers come and go as elsewhere, but they continue to have a voice in the Council of 'Elder Statesmen.' In all questions, in all decisions to be taken, this Council has the final word. The Cabinet must bow before its fiat. The Cabinet has no competence if it has not the covering authority of the Elder Statesmen. Viscount Aoki did not belong to the Council, but Marquis Yamagata entered it, and there represented the ideas and the policy of the Viscount. The Viscount pressed the whole matter on the attention of the Chargé d'Affaires once more before his departure. It had been meant as an invitation to Germany; but, he said, Germany had made no reply, and meanwhile time was pressing. Japan would soon have to conclude the treaty with Britain without waiting, though she would gladly have seen the treaty with Germany well forward before the British affixed their signatures. With Germany Japan would be in a stronger position in face of Britain. The same was true of Germany. The Japanese statesman had put forward all his representations in a masterly manner. He had made the most of every card he held. He had made no false move in his play. He had sought to bring all the players together; he had assessed the importance of each; he had bound no one down. All were to see all his cards and to appreciate their great importance in this world game. He had exposed no one. Now the decision lay with Berlin.

Count Wedel travelled to Germany in great excitement. The vast implications of the Viscount's communication did not escape him. In Berlin, however, he failed to secure an opportunity of speaking to the Chancellor about the Japanese offer. The Reichstag was taking up all Count Bülow's time with its meetings of 'fractions' and its meetings in full house. The new Secretary of State had gone away. Finally Count Wedel found himself in the presence of Baron von Holstein. The Japanese overtures had not escaped the *Geheimrat's* acute observation. But to his great regret he was unable to enter into them. Sometimes the *Geheimrat* liked to give the younger members of the German diplomatic corps a little private instruction in the fundamentals and the determinants of his foreign policy. He did this with Count Wedel. Never, he explained, would Russia forgive a German rapprochement with Japan. France had to be separated from Russia, and if Germany were to join Japan, it would only consolidate the Dual Alliance. Count

Wedel objected that if Germany rejected the Japanese offer, Japan would conclude her alliance with Britain alone. No misfortune, in the eyes of the *Geheimrat*, could be more trivial. There was no harm in the 'whale' joining the Orientals. Japan would never venture to tackle the Russian 'bear.' So the *Geheimrat* went on with his accustomed multiplications and divisions, his similes and his mammals and his schemings.

'All bluff and big talk!' he said.

The Counsellor of Embassy stuck to his opinion: within a decade there would be war between Japan and Russia. At that Baron Holstein laughed outright: ridiculous! Yet, very few days later, the inevitability of the collision between the two rivals in the Far East was mentioned by Emperor William, at the banquet in honour of the heir to the Austro-Hungarian throne, Archduke Francis Ferdinand. Count Wedel had been at the banquet, but had had no opportunity to embark on the subject.

Chancellor and *Geheimrat* had no prevision of the future. They had no eyes even for the things around them. It might have been natural to ask themselves whether there was not some connexion between these offers, almost in the same breath, from Britain and Japan. But they were too busy with their bright talk of the whale and the bear.

In the latter part of March 1901 Lord Lansdowne had put the direct question to Baron von Eckardstein, Counsellor of Embassy, whether Germany was now prepared to enter into a defensive alliance. The Baron had sent one warning message after another to

Berlin that Britain would turn towards Russia and France if Germany rejected her offer. Lord Lansdowne was concerned to show that his question had been put in all seriousness, and finally he set down in writing the essential points on which negotiations might be based. He had obtained the concurrence of Lord Salisbury and Mr. Balfour in his draft. If Britain handed over such proposals in a written document, surely Germany must at last grasp the situation.

But Chancellor and *Geheimrat* persisted in their demand that Germany's partners in the Triple Alliance must be included in the agreement. The treaty with Britain must, moreover, be no secret treaty: it must be ratified by the British Parliament. As for Lord Lansdowne's desire to bring in Japan as well, the Chancellor had no objection to that:

'Japan is inclined to a policy of expansion, and may, therefore, see no direct advantage in a defensive alliance. She will, however, draw from it the advantage of being brought into good political society.'

As the Chancellor and Baron Holstein regarded 'Chamberlain and Co.' as the men behind 'an utter fraud,' the 'good political society' could only refer to themselves. Now, however, the British had had enough. The diplomatic skirmishing continued a little while longer; but by May it was already acquiring on the British side rather the appearance of rearguard skirmishing. Lord Lansdowne held firmly to his view that Britain could only conclude an agreement with Germany and not with Austria-Hungary and Italy; he suggested, however, that the complete draft of the treaty should be put on paper. He had a

stronger sense of the objections to an express ratification of the treaty by the British Parliament than Mr.
Chamberlain had had. He knew as well as Chamberlain that no British Cabinet could conclude a treaty,
public or secret, with a foreign Power without first
making perfectly sure of the assent of the leader of
His Majesty's most loyal Opposition. It was the
function of the leader of the Opposition in Parliament to watch the activities of the Government, and
he actually drew from the Government with all due
formalities a princely salary, greatly exceeding that of
the German Chancellor. He had at once to take over
the duties of the Government when he had over-
thrown it. He was constitutionally and statutorily
bound to assume responsibility if he had persuaded
Parliament that he was better fitted for the control
of affairs than the leaders in office. No Government
in England would perform or envisage any act
of state without first consulting the Leader of the
Opposition. And, conversely, no Opposition taking
over the Government could upset things which had
been done with its prior confidential assent. Whether
an act of state was publicly announced in Parliament
or was kept secret, the Leader of the Opposition was
informed of it in advance, and no British Cabinet
could venture on an act of state against which the
Leader of the Opposition had set himself from the
first. If, on the other hand, he had not done so, he
could not reverse the decision arrived at when he
himself entered office. The Cabinet of the morrow
was thus gradually and almost unceasingly associated
with and committed to the actions of the Cabinet in
office: it had been initiated into them as Opposition,

and it took over the responsibility from them when it became a Government. Consequently Chamberlain was able to offer the certain prospect of Parliamentary assent if he ever actually concluded the agreement. Chancellor von Bülow, however, and *Geheimrat* von Holstein, in their entire ignorance of British traditions, knew nothing of all this. Thus, well-grounded as was the Kaiser's demand for formal Parliamentary ratification, they were unable either to gauge or confirm its force or to take the measure of its real significance. Lord Lansdowne knew exactly how much importance to attach to the Kaiser's demand. But he seized the opportunity of the demand, and replied that he saw difficulties in meeting it. For he was now drawing back.

'If they are so shortsighted,' said Chamberlain of the German statesmen in June, 'as to be unable to see that what is at issue is the possibility of an entirely new grouping of forces in the world, then the men are beyond helping.'

All the German statesmen saw of the 'entirely new grouping in the world' was the opportunity afforded by the cordial atmosphere of alliance negotiations for pressing for British support for the increase of the Chinese maritime customs duties and the fixing of the costs of the Chinese campaign, and for British agreement to the amplest possible compensation of the Germans who had suffered damages in the Boer War. More important in British eyes was the great problem, growing ever more menacing, of the restoration of order in Morocco. The French had occupied the oasis of Tuat, and were preparing to advance on Yuman. A year before the Chancellor had himself indicated to Lord Salisbury the great importance which

Morocco, 'the nerve centre of our earth,' had for Germany. Chamberlain had then asked for the Chancellor's suggestions and views as to the future of this Sultanate. Bülow had made no suggestions to Chamberlain, but had invited the Russians to warn the French against further penetration into Morocco.

'In this matter,' he considered, 'we must maintain for the present a position of entire reserve, a Sphinx's attitude.'

All the British statesmen were calling for the withdrawal from dealings with the Sphinx. Lord Salisbury admitted in July to Lord Lansdowne, his Foreign Minister, that he had 'rather lost interest' in it all. Chamberlain declared that 'it is difficult to do business with Berlin.' King Edward VII and his Ambassador, Sir Frank Lascelles, listened courteously in Homburg in August to the Kaiser's ideas concerning Britain's adhesion to the Triple Alliance; they even seemed to agree with him. Nor did the question of Parliamentary ratification seem to them to be insoluble. They assured the Kaiser that no one was working harder than Lord Lansdowne to bring the Alliance into being. (Yet, from then on, whenever the German Ambassador sought out Lord Lansdowne he always found that he had gone away.) The Kaiser listened to all this with a little discomfort. All this unexpected, unreserved assent on every point was rather too good to believe. It looked as if King Edward was just out for a quiet life.

Joseph Chamberlain, however, made once more, as three years before, a big speech as Colonial Secretary, at a public meeting in Birmingham. The atrocities, he said, which had been laid to the charge of the British

in their African campaign were nothing to the things
done by other nations in like case; and he spoke of
actions committed by the Germans in the campaign
of 1870. Here was a sudden change of tone, another
Chamberlain standing on the platform. Chancellor
von Bülow determined quickly to set him right in a
speech in the Reichstag. Before doing so he had a
secret and confidential enquiry made of the Colonial
Secretary whether he would not take the opportunity
of his next speech to withdraw or at least modify his
attack on Germany. No—the Colonial Secretary had
no intention of doing so. And he told the Austro-
Hungarian Ambassador in London that he despaired
of any friendship with Germany. Further, the British
Ambassador in Berlin was instructed to mention the
objections which a treaty of alliance with Germany
would be sure to meet with in the British Parliament.

At once it was clear to the Kaiser that all the years
of effort and negotiation had been in vain; great were
his dismay and grief. Much of the whole course of
events was mysterious to him, as the Chancellor had
kept from him all the connecting links in the negotiations and almost every crucial detail. He had constantly ordered everything to be done to bring about
the alliance, and Chancellor and Foreign Ministry
had never tired of assuring him of their passionate
pursuit of the goal the ruler had pointed out to them.
As required by the Constitution, he had always
listened to the Chancellor's advice, had never put
obstacles in his path; but he had always toned down
the sharp messages that Count Bülow had desired to
put into his mouth. Consequently he assumed that the
whole blame for his failure lay with Britain. He did,

indeed, see an 'entirely new grouping in the world':
he saw it in depression and deep anxiety. His dream
had come to an end—Britain's friendship was lost.
All the wooing of her had been in vain. The policy of
the approach to her through Russia had also failed.
That detour must now be converted into a direct
path to Russia—an attempt full of dark possibilities
and dangers. He did not yet know that a German
Chancellor and his adviser, working with an un-
scrupulousness beyond all measure and an arrogance
to match it, with a falsity beyond plumbing, with
methods of pretended craftiness and real lying, and
above all with a narrowness without parallel in all
history, had destroyed the good relations of two great
nations and the peace of the world.

All that the Kaiser could see was the formidable
piling up of coming storms. No further word of
friendship came from Britain. Three times she had
offered her hand in alliance. Three humiliating re-
jections had been the reply of the German statesmen.
The British had no difficulty in changing their course:
they had said in advance that their alternative
approach lay to Russia and France. At once they
changed their course. For Britain there was thenceforward only one enemy. He had shown his mentality.
To every attempt at a real and friendly understanding he had replied with threats and exactions. From
now on Britain would be on her guard against him.
She would prepare every means, guns and ships,
alliances and war-preparedness, for the utter destruction of this unmasked enemy, once he raised his head.

Britain would be on the alert every second in
future. The enemy was Germany.

Chapter VI

GERMANY AT THE ZENITH OF HER PSEUDO-POWER

THE LAST negotiations that were attempted for an alliance between Britain and Germany had no sooner failed than Mr. Chamberlain changed Britain's course. At once, in January 1902, he began to try to pave the way for the rapprochement with France which he had foreshadowed. And now this statesman, disillusioned and thrice rejected by Germany, aimed move after move, blow after blow against her. The British-Japanese agreement was concluded; Germany had missed her chance to come into it. Fresh negotiations began in London on Morocco; but they were no longer carried on with Germany but with Paul Cambon, the Ambassador of the French Republic. The British Cabinet moved tentatively and cautiously at first. No precipitate solution, the French Ambassador was told, of the Morocco question was possible; it would only produce discord. But not a word was said to suggest to the Ambassador that Britain would decline to discuss the subject with France. Chamberlain informed the two leaders of the Opposition, Mr. Asquith and Sir Edward Grey, of his conversations with Cambon. The French Ambassador understood at once.

Rumours began to reach Germany from London in the spring of 1902, but neither Chancellor von

Bülow nor his adviser Holstein was disturbed. But Russia, France's ally, began to be suspicious, and Emperor William grew anxious. Russia saw her ally joining in festivities with Britain, her mortal enemy. Her mortal enemy was fraternizing with Japan in Chihli, at the gates of Peking, and in Persia. Count Lambsdorff hurriedly proposed to Berlin an alliance to maintain the *status quo* in the Far East. But Chancellor and *Geheimrat* were not in the habit of plunging into friendships as hastily as all that. If Britain had barely been dismissed when Russia came, that was one more sign of Germany's power and importance. Moreover, in Baron Holstein's view an agreement with Russia would merely cost Germany her field of enterprise in Japan. The Russians were sent away. The Russian Foreign Minister referred to Emperor William's friendly attitude at the time of Kiaochow. He was told that Russia would receive a general support of her policy in Asia; but a Kaiser's word did not bind his statesmen. Emperor William was able to calm the Tsar by pointing out that he could be of more service to him in Europe than in Asia: Count Lambsdorff, injured, lapsed into silence.

Chancellor and *Geheimrat* continued to insist that Germany could not 'commit herself'—either in the East or the West. Germany in her glory, striding forward in trade, blessed with prosperous industries, protected by the best soldiers in the world, soon to be defended also by a great navy—Germany remained in their eyes, in spite of all that was happening around her, the mighty Mistress of the Centre, bestowing her favours where she herself chose. The Kaiser also saw the power and the growing prestige of his Empire, and himself furthered both. But he saw, to begin with, that there was an end of friendship with Britain. And Italy had made a strange amount of difficulty over the renewal of the Triple Alliance. She wanted Austria-Hungary to agree to an eventual Italian occupation of Tripolitania; Austria-Hungary herself, however, was to undertake no enterprise in the Balkans. Albania was to become an autonomous State. The Viennese Cabinet was ready to meet the Italian wishes, and they thus brought no danger to the Triple Alliance. But the Italians also demanded that no provision should be included in the new treaty which might imply any danger to France, and they wanted expressly to inform the French of this. The Chancellor succeeded in getting that demand waived. But, taken with the unceasing bitter struggles for many years past between the nationalities of the old Habsburg Empire, the Italian demand flashed a vivid light on the value of the Triple Alliance. The Kaiser's conviction was confirmed that only the path to Russia remained open—even though Count Lambsdorff had just been turned away.

He put his views to Tsar Nicholas in Reval. He suggested that the Triple Alliance should join Russia and France in a single great coalition, against which Britain would be powerless in spite of her new friendship with Japan. The Tsar could see the advantage he would gain in a strengthened position in the Far East; the Kaiser's purpose was to increase Germany's security. He would point out during a coming visit to London that it was quite obviously to the advantage of the five Great Powers on the Continent to be able to take joint action in the future. Emperor

William had the feeling that the Tsar agreed with him. He might be able to win him over if he demonstrated to him with sufficient energy the reality of his gain from the proposal, and if at the next opportunity Germany rendered him genuine and important services.

The European Powers made one effort after another to arrive at a new grouping of world forces. France had rightly gauged the cooling of British-German relations. Britain no longer seemed entirely disinclined to carry on friendly discussions with the French. France negotiated openly with Spain over Morocco as the preliminary to an agreement with Britain; a Franco-Spanish agreement was arrived at. In March 1903 King Edward went on a visit to Paris. He was received with great acclamations, in sign of the coming fraternization. The President of the Republic went to London to return the visit. There Delcassé, the French Foreign Minister, at last had the opportunity of a discussion that cleared away all difficulties. France, he said, intended to make an end of the unrest in Morocco. And she would tolerate no other Power in Morocco. The problem was no longer one which Lord Lansdowne was unable to touch without disturbing a hornet's nest. Let France, he said, declare herself uninterested in Egypt. Let Egypt become entirely a British interest, and Morocco French. Cambon, the French Ambassador, could negotiate further details in London. That was not merely a victory in Morocco but a change of front: Britain had been detached from Germany and stood side by side with France. The change of front was signalized by Britain on the high seas: the new British Home Fleet was attached to the North Sea Command.

In the Foreign Ministry in Berlin *Geheimrat* von Holstein talked at length to the Chancellor, about this time, on the spectre of the Anglo-French understanding. He had the feeling, it was true, that even a union of all the Continental Powers against Great Britain could effect nothing. There was thus no purpose to be served by attempting to bring the union into being. But he saw no cause for concern:

'Time is working for us.'

'The Chancellor agreed. There was no seeing through all these developments, as yet, but there was not the slightest reason to panic about them. When the Queen of Spain received the Chancellor, however, in Vienna, she rather startled him with an allusion to the new treaties concerning Morocco, already complete in outline. He determined at once to ask in Madrid whether it might not be possible for Germany to receive some compensation. He had not yet grasped the facts that the complete partition of Morocco had long been decided on, that Britain, France and Spain had come to a full understanding over it, and that the Chancellor and the *Geheimrat* had lost Germany her chance of a share in the good things going. In October 1903 the world learned that Britain and France had agreed in future to entrust unreservedly to the Hague Court of Arbitration all differences of opinion which did not touch their vital interests. Four weeks later Lord Lansdowne declared to the German Ambassador, Count Metternich, that no one could prevent France from making use of her privileges in Morocco. The British Cabinet took the expert advice of Sir Arthur Nicolson, the Minister in Tangier, as to the details of the Morocco agreement.

Britain and France had cleared away every difference between them; and still the Chancellor remained unconcerned. His attention was monopolized by the events that were making history in the Far East. A Dutch banker had invested large sums of money on behalf of the Tsar and the King of Denmark on a forest concession by the Yalu River. The Japanese had no objection to a mere timber deal. But when the Tsar stationed a cordon of troops to protect his property they feared that it would come under Russian occupation. At that the latent tension was discharged. The 'Yellow race' had actually begun the war between Russia and Japan, of the coming of which Nicholas II had spoken to the Kaiser, and Count Wedel to *Geheimrat* von Holstein—the war anticipated by the Kaiser as the great parting of the ways, and laughed away by the *Geheimrat* as incredible.

The Chancellor noted the outbreak of the war. Count Bülow was a statesman who was instantly equal to every turn of events. Even the publication of the agreement of April 8, 1904, between Britain and France, under which all questions outstanding between the two countries were disposed of and an Entente Cordiale concluded, found the Chancellor armed at all points. He was not to be caught out by events of that sort. The British Secretary for the Colonies had repeatedly let him know that it was impending. Only, he had not believed Mr. Chamberlain. However, he welcomed the new alliance as of good omen for the peace of the world. It might have been imagined that he had been wishing for nothing better. Not for a minute did he fail to keep on smiling. He filled the air with polished and placid phrases entirely irreconcilable with the menace of the new development. He knew the value and the effectiveness of pleasing and neatly concocted untruths in the Reichstag, in the Press and among the mass of the people. Once more the Kaiser was alone in viewing the matter differently.

For three years the Kaiser had been urging the negotiation of an Alliance with Britain. As far back as when Bülow was Secretary of State, he had pointed out to Bülow the advantage he had in negotiations with England in being Queen Victoria's grandson. For more than ten years he had pursued every possible path to Britain's favour. One after another his statesmen, Baron von Marschall and Count Bülow and the rest, had shaken their wise heads at the idea. Bülow especially had continually painted in vivid colours the Russian enmity that would follow a German approach to Britain. Britain, according to Bülow, was quite determined on no account to enter into any agreement with Russia. It had been axiomatic with Bülow and Holstein that she would never join France. Now her union with France was an accomplished fact. And, after all, Russia showed not the vestige of any intention to make an end of her friendship with France. All the vast accumulation of the over-clever speeches of the Chancellor, and his incessant appeals to the Kaiser to waste no civil breath on Britain, were reduced to a miserable fatuity in face of the devastating reckoning that the facts now imposed. The Kaiser's mistrust of Britain did, indeed, remain active. It might be that the Chancellor was, after all, right in his contention that Britain was not genuinely seeking an alliance, that she had been merely playing with Germany. Thus the Chancellor's failure did not stand unmistakably revealed; though the discovery that Russia was remaining quietly at France's side even after the French had allied themselves with the British exposed the Chancellor, in the Kaiser's view, in one obvious and profound miscalculation. That alone certainly counted for much, with all its devastating consequences, and its proof of want of due foresight. Yet the great mistake was the Kaiser's own—he retained this Chancellor.

In face of the Kaiser's displeasure with him, Count Bülow found the war between Japan and Russia really a godsend. Again and again he brought up that subject with the Kaiser. Britain was allied with Japan, France virtually allied with Britain. When the time came for peace negotiations, France must offend either the Russians or the British. Then all the friendships would burst like soap bubbles—one more instance showing how Germany's true power lay in her ability to choose sides and so keep the upper hand. So convinced was the Chancellor of the inevitability of that development, that he soon regained his peace of soul and lightness of heart. If it gave the British any pleasure to conclude alliances, by all means let them enjoy themselves—even if they brought a Home Fleet into the North Sea, let no one grudge them their satisfaction. What did it matter, thought Count Bülow, which way they pointed their guns?

For Emperor William the war in the Far East came as a signal and a stimulus: now Tsar Nicholas should see where were his true friends. The Kaiser was no longer concerned for the effect on Britain. He was sick of the empty phrases about '*arbiter mundi*,' 'no commitments,' 'preservation of freedom of action.' Up to now, in spite of all the phrases, all the rest had done simply what they wanted. He wanted now to get Russia to commit herself. At that price he was perfectly prepared to commit himself. Naturally Germany must preserve neutrality in the conflict between Russia and Japan. For all that, it was possible amid the neutrality to show such chivalry and, so far as was permissible, such readiness to be of assistance, that the Tsar could only be filled with gratitude. The Kaiser promised to preserve Russia's flank from any attack from Europe. He would see to it that Austria-Hungary kept quiet, and that there were no disturbances in the Balkans. If the Russian fleet should sail, German coaling stations and German ships should assist it with their own fuel and stores on its endless voyage to the Far East. Albert Ballin, the creator and director of the *Hamburg-Amerika Linie*, undertook to be responsible for this. The incidents of the war might offer various other opportunities of showing the Tsar Germany's sympathy in Russia's fate.

Meanwhile the shipyards in Kronstadt were working feverishly. Admiral Rozdjestvensky was to sail with the Russian fleet in October 1904, to go to the relief of Port Arthur, which the Japanese had blockaded. But Russia's fleet was not ready. Almost half of it had to be re-created; old ships had to be refitted and re-armed—and all this in the midst of war, in haste and anxiety and under pressure, as shipyards and Admiralty, Ministry of War and the ships' commanding officers, had the most precise of information, before the fleet was half ready to sail, of the attacks which were to be made on it on its way out.

The Japanese, so it was said, were going to make their first attempt against the fleet before it left the North Sea. They had sent torpedo-boats from the Pacific to lie in wait for the Russians. Other messages spoke of torpedo-boats lying in British ports, with the tacit permission of Japan's ally. Shortly before the Admiral sailed a report came in of enemy vessels sheltering in a secluded inlet on the shores of the Baltic. The Russian Admiralty grew more and more alarmed, and in Berlin the Russian Ambassador, Count Osten-Sacken, sought an audience of Emperor William. He asked that a watch should be kept on Japanese in Germany, and particularly in the great Hansa cities. According to his information, said the Ambassador, there was irrefragable evidence of Japanese preparations for a blow against the Russian fleet either in the Baltic or the North Sea.

Emperor William gave orders that Russia's desire should be acceded to. All Germany's police hunted out suspicious Japanese and watched what they were up to. The naval stations searched the Baltic day and night, and the North Sea, and the Elbe and the Weser. But the German patrols sighted neither the Japanese war vessels, nor the suspicious steamers of which the reports and enquiries from St. Petersburg had spoken.

At last the Russian fleet was ready. Admiral Rozdjestvensky steamed away from Kronstadt—full of fears unmastered, shaken with visions of horror at the very start, an Admiral on tenterhooks, the despairing leader of a fleet that he regarded as lost.

Cautiously he proceeded in two columns. On reaching the Channel the first group of cruisers was to stop and await the remainder of the fleet. The ships steamed slowly, all the look-out men watching every speck. By night the ships glided on in the light of their projectors. The sailors slept armed by the guns. Every hour there came some fresh alarm. Captains, officers, and crews of the first column were tired out before they reached the entrance to the Channel.

At the mouth of the Channel the column came into fog. The vision was poor, and the over-strained, over-alert lookout men scented danger. The lights of a British fishing fleet showed one by one. For a second the men in the catheads imagined that they had seen through the fog and espied torpedo-boats takingcover behind the fishing vessels. At the next moment there came into the light of the projector, out of the greyness that enveloped all else, the gigantic silhouette of an enemy warship. She fired. Then, in one second, the tremendous tension that had lain over all for months past, and had been yet further tautened amid the terrors of the voyage, broke down. All the Russian ships fired: the first naval engagement raged amid the mists. The second column came up to reinforce the first, obviously in the nick of time. It sailed on, in full sight of the first, right into the bank of fog from which the sound of firing had come. It cleared for action, and fired. A blind cannonade boomed across the sea. Suddenly the enemy retired. The firing ceased. The first naval engagement was over. Admiral Rozdjestvensky sailed on.

The thunder of those guns on the Dogger Bank, near Hull, resounded through the world. Britain declared that there had been no Japanese torpedo-boats among the British fishing vessels. She demanded compensation. Public feeling in Britain was roused against the Tsar. Then it veered round: the whole incident, the story went, had been planned and produced by the Kaiser, in order to get Britain and Russia at one another's throats, or else to bring Russia over to Germany's side. The Tsar's indignation was boundless. He wrote in his diary:

'October 15, Friday. Short conference at midday in my room with Uncle Alexis, Lambsdorff and Avelan, about British impudence and the steps to be taken.

'October 16, Saturday. Our proposal of yesterday to Britain that the affair of the firing in the North Sea should be brought before the Hague Tribunal (*sic*) has had its effect. Our mangy enemies at once altered their tone and agreed.'

Emperor William had instructed the German Admiralty to institute an inquiry into the North Sea incident, so far as could be done from its own observations and the information obtainable. The second column of the Russian warships, it appeared, had been proceeding alone. Hearing the sound of firing in the fog, it could only suppose that an attack was being made on the fleet. The first squadron was due to be at the appointed point at the entrance to the Channel, much farther south, long before this. The second column had accordingly fired on the aggressors. The German Admiralty entirely agreed that a flotilla of fishing boats would have been an admirable cover for torpedo-boats, had there been any. It had itself received news, alleged to have leaked out from British shipyards, that 'torpedo-boats of foreign nationality' had left the British yards in the night before the engagement on the Dogger Bank, and had not returned. On top of this came the detailed report

278

on the matter sent by Admiral Rozdjestvensky to the Tsar. Emperor William was unable to see to the bottom of the matter. There was nothing for it but to wait and see whether the British managed to clear themselves before the Hague Court of Arbitration and to carry through their claim for compensation. After all his experience of them, the Kaiser was ready to believe the British capable of anything, and quite easily capable of an indignant air of injured innocence, supported by a blind eye to what they might have been doing before the indignation came over them. But only one thing really mattered to the Kaiser: the Tsar must be doubly susceptible to every word of friendship that he sent him after the Dogger Bank incident.

Meanwhile Admiral Rozdjestvensky continued on his voyage to the Far East. He had done his duty. Russia's navy had shown its mettle in the moment of trial. The Admiral had reported to the Tsar the courage shown by his ships. His battleships and cruisers steamed southwards in regular formation, bearing their carefully kept logs with the exact entries of what had happened:

'1.35 a.m. The Squadron came into waters in which there was a quantity of fishing boats.

'1.40 a.m. Two warships came into sight of the Squadron, on port and starboard.

'1.41 a.m. Admiral's order to fire on the suspected ships.

'1.43 a.m. The suspected ships replied by signal: they were the cruisers *Dimitri Donskoy* and *Aurora*.

'1.44 a.m. Admiral's order to cease firing.'

After those entries the ghost of the North Sea

battle vanished into thin air. The ships in the first
column had got in amongst one another in the fog.
They had shot at one another, had a battle between
themselves.

The lookout men and signalmen had come straight
on board from Kronstadt Dockyard. All were new to
their work. They did not know a battleship from a
cruiser, or any ship from any other. Cries and signals
which shouted the error were beyond their understanding until the battle was over. The enemy had
had no more reality than a Potemkin village. They
had fought like the heroes of a Gogol farce.

Admiral Rozdjestvensky did not read his ship's
logs; or if he did he ignored them in making his report.
He had telegraphed his experiences to the Tsar. A
war was a thing of long duration; before it was over
the whole Dogger Bank incident would be forgotten.
It was uncomfortable for the Admiral that one day,
while he was still off the coast of Africa, the Hague
Court demanded to see the logs. A naval officer took
them. Amid his vexation the Admiral could only
steam on for the roads of Tsushima.

Emperor William felt that the time had come for
one more discussion with the Tsar of the possibilities
of a Continental alliance. At first, in his bitterness
against the British, Tsar Nicholas lent him a willing
ear, even against the counsel of his advisers, who were
opposed to the ideas of the two Monarchs. The Tsar
was keen at first for the German Cabinet to work out
a draft agreement. He agreed with the Kaiser that
when the agreement was ready it should be communicated to France, who would have no choice but to

come into the alliance. Yet in the end the Tsar's advisers had their way and defeated the proposal. Suddenly the Tsar changed his mind and demanded that France should not be faced with an accomplished fact but should be consulted in advance. If that were done, Emperor William feared that the plan would collapse. It was the accomplished fact that would have influenced France. He withdrew his proposal.

The Kaiser had calculated on Russian readiness to enter into an alliance amid the misfortunes of the war. He had had news from Japan via America which forecast with the utmost confidence the collapse of the Russians. Unlike his General Staff, he expected the Japanese to win. The Tsar, however, was also still hopeful of winning the war. He gratefully acknowledged Germany's readiness to help, and accepted her coal for his warships. Britain saw in these supplies of coal almost a breach of neutrality, although Germany stated that she would permit them only as far as the latitude of Madagascar. Ultimately Britain declared that she would no longer permit German ships to leave her ports to coal the Russian squadrons. On this Emperor William sent to St. Petersburg the inquiry whether, if a conflict were to arise over the coal supplies, Russia would be prepared at least in that case to stand by Germany. Count Lambsdorff had every reason to answer Yes. Emperor William then repeated his great offer yet again. Once more, however, Tsar Nicholas insisted that France must be consulted before the conclusion of a Continental alliance. And once more Emperor William dissented.

Apparently the Tsar had not yet been hit hard

enough by fate to be ready to accept German friendship without haggling. He evidently did not realize
that the time was approaching when Germany's
enormous power on land and her growing navy would
provide him at all times with an ally whose support
would bring the same relief as France's brought
Britain—quite apart from the fact that, faced with the
enormous preponderance of power which a Russia in
association with Germany and the whole Triple Alliance would represent, France would have no possible alternative but herself to come in.

The future had no rosy look to Emperor William if
his plans miscarried. There was no getting rid of the
existence of the Entente Cordiale. The Civil Lord of
the British Admiralty was openly demanding that
Britain should veto the further building of warships by
Germany. Germany's attitude on the occasion of the
Dogger Bank adventure had, in his view, shown
plainly what Britain might expect one day from her.
This was the first time that Britain had stood out in
blunt opposition to the building of the German navy
—six months after Britain's own battle fleet had been
brought to the North Sea. Alliance with Russia seemed
to the Kaiser to be the most essential of assurances.
Port Arthur had fallen. Yet a little while, and the
Tsar would be bound to be much more accommodating.

Emperor William sailed for the Mediterranean. His
first visit on his southward journey was to be to the
King of Portugal. A year before he had sailed down
the Portuguese coast without putting in to port. This
time, on Count Bülow's suggestion, the greeting was

not to be omitted. The rest of the journey was to be one of simple holiday-making. Before the departure, however, Count Bülow had yet another urgent request to make. To all appearance he set quite special store by it. In the course of this Mediterranean cruise he wanted the Kaiser to stop at Tangier.

The Kaiser was very unwilling to do this, and made all sorts of objections. There was nothing to be gained by landing there. Conditions in North Africa were heated enough already. If he were to land in Tangier it would create a tremendous sensation. Let France, Britain and Spain settle Moroccan affairs between themselves. A year before he had expressly assured King Alfonso, when the King visited him in Vigo, that Germany had no intention of interfering or seeking any territorial gain in Morocco. This declaration of his had all the more force and finality since at the time the Chancellor had moved heaven and earth to prevent him from returning King Alfonso's visit and possibly recurring to the subject. Count Bülow, however, would not admit the force of any objection. He came again and again to the subject of the visit to Tangier.

'It is absolutely necessary.'

'I don't at all like doing it,' the Kaiser insisted. 'I am going on afterwards to Gibraltar. That will not be very pleasant for me.'

'Your Majesty really must make the visit.'

The Chancellor brought up the matter again and again, until the Kaiser's departure. He came on board the ship:

'For God's sake, your Majesty, go to Tangier.'

Emperor William agreed, and set sail.

In Tangier the young and ambitious Counsellor of Legation, Richard von Kühlmann, was energetically pursuing a policy of his own. He was filled with the sense of the world-wide importance of a solution of the Morocco question. So far it had defied settlement, but it was not yet necessarily to be regarded as insoluble. He had studied the history of this country, in which the English had tried to establish themselves as long ago as the seventeenth century, in order to dominate the Atlantic trade routes—including then the only route to India—and the shipping of the Mediterranean. They had not entertained the fantastic plans of Louis XIV of securing domination over the Mediterranean through an immense *Canal du Midi* at the back of the Pyrenees: Britain's stout, swift ships served the same end by simpler means. British forts were constructed in Tangier. Then the English discovered that the Rock of Gibraltar offered better service than Morocco. They abandoned Tangier. It was left to Joseph Chamberlain to make the discovery that, from the point of view of the sea route to the newly occupied Egypt, the shores of Morocco had their importance after all. They would assure a safe passage through the Straits of Gibraltar. Alternatively France would assure it, if Morocco were given to her. Counsellor of Legation von Kühlmann considered what could be won for Germany out of this situation.

The Treaty of Madrid, signed by the Powers in 1880, had provided for equal rights and freedom of trade for all in Morocco. What France and Britain, with Spain following suit, were now doing in Morocco was quite clearly in conflict with the provisions of that Treaty. Germany's trade was suffering. The Counsellor of Legation knew well enough what 'spheres of influence' would mean—the determining of all issues by the fact of the presence of the soldiers of the dominant Power. Germany would lose not only her trade but all influence; France and Spain would have new colonies while Germany went empty away. If, however, Britain was making use of Morocco, of which she had no right of disposal whatever, in bartering for the recognition of her power in Egypt, Germany could also make use of the modest rights which she drew from the Treaty of Madrid to drive a political bargain. All she needed to do was to make much of them, to talk big about them, to make them seem of real importance. The Counsellor of Legation showed how Germany's just claims in Morocco were being interfered with and reduced to nought. If the Powers intended to partition Morocco among themselves, they would have to indemnify Germany for the damage to her rights. He thought, and others with him, of the possibility of the cession of Casablanca to Germany. The idea was publicly discussed. But, above all, the Counsellor of Legation reflected that the road to negotiations of this sort almost always led on to still more important agreements between nations and Cabinets. The sharing out of gains was the prelude to great political agreements. That had only just been exemplified in London.

Baron von Mentzingen, the German Minister in Morocco, was not prepared to enter into ideas and projects of such extensive scope. His duties, he considered, were those of a diplomat, not of a statesman. He was not of the school that delved into the mysteries of economic geography and its practical application in bargaining. Counsellor von Kühlmann determined to do what was possible for Germany without the Baron's aid.

Germany, he considered, ought not to tolerate the tearing up of the Treaty of Madrid. She ought to make a noise about it, in order that it might be made worth her while to keep quiet. Any change in the terms of the Treaty required her consent. That consent should be bought from her at a high price. The Counsellor of Legation took six or eight men, correspondents of great newspapers and young diplomats, into his confidence. He had submitted the broad lines of his own Morocco policy in all modesty and with great caution in letters to *Geheimrat* von Holstein. Strangely enough the *Geheimrat* neither objected to the proposals nor dispatched the thirty-one-year-old Counsellor of Legation to another Continent to cool his enthusiasm. Almost every time the Counsellor lunched with one or another of his eight confidants or walked with him in the old English fortress gardens, some confidential piece of news would escape him. Germany, he would go on to say, could not put up with the treatment the French Foreign Minister was permitting himself to inflict on her. Germany would sooner or later announce her standpoint with startling clarity. France's attitude could no longer be submitted to. Germany was going to speak out, in sharp and unambiguous terms.

The Counsellor's indiscretions were all deliberate, and deliberately repeated. Whatever he said to his six or eight confidants was meant to be passed on to the personages in their confidence in Paris and

London. The Secretary of Legation was forming his 'channels.' He got some more than dubious details conveyed to the French Foreign Minister, M. Delcassé.

One day the Counsellor of Legation recommended the representative of the *Kölnische Zeitung* to send a telegram to his paper of which von Kühlmann had himself drafted the text. Germany's interest in Morocco needed to be insisted on with real emphasis, and there could be no better or more impressive way to do this than through a visit of the Kaiser's to the country. He was bound to pass along the coast of Morocco during his coming Mediterranean cruise. Von Kühlmann dictated to the correspondent of the *Kölnische Zeitung* a message to the effect that

'From the standpoint of the population of Morocco it is very desirable that the Kaiser should land in the country.'

The telegram was sent off. But it did not appear. Instead, a telegram came for Counsellor of Legation von Kühlmann from the Foreign Ministry. The publication of his message could not be permitted, though the suggestion it contained would be borne in mind. The Foreign Ministry did not know, however, that the Counsellor of Legation had covered himself against the stonewalling arts of *Geheimrat* von Holstein. The Counsellor had been astute enough to avail himself also in his move of the services of the correspondents of the London *Times* and the Paris Havas Agency, and both of them had sent to their offices the news of the alleged state of feeling in Morocco and of the longing of the Moroccans for a visit from Emperor William. The correspondents had, of course, telegraphed in terms of their own impressions, resulting from independent enquiry.

Chancellor and *Geheimrat* caught with alacrity at this unanticipated invitation. They too had for some time past made up their minds to pursue an independent policy in Morocco. They had thwarted Chamberlain's proposal for British-German co-operation in Morocco, and had gambled away their opportunities in regard to Tangier and the Atlantic coast of Morocco; now the ground that they had recklessly abandoned in North Africa had begun to be, in their eyes, of quite obvious and quite special value. Moreover, the cordial greetings which the Chancellor had extended to the news of the Anglo-French understanding had served merely as a soothing syrup for Reichstag and public: in reality, Chancellor and *Geheimrat* were glad of the opportunity to show the new allies that Germany was not to be intimidated; that it was quite possible to put difficulties in their way; and that no agreement could be come to anywhere in the world over Germany's head. If Chamberlain ventured on negotiations with France after Germany had turned him away, there were ways of making him pay for his audacity. As for France, it was an incredible piece of insolence that she should be concluding further alliances. France was in a miserable situation. Her Russian friend was staggering from one defeat to the next. The 'bear' could no longer be of any possible assistance to 'Marianne.' Morocco had been torn from them, but they would show France, and show her in Morocco, that even Britain was no protection against the millions of bayonets of which Germany could dispose. In any case it would

Hernösand (North Sweden)
1905
Lumbermen, workmen from the sawmills,
charcoalburners and their families
listening to the concert of H.J.M. band on
board H.J.M. Yacht "Hohenzollern"

be a good thing to make France's position thoroughly clear to her. Twice in the past year Chancellor and *Geheimrat* had tried to find an opportunity of action somewhere in Morocco. Baron von Mentzingen had repeatedly reported that the French were beginning regularly to dig themselves in in North Africa. On that the two statesmen had sent Consul Vasal to the Sultan in Fez to stir him up against the French. They had sent the Sultan a written demand that he should insist on the observance of the terms of the Treaty of Madrid of 1880. The Sultan hated the French. He hated the British no less, believing that they had betrayed him. He could understand why Germany was trying to induce him to stiffen his attitude.

The Chancellor himself was less clear as to coming developments:

'Our attitude in this matter,' he said, 'at present is like that of the Sphinx, which amid the curious questions of the tourists around it betrays no secrets.'

All that the Chancellor knew was that he intended that his challenge to France should be on the grand scale. He had found the suggestion put forward by Counsellor of Legation von Kühlmann, intended as the prelude to later negotiations for an understanding, a particularly happy one—that the Kaiser should challenge the French by going to Tangier.

In the peace of the days of the voyage to Lisbon the Kaiser had grown more and more determined not to land at Tangier. He had repeatedly discussed the matter on board with the representative of the Foreign Ministry in attendance on him. He was afraid of complications. He hated having anything to do with

T   289

Morocco. Various German business men were besieging the Chancellor with claims for the protection of all sorts of interests of theirs, but the Kaiser saw no reason why the advantage of a few individuals should be pursued at the cost of setting two nations by the ears. A year before in Tangier there had been some utterly insignificant trouble over a few Arabs or negroes employed by a German merchant. The Chancellor had managed to twist the affair into some sort of breach of treaty, and had proposed to send a warship to Tangier to defend Germany's prestige. The Kaiser had vetoed the idea. On another occasion later on the Chancellor had made plans for a naval demonstration off Morocco. This adventure also the Kaiser had prohibited. He scented the danger of war. He believed Delcassé, the French Foreign Minister, to be capable of anything. Moreover, he did not know how far the British assurances to France of April 8, 1904, went. They had certainly gone further than a mere promise of diplomatic support. The Kaiser had no desire at all to irritate France. He had his plans in regard to the Tsar, and France played an important part in them. It would be absurd, when their aid was needed, to begin by upsetting the French. He had the Chancellor informed by telegraph that the landing in Tangier had been abandoned. Then he broke his journey in Lisbon.

He had pictured this holiday visit a little differently. The King and Queen drove him from the port of Lisbon, in four-horse carriages of the seventeenth century, gilded and glazed, for four hours along frightful roads over which the carriages danced rather than rolled—danced till they threatened to splinter—to the ornamental castle of Belem. It was an endless swaying and rocking on squeaking boards that had not been renewed since the days of the Roi Soleil. Fat King Carlos calmly smoked his Havana until in the end the state carriage became a jogging glass ball filled with smoke.

'You must not suppose,' the King said after two hours of silence, 'that this procession has taken place for your special benefit. The people insist on having it. Every ruler who comes to us for the first time has to travel in this way.'

The Kaiser adapted himself courteously to the usages of this Court and country. He joined in the festivities in tropical heat, from 3 p.m. to 3 a.m., in his full dress uniform as a Portuguese cavalry commander. He smoked cigarettes with the Queen during the gala performance at the Opera: the King would not abandon his cigar even in the Opera House, and the Queen feared trouble if she failed to induce her imperial guest to smoke. The Kaiser was astonished at the disorder and confusion at every turn. He had never been at such a Court.

'In Portugal,' Herr von Radowitz, the German Ambassador, assured him, 'your Majesty must not be surprised at all this. I have long given up being surprised at anything here.'

Emperor William got back to his ship at last, amused but thoroughly exhausted.

There, however, he found telegrams from the Chancellor awaiting him. The Chancellor was upset; his tone was categorical. His Majesty must have regard to the feelings of the nation. The *Times* and Havas Agency telegrams had been quoted in the German papers. The Reichstag was demanding that the Kaiser should land. Public opinion had 'now become enthusiastically in favour of the step.'

The Kaiser had no means of judging; he only knew how he felt about the whole affair. Count Bülow must have discussed it with the Secretary of State and with *Geheimrat* von Holstein. He formally claimed to speak for the Reichstag, for public opinion, for the whole of the German nation. Once before the Kaiser had found all these ranged against him and had still acted according to his own judgment—he had visited England, as an ostentatious mark of friendship, during the Boer war. He had smoothed away many of the difficulties between Britain and Germany on that occasion. But public opinion throughout Germany had at once turned against him, and he had merely found his position weakened.

He hesitated as to what he should do. He continued on his voyage. But the weather had changed. He sailed on now through rain and storm.

Meanwhile Counsellor of Legation von Kühlmann had made preparations for the Kaiser's landing. He had received confidential telegrams from the *Hamburg*, on board which the Kaiser was travelling as Albert Ballin's guest, when the ship was at Lisbon. They reported sharp opposition to the landing and a doubt whether Emperor William would agree to it. A telegram came at the same time from Chancellor von Bülow. The landing, it said, was already known by the public to be going to take place, and, as German Chargé d'Affaires, von Kühlmann would be held personally responsible for seeing to it that the Kaiser did land.

In the night before the arrival of the *Hamburg*, the storm had grown much worse. The sea ran high under angry skies; landing might prove difficult. Very likely the Kaiser's entourage and the Kaiser himself would make use of this to escape from the necessity of landing. The Counsellor of Legation determined at once to overcome any objection on the score of the difficulty of landing. He put on his full dress uniform of the 1st Uhlans, and went in his patent leather boots and sash and plume on board a small open tug, to meet the *Hamburg*. At that time Tangier had only one landing pier; one landed from the open roads. It was certainly no pleasant experience to land under such conditions in a heavy sea. But the Counsellor of Legation in his full dress uniform on board an open tug-boat was living evidence that to come off and land again was quite practicable.

The Head of the Criminal Investigation Department had been sent from Berlin in advance, on account of information received that there were anarchists in Tangier. The Counsellor of Legation took him on board the tug. The criminologist was seasick; the little vessel tossed and plunged. At last the *Hamburg* was sighted. The Counsellor of Legation demanded to be taken on board. But the two vessels moved so violently that he was only able to climb on board by means of a pilot's rope ladder thrown out for him. For some little time he was whirled about in the air on the rope ladder. It slapped and bumped him against the ship's side. At last he came up on board, with not a dry thread of clothing on him.

The Kaiser had watched the Counsellor's acrobatics from the Captain's bridge. He received him most

cordially, but declared at once that he had given up
the idea of landing. Now the Counsellor of Legation
played his cards boldly. The whole world, he said,
had its eyes on this visit of the Kaiser's to Morocco.
It had been announced everywhere, and nothing else
was being talked of. There had been tremendous
preparations in Tangier. The Sultan's uncle was waiting there. A most distinguished special mission had
been delegated to greet the Monarch. If the Kaiser
were to sail past without landing, it would be a ter-
rible discourtesy to the Sultan to begin with. It would
be felt to be beyond forgiveness. It would naturally
have its effect on the Sultan himself. And the world
would simply be furnished with food for derision.
Doubt might be thrown on the Kaiser's personal
courage. It was conceivable that complications might
arise of which no one could foretell the end.

The Kaiser listened in vexation. But the dripping
Counsellor of Legation had the impression that he did
not entirely reject his arguments. At this moment the
Senior Officer of the French warships lying off Tangier came on board to pay his respects to Emperor
William. The Kaiser asked him what possibility there
was of landing. The French officer painted the operation in the blackest of colours.

A small group from the Kaiser's entourage, it was
finally decided, should go first in order to see
whether it really was difficult to land, and also to see
for themselves what preparations the Sultan had
made. The sea had grown a little calmer. The group
went off with the Counsellor of Legation; they returned with assurances that all was in order. It was,
in fact, true that an immense reception had been pre-

pared for the Kaiser. The horses on which he and his party were to ride in the procession had also been selected with the greatest care.

The Kaiser's vexation had not diminished. His entourage stood by, dumb and none too anxious to put in a word. At last the Kaiser, with an abrupt gesture, put on his helmet:

'We will land!'

He went ashore in Field Marshal's uniform, with an army revolver at his side.

The Sultan's uncle stood waiting on the landing pier. The Sultan's mission from Fez had assembled in splendid array.

The Kaiser spoke the short address asked for by the Chancellor: Germany would give her unqualified support to the Sultan's independence. The company mounted on horseback. Crowds reaching as far as the eye could see, brown and black, almost all natives, in their bright, fluttering burnous, stood some way off, in packed masses. The procession through the suburbs began.

The Kaiser rode slowly, in pace with the procession, through steep, stony, narrow lanes. Before him there rode a Moroccan General in a bright red uniform. This was Maclean, the Sultan's British confidant, formerly a non-commissioned officer in England—a magnificent bagpipe player. He was accompanied by a gigantic, deep black Arab, his adjutant or secretary. Alongside the Kaiser went, on foot, General von Scholl on his right, General von Plessen on his left. They were determined to be at his side whatever might happen. Then, on either side, came the Arab soldiers whom the Sultan had sent as escort.

They kept up a lively conversation as they marched, and time after time turned this way and that to greet friends as they passed them. They continually brandished their loaded guns in the air; at times their bayonets were almost under the Kaiser's nose, at times they stung the flank of the white horse that the Kaiser rode. The beast was good-natured, or used to such attentions: it had been sent by the Sultan as a symbol ('the dove of peace', said von Kühlmann in his report) and in concern that the Kaiser should be well-mounted. From all around there came an indescribable uproar. The procession passed the market place; here a large number of rather ragged men waved Spanish flags amid a great clamour. They threw their caps into the air. The Kaiser asked:

'Who are these people?'

'Spanish anarchists, your Majesty,' replied the head of the C.I.D.

'But what are they up to,' asked the Kaiser, 'in letting me live?'

The Sultan's soldiers stood with loaded rifles at the ready. They let no one pass, with the single exception of an aged Englishman. He was the doyen of the British trading community in Tangier. He approached the Kaiser:

'I am an Englishman, and have come in the name of the British merchants to thank your Majesty for landing here. Your landing has saved the British from being thrown out by the French. We had already packed our trunks.'

He handed the Kaiser a number of picture postcards as mementos. The Kaiser thanked him; the Englishman took respectful leave of him and withdrew. No one else was permitted to approach the guest. The head of the C.I.D. had been informed of the Sultan's order to his soldiers that the anarchists should be exterminated if the slightest trouble occurred.

At last the procession reached the German Embassy. The Kaiser turned into the Embassy garden, and Counsellor of Legation von Kühlmann, who had already paid out the necessary coins, gave the sign for a *feu de joie*. The rifles of some thousands of Arabs ranged in front of the Embassy went off with a roar. At once the Kaiser's horse leapt high up, directly in front of the stand in which the foreign diplomats were waiting. They jumped up from their seats, but the Kaiser pulled up 'the dove of peace' and dismounted.

The French Chargé d'Affaires, Count Chérisey, was received by the Kaiser. The diplomatic corps of Tangier waited on him. There was a quick lunch, and then the Kaiser witnessed the march past of the Moroccan troops. The first column was led by the Englishman who was a Moroccan General. The second section was commanded by a French officer. The Counsellor of Legation suggested that the French Commanding Officer should be decorated with the Order of the Red Eagle, of the grade corresponding to his rank. The Kaiser's military entourage opposed the decoration. Once more the Sultan's uncle, a man of eighty years, asked an audience of the Kaiser. It had occurred to him that he ought to apologise for not having come right out to the Kaiser's ship. Until now, however, he had lived entirely in the heart of the country, and he had now seen the sea for the first time. He had felt that the water was too rough.

297

Native riders then came up to the city to prepare a 'Fantasia' of dances and combats on horseback. But the Kaiser declined: there was no time for the spectacle. The procession returned on board in the same theatrical and tiresome way as it had come. The Kaiser rode with a gloomy expression, all the gloomier for the absurdity of the cavalcade, which was exasperating him. The Sultan of Morocco, whom the Kaiser was to have visited, had been seen by no one.

The Kaiser crossed to Gibraltar. A year before he had been received there with all the attention and geniality which Englishmen show to welcome guests. This time the British Admirals and Generals stood coldly and stiffly to receive him, without a single word more than was necessary—the first result of the visit to Tangier. The Kaiser hurried away.

When he got back to Germany he was met by a Chancellor trembling with emotion, and showing in every word and gesture his devotion and affection for his ruler and the relief he felt at last from long-suppressed anxieties.

'I shook with fear!' he confessed, abandoning all reserve. 'When the news reached me that your Majesty had come away alive out of Tangier, I broke down and sat weeping at my desk while I uttered a thanksgiving to Heaven.'

'But why did you send me there?' the Kaiser asked. 'It is all incomprehensible to me.'

'It was necessary for my policy,' the Chancellor replied. 'Through your Majesty I threw down a gauntlet in challenge to the French. I wanted to see whether they would mobilize.'

The Kaiser could find no answer to make. So, the

Chancellor had himself wanted war; or had toyed with the possibility of it. There was no salvation that way. The Kaiser had seen Gibraltar once more. A war which might bring Britain into the field against Germany would be madness. He spoke at length to the Chancellor, impressing on him that he was set on maintaining peace, that he wanted peace and nothing but peace—no complications, and certainly none with France. He could understand that it would not be so easy for the French to become friends of Germany once more, however much Germany might wish for peace; but he was determined at least to get back to terms of ordinary civility with them. He knew of various ways in which some measure of understanding at least could be brought about with them. He meant to try every one of them.

And to try them, moreover, as quickly as possible.

The Kaiser's visit to Tangier brought the fall of the French Foreign Minister, M. Delcassé. Germany's whole attitude over Morocco had beyond question been one of deep and deliberate provocation. Nevertheless, Delcassé had hesitated for a long time to take up her challenge. The agreements with Britain had brought the French new strength and new prospects of successful resistance to their neighbour Germany. Apart, however, from her nationalist fighting-cocks, whose whole life was filled with the dream of revenge for 1870, France did not want war. The French Prime Minister, M. Rouvier, was one of those who held that a fresh conflict between the two nations would be criminal lunacy. The Foreign Minister was filled with anxiety as to how he could remain in power. He had accordingly managed to get proposals for a reconciliation brought by indirect means to the notice of the German Cabinet: they were confidentially communicated through an Italian intermediary to the German Ambassador in Rome, Count Monts, who transmitted them to Germany. Delcassé offered Germany the port of Casablanca, and a second port on the Atlantic coast of Morocco. France would also support Germany in Asia Minor; and she would lend her aid to the construction of the Bagdad Railway. Germany might also state any further desire, might herself indicate what more she wanted, and if it was within the realm of the practicable France would lend Germany her support for its attainment.

Chancellor von Bülow was greatly embarrassed. He had encouraged the Sultan of Morocco in his resistance to the French. He had had definite promises made to him. Counsellor of Legation von Kühlmann had suggested the idea of a conference of the Powers before that solution of the Morocco question had been thought of in any other quarter. Von Kühlmann had persuaded the Sultan that the best way of rejecting the French demands *en bloc*— they had been presented virtually in the form of an ultimatum—would be to declare that he would only accept the ultimatum if all the Powers supported it as reasonable. The Sultan had at once turned to the German Cabinet and asked whether if he adopted that attitude it would support him. Lacking ideas of his own, and lacking even the capacity to think out to the end the ideas of other people when he took them over, Chancellor von Bülow had seized on the new

plan with enthusiasm. He had sent word to the
Sultan that Germany would support him in the proposal of a conference. At that stage Count Monts had
reported the French offers. The Chancellor could not
accept them without leaving the Sultan in the lurch.
It also occurred to him that in Vigo, in talking to the
King of Spain, the Kaiser had opposed all ideas of
acquisition of territory in Morocco. Count Bülow had
not at the time been pleased with the Kaiser's attitude. His return visit to King Alfonso would have
provided the opportunity of a second discussion, in
the course of which his attitude could have been
modified to meet the Chancellor's wishes; but instead
of this the Chancellor had frustrated the return visit.
Thus the Kaiser's statement stood. The Chancellor
was at a loss what to do—whether to have a settlement of all issues with France, or to acquire fresh
colonial territory, or to go to war. Only the idea of
humiliating France returned again and again to his
mind.

His adviser Baron Holstein came round gradually
to bolder views. He was influenced by Count
Schlieffen, the Chief of Staff. The General was much
more of a calculating machine even than the eternal
calculator Holstein. For the moment Russia, as he
figured it, could not move. But in five or ten years
she would have recovered from the wounds Japan
had inflicted on her. Then there would perhaps be a
Russian army on Germany's eastern frontier. It was
true that, if war came over Morocco, Britain could
really send to France's aid the hundred-thousand men
of whom Delcassé spoke so often in dead secrecy that
in the end the German agents were able to transmit

the news to Berlin. But, as things were at that time, that reinforcement did not count for much. The Chief of Staff was in favour of the earliest possible thorough clearing up with France—at arms. No waiting ten or twenty years for a world war, but so thorough a settlement that thereafter there should be no fear of a world war. France should be provoked until she had no course left but to take up arms.

'If the French will not give way,' Count Schlieffen concluded, 'let them come at us! They will run straight into our guns.'

Baron Holstein was not yet ready to go so far. Decisions should never be made precipitately. It was possible that the French might capitulate without a war. For the moment it would be enough if they were subjected to humiliation. It was certainly a nuisance that Emperor William's assurance to King Alfonso and the assurance given to the Sultan made it difficult to accept the French offer; all the more since no one would understand why they were upsetting the French or what they really wanted from them. For all that Chancellor and *Geheimrat* were agreed that for the present the French should be kept on tenter-hooks. Count Bülow declined Casablanca and the other port, the concessions in Asia Minor, and the opportunity to state any other desire. The first thing needful was that the *status quo* should remain unaltered in Morocco. Then the conference would be due to begin. Later everything might go again into the melting-pot.

Count Monts was amazed. It would have been impossible to ask more than the French had actually offered. Apart from that, the offer had implied almost

everything that a statesman could desire: an understanding upon the principal colonial issues, similar to
the Anglo-French agreement. This first step could
have been followed by a general settlement of all
African questions, in so far as Britain was not affected.
'But,' wrote Count Monts, 'to all this Bernhardus
Magnus was blind.'

In the first days of May 1905 Count Monts and
Baron von der Lancken, Counsellor of Embassy,
were staying in the Palazzo Fossanova as guests of
Prince Borghese. Count Monts spoke in sharp
criticism of the Chancellor. He asked at least to know
what were Count Bülow's reasons for rejecting Delcassé's offer. The reply came:

'It is impossible to accept the offer from considerations of the monarchical principle. The monarchical
principle would be gravely infringed if the Sultan
were made in this way into a Shadow Prince.'

The Ambassador had to convey the refusal of the
offer to the Italian intermediaries, for transmission to
the French Foreign Minister; but it is doubtful
whether he conveyed it in that form. Count Monts
was always witty, and generally caustic. But he had
no ambition to play the clown.

Delcassé saw only one way out of the situation, if
he was to remain in power: himself to work on
France's sense of national honour, and to put up the
most determined opposition to Germany. He would
put it to the test now whether the Moroccan question
was to lead to war. He would reject the idea of a conference. But he had taken insufficient account of the
feeling of the nation, which was against war, and still
more against a war of which the issue was doubtful.

Moreover, Delcassé was still entirely unaware of the way in which his position had been weakened by the many warnings to the other Ministers so adroitly distributed by the German Legation in Tangier. At a Cabinet meeting he declared his reliance on British friendship, and proposed the rejection of the proposal of a conference on Morocco. He was prepared to accept the responsibility of a war with Germany. But all the Ministers opposed him with one accord. The Minister of War showed that France was not prepared for a war; the Foreign Minister, in his view, misread the whole situation, and had done so from the first. He had failed entirely to foresee the coming complications in Morocco. He had paid no heed to any of the warnings that he had received. All his colleagues had had news of the impending visit of Emperor William to Tangier; Delcassé alone had regarded the news as a *canard*. Everything had then happened as the warnings had indicated; the Kaiser's visit had taken place, and the complications had come. No one in the whole Cabinet had confidence any longer in a Foreign Minister of such irresponsibility.

In a moment Delcassé had fallen. Rouvier, the Prime Minister, took foreign affairs into his own hands.

Chancellor von Bülow was filled with pride. He had always known how to deal with these Frenchmen. He had simply hinted to the French Prime Minister that there would be no improvement in Franco-German relations until Delcassé had been removed from the scene; and immediately Rouvier had set out of his own accord to remove Delcassé. The real

Björkive Summer 1905
The Zar inspecting the German Cruizer

Björke Sommer 1905
Tartar inspecting the German Kaiser

fact was that Prince Albert of Monaco had urged the Prime Minister to take that step. He was on friendly terms with Rouvier, who was himself by nature conciliatory and a man of peace. During Kiel week and on other occasions the Prince was frequently the guest of the German Emperor. He had told Emperor William of his relations with the French Premier and had made use of them in the service of an improvement of Franco-German relations. The Kaiser had made it unmistakably plain to the Prince that he had no desire for war or conflict or unpleasantness with France. The Prince had then used his influence with Rouvier. If it was really true, as the Prince of Monaco insisted over and over again, that the Kaiser wanted friendship and decent neighbourliness with France, then Delcassé should not be allowed to stand in the way of it. So Delcassé fell.

About the same time Emperor William had a talk with Prince Radolin, the German Ambassador in Paris. He pointed out to him the excellent opportunities opened out by the friendship between the Prince of Monaco and Rouvier. The Ambassador must make the most of them. The Kaiser definitely requested him to work for an understanding. Yet Prince Radolin had scarcely returned to Paris when he spoke hotly to Rouvier, assuring him that Germany stood 'with all her strength' at the back of the Sultan of Morocco. The French Premier had supposed that after the sacrifice of Delcassé Germany would at least show some measure of friendliness; but Prince Radolin warned him of coming 'remonstrances and menaces,' and confirmed the warning in writing on his return to Berlin.

'What stupidity are you up to?' the Kaiser asked angrily the next time they met. 'I gave you absolutely definite instructions, and you are doing the exact opposite!'

The Ambassador paled.

'That is so, your Majesty! But here are instructions to the contrary effect which I received.'

'I surely made myself perfectly plain?' the Kaiser thundered. 'What is up? Where did you get these instructions?'

'From Baron Holstein. I could only assume that these contrary instructions came from your Majesty.'

The *Geheimrat* had not been alone in upsetting the Kaiser's command in his letters to Prince Radolin. The Chancellor too had commissioned the French Ambassador to speak sharply in Paris. Both had expressly stated that they were acting in accordance with the Kaiser's views and command.

Chancellor and *Geheimrat* intended to maintain their harsh and domineering tone until France had agreed to the calling of the conference, which the Sultan himself had proposed a week before Delcassé's fall. The French Premier was ready to agree to the conference if an agreement could first be arrived at as to the concessions which Germany would make to France. To this, however, the Chancellor would not agree. France must first submit, unconditionally and without laying claim to any rights whatever; then it might conceivably be possible to negotiate in a more gracious spirit. The French Premier hesitated once more. There were limits to the strain which he could put on the French sense of national honour. Then, in spite of their exultant sense of power, Chancellor and

Geheimrat were suddenly seized with alarm. Matters would grow serious if Rouvier broke off negotiations entirely. The Premier, however, made one more effort. France had a long common frontier with Morocco. She had a right to see peace and order maintained at least on the borders of Algeria. Rouvier proposed that the conference should be authorized to permit France to adopt measures of policing.

Chancellor von Bülow and *Geheimrat* von Holstein studied this new communication from Rouvier. They asked for changes in its wording. The French Premier made alternative proposals. Neither Bülow nor Holstein saw that they amounted to a French claim to come to the conference at all events with some rights admitted by Germany. The ultimate outcome of the conference would depend, Rouvier hoped, on France's adroitness in its course and on the support accorded by the Powers—a support for which she would seek in advance. But all that Chancellor and *Geheimrat* saw was the triumph that Germany would be securing if she compelled the French to accept the European tribunal that was so distasteful to them. They agreed at last to Rouvier's demand. That would be the final defeat of his efforts to save France from the conference.

Germany's new Minister in Tangier, Herr Rosen, stayed a short time in Paris on his way to Morocco to negotiate concerning the subjects and the venue of the conference, and also concerning all the further alternatives still suggested even at this late hour by M. Revoil, representing the French Prime Minister. But it did not matter how far M. Revoil went, or what offers he now made in regard to German protection of the Christians in the Levant or to privileges in

connexion with the Bagdad Railway or in Cameroon—
Herr Rosen rejected every advance. Every offer
seemed to him to be trivial in comparison with the
German sacrifice in foregoing the humiliation of
France.

'Your Excellency,' he declared to Prince Radolin,
the German Ambassador, 'I have my career to think
of. I cannot pass such suggestions on to Berlin.'

Then the French Prime Minister definitely agreed.
Yet, after all, the settlement arrived at concerning
measures of police protection had meant that in the
end France and not Germany had gained the advantage. Not that either the Chancellor or Baron
Holstein noticed it.

The two statesmen were deeply moved. It seemed
to them that much more had been achieved than their
triumph in the fight for the conference: they saw the
rosy dawn of the day of an alliance with France.

'So, then,' wrote Baron Holstein on July 2, 1905,
to Prince Radolin, 'if you are not out of sympathy
with this line of thought, you might discuss it with
D., presenting it in an entirely non-committal and
unconcerned way as your own personal idea, as a
"dream of the future as it should be." '

The dream of the future seemed no less rose-red to
the Ambassador. Neither Chancellor nor *Geheimrat*
nor Ambassador allowed the vision to be disturbed by
the fact that France meanwhile was thoroughly exasperated, clenching her teeth in painfully suppressed
hatred.

The agreements in regard to the calling of a Morocco Conference were embodied in an exchange of

Notes between M. Rouvier and Prince Radolin on July 8, 1905. The Chancellor had pressed specially for signature; Emperor William was setting out on his northern tour, and the work must be completed first.

The Kaiser noted with satisfaction the news that the Chancellor sent him of the final smoothing away of all difficulties. Now he would build further on that foundation. He had ambitious plans in view. It was precisely for these that he needed a France at peace and reconciled with a Germany that had set out to meet her wishes. His Ambassador in Paris knew that he wanted good neighbourly relations with France. Emperor William assumed that Prince Radolin would at least obey his instructions in the future. He had seen the Prince of Monaco again during Kiel Week. Prince Albert had telegraphed to the French Prime Minister about Emperor William's friendly attitude— at such length that Rouvier complained loudly of the burden of the unending messages, and almost collapsed under them. But the Kaiser regarded this completed work of accommodation with France as only the preparation and prior condition for his new plans. The Tsar had lost the war with Japan. He would have to sue for peace; he was in a grave situation.

'The war must end,' Grand Duke Michael had admitted during his visit to Berlin. 'Opinion in Russia is all against it, even in the army. My brother will have to make an end of the war.'

'Would you think it would carry weight,' the Kaiser asked, 'if I wrote to your brother?'

Grand Duke Michael had come to Berlin specially in order to hear the Kaiser's views of the war and the way out. The Russian Ambassador, Count Osten-Sacken, asked:

'Will your Imperial Highness simply repeat what you have heard, acting as His Majesty's mouthpiece? Or will you convey it to your brother as your own firm opinion, and urge him to follow the advice?'

'Yes, I shall certainly do that,' the Grand Duke replied, 'and communicate it as my most sacred conviction. My brother absolutely must accept the Kaiser's proposal; for it means the salvation of my country.'

Count Osten-Sacken was profuse in his thanks to the Kaiser. He had tears in his eyes when he kissed the hand of William II:

'*Sire, vous êtes l'ange gardien de la Russie.*'

The Grand Duke took with him a letter from the Kaiser to the Tsar. Nicholas II decided, on the strength of Emperor William's advice, to accept the proposals which had reached him some time before for mediation by President Roosevelt. The plenipotentiaries were to meet in Portsmouth.

The Kaiser's sympathy and readiness to help would be bound to have a redoubled effect on the Tsar in his misfortune. Once more William II determined to make the offer of an alliance—actually to the conquered nation.

In the Norwegian waters Emperor William thought over the broad lines of the new agreement.

Chapter VII

ISOLATION

Before setting out on his northern tour, the Kaiser had a farewell talk with the Chancellor on the general situation. He pointed out the advantages which Germany still stood to gain from an agreement with Russia. The Chancellor agreed. Subsequently the Kaiser sent from Hernösand a request for the transmission by telegraph of the text of the draft treaty which had been under negotiation in the preceding autumn, until the negotiations were rendered abortive by the objections of the Russian Ministers. He told the Chancellor at the same time that he had made arrangements for a meeting with the Tsar. No howl was raised to prevent the meeting or the discussion of a Russo-German agreement; on the contrary, the Chancellor entered into the matter thoroughly and with interest. He also undertook to see that the meeting should be kept entirely secret for the time. Emperor William left Hernösand in his yacht for Björkoe.

No one even in the Kaiser's entourage, except Minister of Legation von Tschirschky, had any knowledge of his purpose or even of the rendezvous for which he was sailing. When the yacht was moving off, the fishermen of Hernösand brought their boats and skiffs alongside the *Hohenzollern*, as always on such occasions, and sang their mournful folk-songs. The

entourage threw sweets and fruit into the boats, rare
dainties in the North; then the ship's band struck up.
On deck above, the Kaiser was going to and fro with
the Minister, deep in an endless conversation. The
Hohenzollern glided away and got up speed, but the
conversation on deck went on and on. The Kaiser
was discussing the new programme that he intended
to lay before the Tsar. Scarcely four weeks had passed
since the destruction of the Russian fleet at Tsushima.
Now the details of the disaster were coming through
in all their horror. The Kaiser considered the situation and the feeling in Russia: both were likely to
further his purpose. He went over the whole position
with von Tschirschky:

1. Britain stood behind Japan.

2. France had refused all aid to the Russian fleet
on its outward journey.

3. There was grave unrest among the Russian
people and in the Russian army over the defeats in
this very unpopular war, which

4. might become dangerous for His Majesty personally and his dynasty.

5. Thus the Tsar, in his complete isolation, ought
to be offered sympathy and encouragement and the
opportunity of finding a support in the world.

6. This could only be offered now by Germany,
since she alone had shown truly benevolent neutrality towards Russia, up to the limits of what was
possible—including the coaling by Ballin of the
outward-sailing fleet, but for which the fleet could
never have got out to the Far East.

The Kaiser built up the agreement which he proposed to conclude with the Tsar only partly on the

basis of the rejected draft of the autumn of 1904. The new treaty was to be binding on the signatories from the day of the conclusion of peace between Russia and Japan.

The *Hohenzollern* entered the Finnish waters on the evening of July 23, 1905. A dignitary in full uniform, with a large feathered hat, came on board. The imperial entourage prepared to receive this admiral.

'No,' laughed the Kaiser, 'it is the pilot. In two and a half hours' time, gentlemen, you will meet His Majesty the Tsar.'

The Tsar's yachts *Standard* and *Polar Star* lay at anchor in the roads of Björkoe.

Emperor William gained the impression that his arrival was greeted with sincere pleasure by the Tsar and his whole entourage. Nicholas II embraced his guest again and again. The old Minister in attendance, Baron Fredericks, who had been a friend of the Kaiser's for many years past, was overcome with emotion:

'At the moment when we are abandoned by all the world, ay, despised, and not even a dog will take a bone from us, your Majesty has come as a true friend to comfort us and lift us up again !'

The Baron, too, on the impulse of the moment, embraced the Kaiser.

'Above all,' he continued, 'your Majesty is giving such pleasure to our poor, sorely proved master by your visit! When he told us the news of it, we all breathed once more, and someone cried: "*Enfin un rayon de soleil! un ami!*" We look on your Majesty as our saviour in distress. Russia will never forget it.'

It was plain that the Kaiser had chosen a good moment. The Tsar was unrestrained and jovial. He remained on board the *Hohenzollern* until the early hours of the morning. The Kaiser cautiously approached his subject on the very first day. The Tsar responded at once. He was filled with immeasurable rage against Britain. He himself declared that the best way to secure the well-being of Europe would be for the three great Continental Powers, Russia, Germany, and France, to come together.

Next morning, on board the *Polar Star*, the Tsar shut himself in with the Kaiser in Alexander III's writing-room. To all appearance he was himself impatient to speak alone with his guest on this very important matter. He came at once to the subject of the practicability and the advantage of an alliance. His gaze reflected every emotion. He looked dreamily into the distance while the Kaiser told him of his own dream of the great Continental coalition of the future. His eyes blazed with hatred at any mention of Britain. Hatred of Britain was his one dominant feeling. She had prevailed even on his ally to leave him in the lurch in the moment of supreme danger. Emperor William considered that France would certainly put no difficulties in the way of an agreement such as the two rulers had in view; he believed that she would join in. He produced the draft treaty. The Tsar read the text three times, slowly and carefully. He proposed only one alteration—the alliance should be applicable only to Europe. Emperor William discussed this proposal thoroughly with the Tsar; they both came to the opinion that the restriction was in the interest of both Powers.

'That is simply splendid,' the Tsar finally exclaimed—'I entirely agree to it all.'

314

'Would you care to sign it?' the Kaiser asked, in the same casual way in which the whole thing had been put through; though he knew how greatly excited he really was. 'It would be a jolly memento of our meeting.'

'Yes, I will,' said the Tsar.

Emperor William inserted in the draft the words '*en Europe*.' Then he passed the pen to the Tsar.

The agreement in its final form indicated its main objective, a defensive alliance, and developed four points:

'Their Majesties the Emperor of all the Russias and the German Emperor, desiring to assure the maintenance of peace in Europe, have laid down the following Articles of a defensive alliance:

'*Article I*. In the event of either of the two Empires being attacked by a European Power, its ally will come to its aid in Europe with all its land and sea forces.

'*Article II*. The high contracting parties bind themselves not to conclude a separate peace with any common antagonist.

'*Article III*. The present treaty will come into force as soon as peace has been concluded between Russia and Japan, and will remain in force until the expiry of twelve months' notice of its termination.

'*Article IV*. After this treaty has come into force, the Emperor of all the Russias will take the necessary steps to convey to France the fact of its existence, and to invite her to adhere to it as an ally.'

The Tsar signed 'Nicholas'; then he rose and took his new ally into his arms:

'I thank God and I thank you! It will be of the

315

most blessed significance for my country and yours!
You are Russia's only true friend. I felt that right
through the war. And I know that it is so.'

Some sort of countersignature was needed on the
document. Neither Emperor William's Chancellor
nor the Tsar's Foreign Minister, Count Lambsdorff, was there. Emperor William had informed the
Chancellor of his intention; as for Count Lambsdorff, the Kaiser had particularly wanted the secret
to be kept from his knowledge for the time. Since
the day when the Chancellor had refused to enter
into the Far East pact desired by Count Lambsdorff,
the Count had had no good word for Germany. It
had been mainly his objection that had wrecked the
effort to arrive at an agreement with Russia in the
autumn of 1904. Count Lambsdorff should learn
the great news of the new alliance only after peace
had been concluded with Japan. The Tsar himself
agreed that that was best.

For a moment Emperor William was faced with
the difficulty that the Tsar's act was supported by no
responsible Russian statesman. The Tsar was, however, an autocrat, the head of an absolute regime. No
Chancellor, no Minister could upset his signature. It
seemed sufficient to the Kaiser, since the Chancellor
was in agreement with the treaty, for von Tschirschky to affix his countersignature for Germany. The
Tsar's signature was equally binding on Russia
whether there were a countersignature of some Russian dignitary or not. It was thus more as a matter of
form than for any practical purpose that Admiral
Birilev also countersigned.

The document now had its four signatures. A copy

was made by the Tsar's brother on the *Polar Star's* notepaper. The Admiral kissed the Kaiser's hand; in his emotion all he could say was—

'*Quel honneur pour moi de pouvoir signer un tel document! Sire! Dieu vous bénisse—vous êtes un ange gardien de la Russie.*'

Emperor William thought of his journey home with a happiness which he had never before experienced. The Tsar kissed him on parting:

'Dear Wilhelm, if ever you are involved in hostilities with another State I shall never take up arms against you. I shall either remain neutral or stand at your side. As sovereign and as a gentleman I give you my sacred word of honour that, definitely, I shall never in my life help the English in a war against you, should they attempt it as they may.'

Tsar and Kaiser parted. The two yachts steamed off. Nicholas II had given his word of honour in the same sense once before, in Reval, to Admiral Tirpitz.

Emperor William's aspirations had been more than amply fulfilled. He had no doubt that France would adhere to the agreement. It was doubly satisfying to him to reflect now that he had rejected a policy of unfriendliness towards the French Government. The agreement with the Tsar seemed to him the completion of the foundation for the league of European nations which he had pictured to himself. All friction would in future be smoothed away without resort to arms. The Tsar could speak as mediator with the Dual Alliance and he himself with the Triple Alliance. And this above all had been achieved: British influence had been shut off from the Continent. Britain could join the five-Power alliance if

317

she chose. It might be assumed that the small nations would also join. There was not much else for them to do. France could continue to develop in peace her settled relations with Britain. One thing, however, was smashed by the agreement with the Tsar: Britain's play with the Balance of Power, to which the Continent had been subject for centuries, was at an end. Britain could rule her own world; and she could have her part in Europe. But for the future the Continent would be master of its own destiny.

It was unlikely that France would refuse to join the alliance, but the Kaiser, in spite of his confidence that she would not refuse, had taken that possibility also into consideration. Russia was bound to defend France if France were attacked. In Björkoe the Tsar had bound himself to defend Germany if the Germans were attacked. In either case Russia had to fight only in defence of an ally.

Germany and France would alike have to think twice before taking up arms. A new reinsurance treaty had been arranged with Russia, this time with no betrayal. The secret treaty of 1887 had been concluded against Germany's own ally, behind her back, and had shut her out from participation in it; Tsar Alexander III had desired from the first that the dark deed should be kept secret. The treaty of Björkoe called for straightforward dealing with France. It set out to bring her into the alliance.

Neither Austria-Hungary nor France was paying for the treaty by sacrifice or risk or any exaction. Neither Russia nor Germany was making in connexion with the treaty any concession which would kindle fires of resentment across the frontiers. Peace was imposed on Europe—the end that Britain had sought, that the Kaiser had first endeavoured to reach in co-operation with her, and that had only been attained now by an effort in the opposite direction. Anyone who thought of going to war would find at once such an army of weapons bristling in front of him that he would prefer to put up his sword. The voice that ruled now was that of the arbitral court of the nations—Tsar and Kaiser in its supreme division.

Emperor Nicholas had wanted the agreement to be confined to Europe. If Britain went to war with Russia, the Far East theatre would certainly be an important one. As things stood after the Russo-Japanese war, the British would be certain to invade eastern Siberia. A march on Persia and India would be a threat which would immobilize British troops, but it would be a very difficult and laborious movement. If the decision with Britain was some day to take place in eastern Siberia, or perhaps in north China, it was necessary that she should be faced by a Russia entirely recovered and reinvigorated. The great Siberian railway would have to carry eastwards quite different troops and war material. But Russia would be able to feel entirely secure in her rear. The Baltic shore and the capital, St. Petersburg, would be covered by the German navy—for Russia no longer had any navy at all. And Russia's western frontiers would be under German protection.

The agreement gave Germany no claim to Russian armed support in the form of activities in the Far East or of a march on India if Germany were at war with Britain. Nor could Russia make any corresponding demand on Germany. Emperor William could see no difficulties at all. He had attained the maximum of security for Germany. Campaigns of great German armies at the gates of India, clashes on new Manchurian battlefields, would have been simply fantastic adventures. Emperor William himself wanted the treaty to be confined to Europe. Germany was now secure on all her frontiers. More than this the Kaiser had never dreamed of attaining.

He informed the Chancellor on the same day of the signing of the agreement. The Chancellor replied from Norderney—overcome by the greatness of his Monarch's achievement in statesmanship:

'Your Majesty's gracious telegram from Björkoe received with deep emotion and heartfelt thanks. The credit for this success belongs to your Majesty alone, for your Majesty alone has made this turn in affairs possible and brought it about.'

Two days later the Chancellor was still filled with admiration:

'Your Majesty has made a great *coup* in the conclusion of the treaty. Now the main thing is that the Tsar shall have a long life and remain at the helm.'

Yet on the day before this he had put a question to Baron Holstein:

'Do you consider that the addition of the words '*en Europe*' to the treaty makes it worthless to us, seeing that in Europe Russia can give us no help whatever with her remains of a navy and no help against Britain with her army? Under these circumstances shall I render the treaty invalid by refusing my countersignature? Or do you think that even in this form the treaty is of value to us as a breach in the Dual Alliance?'

Björköe Summer 1905
The Zar talking to the officers of the German
cruiser escorting the German Emperors
Yacht.

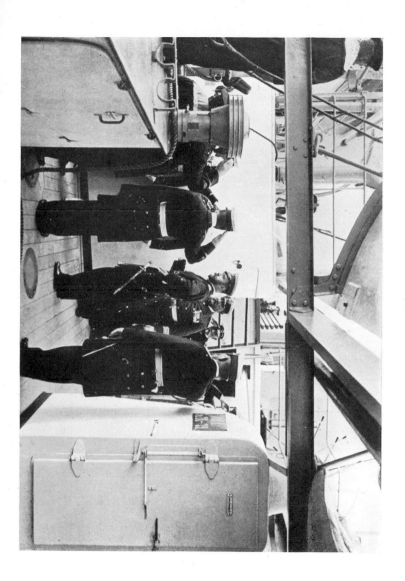

The Chancellor was uneasy about the whole agreement. The thing that mattered to him was not the peace of Europe. Nor was he troubled by any fears lest France should after all be able to upset the treaty. The thing that mattered seemed to him to be the march against India. If Germany was to be unable to ask Russia to make trouble for Britain in India, the whole agreement was valueless. He overlooked the counter-demand that the Tsar would then have been able to make—for a whole series of army corps to be sent into Asia.

Baron Holstein had a better opinion of the agreement. It brought in any case a rapprochement and a measure of protection. If there was anything that he regretted, it was the fact that the Kaiser had not obtained more while the Tsar was in a mood for giving. Suddenly, however, the Chancellor passed at a bound from admiration to indignation: the Kaiser should not have concluded any agreement at all. Forgetting his telegrams to Hernösand, he abruptly turned against the Kaiser, in defiance of logic and of the immediate past. William II was not the Tsar (and the counter-signature of acts of state was the Chancellor's business: he would make that very clear indeed to von Tschirschky). The moment had come to rob the Kaiser once for all of all taste for putting his finger in the pie. Without a word of preparation the Chancellor tendered his resignation.

The Kaiser was stunned. His own impression had been that a great success had been achieved for Germany and a real advance made. He failed to understand what could be wrong with the agreement. The restriction of the treaty to Europe simply relieved

Germany of responsibilities. It was Europe, too, that mattered: never again should the guns thunder across civilized countries. Germany's real colonies were in Africa and in the South Seas. Outside Europe Russia could be of no assistance to her—probably not even in Kiaochow. Only the great European coalition could do anything against Britain, even, through its influence, in other continents. The Chancellor disagreed; he held to his objection in regard to India. The Kaiser sent for the Chief of Staff, Field Marshal Count Schlieffen. The Field Marshal shared the Kaiser's view:

'It is absolute rubbish!' he exclaimed. 'What could we do with our troops in India?'

But even Count Schlieffen was unable to convince the Chancellor. Gradually the Kaiser became quite beside himself. So, once more he had made a mess of everything. It was the same story as in his youth, the story his parents told, and Prince Bismarck. He was utterly downcast; he began to doubt his capacity to deal with matters of high policy, with the international problems of the day. The William II who spoke to all the world amid the glamour of his imperial tasks, perhaps to be carried away by the winged words of his passionate oratory, was quite another person to the doubter and brooder of other times. The longer the Kaiser thought about it the less he was able to conceive what the Chancellor was really after, where the point of danger lay, why the agreement with the Tsar was worthless. Count Schlieffen was a soldier. Perhaps in agreeing with the Kaiser he was relying on wriggling out later on the score of technical difficulties. But search as he might for the possible grounds of criticism of his action, the Kaiser was unable to follow the Chancellor's line of thought. In his depression he gave himself up as intellectually lost.

Whatever troubles might come, the Chancellor was always a loyal and devoted friend. His face brightened whenever he approached the Kaiser. He was capable of weeping for concern and anxiety over the Kaiser. There were no secrets between Kaiser and Chancellor. The Kaiser had showered on the Chancellor evidences of his gratitude and devotion to him. It was only a little time since the Kaiser had raised the man who had started as plain Bernhard von Bülow to the rank of Prince. The Chancellor was entirely indebted to him for his unprecedented rise in the world. Such favours conferred and such favour shown could not but of themselves attach the Chancellor to him. And up to now the Kaiser had had nothing but proofs of attachment. If now the Prince wanted to part from him, if he preferred to abandon all his unexampled distinctions rather than continue at work with his friend, the cause of such a change must be of the most grievous nature. The Kaiser must really have made a complete mess of the whole matter. But he could not lose the one friend that he had in a Court that he was never quite able to trust. Philipp Eulenburg was far away; and in any case his visionary romanticism put a barrier between the two in the last resort. Prince Bülow was with the Kaiser every day, working and contriving with him for Germany's welfare. If the Prince went, he felt that his life was destroyed. He would not go on living it. He wrote so to the Chancellor. If he left him, the darkness would have

returned: obedient soldiers, Ministers with their life-
less reports. Prince Bülow was the glowing spirit that
poured life and light over all. Certainly, too, he had
more ability than the Kaiser. The Reichstag was un-
failingly loyal to him. He was loved by the people.
Every day Press and public spoke of the great gifts of
this great statesman. He would not allow Prince
Bülow to leave him. He would rather admit his error.
He had made one more mistake. The agreement with
the Tsar was a beautiful dream with a cruel awakening.

Emperor William promised Prince Bülow that he
would not again attempt to undertake any business of
state independently. The Chancellor allowed himself
to be mollified, and withdrew his resignation. As for
the treaty with the Tsar, the attempt might certainly
be made to turn it into an agreement applying also
outside Europe. All that was needed was to remove
the two words 'in Europe.' It did not occur to the
Chancellor that that might mean the whole treaty being abandoned. The agreement was of too much
value for that; in the end some concession would be
made by the Tsar. Besides, the two words 'in Europe'
were not in the least of sufficient importance to war-
rant the negotiations being allowed entirely to collapse for their sake. For the time the Chancellor would
say nothing more at all about them.

The Kaiser had become perfectly quiet—quiet as
Prince Bülow had hoped to get him. In his inmost
heart, however, he still hoped—and he noticed that
the Chancellor's view seemed suddenly to be changing—to save his treaty. He found it impossible to believe that he had gone entirely wrong in Björkoe.

Six weeks later Witte, the Russian Minister of

State, fresh from the peace negotiations in Portsmouth, came to *Schloss* Rominten to visit the Kaiser. The two had met in Peterhof in 1897. Witte was a man from whom enormous power seemed to emanate —one of the big, strong-willed Russians of German origin whom the Tsar always liked to draw into the service of the State. The Kaiser took him into his confidence over the treaty of Björkoe. The Minister of State was profuse in his declarations of boundless enthusiasm.

'That is just,' he exclaimed, 'what I have always been working for.'

Prince Bülow considered that the Russian statesman should be committed in some way to the plan. The Kaiser gave him the chain of the Order of the Red Eagle, a very high distinction, quite out of proportion to the Minister's rank.

'That is a stroke of genius! A very valuable one,' chuckled the Chancellor. 'We are counting, to be sure, on Count Witte for so much.'

The Russian Minister of State departed, taking with him as a further memento a portrait of Emperor William. On it there was written:

'Portsmouth—Björkoe—Rominten. Wilhelm Rex.'

Immediately after reaching St. Petersburg, he discussed the agreement with Count Lambsdorff. He was in high spirits; not only had Emperor William loaded him with distinctions, but the Tsar had raised him to the rank of Count in consideration of his conduct of the negotiations in Portsmouth. He never lacked self-confidence, but in these days he lacked it less than ever, and he brought the whole force of his personality into play on behalf of the union of the

325

three Powers which the treaty of Björkoe contemplated.

'But,' asked Count Lambsdorff, 'have you read the treaty of Björkoe?'

'No,' admitted Count Witte, 'I have not read it.'

'Wilhelm and the Tsar did not give it to you to read? Have a look at the masterpiece.'

Count Witte read. He quickly skimmed the introduction—he dismissed it as 'mere words.' As for the treaty—the treaty for which he had always been working—he found it at once quite hopeless. If France and Germany went to war, Russia, under the treaty of Björkoe, would have to go to the aid of the Germans. It would be a Russian betrayal of France. The treaty was 'dishonourable.' It would have to be abandoned. That the 'mere words' in the agreement included the term 'defensive alliance,' that her alliance with France entailed no obligation on Russia to support the French in a war of aggression, that in spite of her commitments she could oppose the French if the French themselves launched a war—all this Count Witte failed to grasp. No doubt Russia might under certain circumstances be failing to observe the spirit of her alliance with France, in spite of her indisputable right to a free hand in the event of a French attack on Germany. In any war with Russia, Austria-Hungary would be compelled for military reasons to be the aggressor, and similarly France might be the one that had suffered provocation and might still be compelled to be the aggressor; in that event Russia would obviously be bound to go to her aid. But even that eventuality was excluded from the operation of the treaty of Björkoe. The Alliance was to be no

secret to the French. They were, on the contrary, to
be equal partners in it, and equally under its protection. Germany and France were to be placed by that
treaty in a position in which neither of them could
venture on any attack whatever without running into
the gravest danger. War under the treaty was to die
out. If France wanted to go beyond the guarantee
of peace contained in the treaty of Björkoe and to reserve liberty to attack, or if she refused altogether to
sign the treaty, she would by so doing release Russia
from the moral obligation to stand by her ally.
Russia had made no alliance with a France lusting for
aggression. As aggressor, France could have no knowledge of what Russia would do, and no right to com-
plain of any action of her ally's. The whole spirit and
purpose of the treaty of Björkoe was constructive. It
took account of every eventuality and every objection
that could be raised. And its basis was ethical. All
this, however, was far beyond Count Witte's range.
His opinion was that Russia was bound to aid France
in any war—aggressive or not. Accordingly, the
treaty must go. One could not possibly commit a
dishonourable action.

Count Lambsdorff's view was that Russia should
adhere to her treaty with France, but should enter
into no agreement with any other Power. He knew
that the Russian alliance with France was in no way
formally incompatible with the treaty of Björkoe. He
knew, moreover, that the spirit of the agreement with
France was quite compatible with that of the new
agreement. But he wanted no bridges built, would be
no party to them, simply because he was against the
conclusion of any alliance at all with Germany. He

took up his stand behind the claim that Russia was morally bound to France. The fate of the treaty of Björkoe ought to be made dependent on whether France accepted or rejected it. Count Lambsdorff confidently anticipated its rejection. There was no need for him to consider the possibility or the value of any league of the nations, for he regarded it as out of the question for France ever to come to Germany's side. He was thus quite in agreement with the strange verdict at which Count Witte had arrived after two minutes' study of the treaty.

Count Witte talked to Grand Duke Nicolai Nicolayevitch, of whose influence with the Tsar he knew; that influence had for some time been growing into a stronger power than the Tsar's own. The Grand Duke was ill-inclined towards the Germans: he was the leader of the Pan-Slavs in Russia. Count Witte was on friendly terms with him, but he had no trouble in guessing how long that would last if he took Germany's part. He forgot all about Rominten. Together with the Grand Duke and Count Lambsdorff, he pressed their common view on the Tsar. Nicholas II had not the strength to break through the network of considerations which the three enemies of the agreement wove around it. They worked steadily on him and steadily unsettled him. Finally he gave way. He summoned the three to a Council to decide the question, on October 1, 1905. The treaty, it was resolved, must be rescinded, or, if France would agree to come in, it must be further amended.

Count Lambsdorff, as Foreign Minister, was kept thoroughly well informed as to opinion in France by the Ambassador in Paris, Count Nelidov. It was left to Prince Bülow and Baron Holstein to indulge in their dream of a better future born of their statecraft. Prince and *Geheimrat* were counting on still saving the treaty of Björkoe in some form or other; yet at the same time the *Geheimrat* was once more getting fits of bellicosity against the French. He had no knowledge of the fact that between Tangier Day and the autumn Britain had given the French definite assurances of aid in the event of a German attack. He believed France to be thoroughly weak and nervous. The German Chargé d'Affaires in Tangier, Counsellor of Legation Richard von Kühlmann, ventured to express a different view:

'French panickiness might have yielded a pleasant drink in spring, taken when it was fresh; but now in autumn, bottled and flat, there is no enjoying it.'

In those intervening months, the Counsellor of Legation had had many useful talks with the French Chargé d'Affaires, Count Chérisey. The two diplomats agreed that it would be useful if Germany and France went to the Conference with exact knowledge of the mutual concessions which they could make. They wanted to have no more than a stage battle at the Conference: they proposed to have its agreed resolutions drafted and settled in advance. If France were to obtain from the other Powers a sort of mandate for Morocco, with control of the police, Germany would not be bound to give her assent. If, however, that system were to last two more years and then to be accepted as a permanent arrangement by the Powers, there was no reason why Germany should then veto it. In consideration of her assent, Germany might then receive French Congo and the right of pre-emption of Belgian Congo. These conditions Chérisey found entirely acceptable:

'I will talk to my friends. You talk to your friends in Berlin. If they agree, we will make a secret treaty.'

In Paris the Counsellor of Legation had one more talk with the Count. An adroitly chosen excuse that would excite no curiosity had been found for calling Count Chérisey urgently to Paris from Tangier for this interview. He showed a confidence of success that could only be explained by the knowledge that the French Foreign Ministry was already won over. The two diplomats agreed on phrases which Counsellor of Legation von Kühlmann should employ to indicate the results of his coming discussion with *Geheimrat* von Holstein. If all went well, he would telegraph: 'Weather fine.' If doubtfully, 'Weather dull.'

The German Chargé d'Affaires went off to Berlin. He first saw Ambassador von Radowitz. The two went together to see *Geheimrat* von Holstein. The *Geheimrat* listened in silence; then he declared, in icy tones, as was his habit when taken by surprise in this way:

'I cannot decide that. I shall have to consult the Foreign Ministry.'

Ambassador and Counsellor of Legation returned next day. The Counsellor of Legation telegraphed to Count Chérisey:

'Weather very cold. Cannot travel at present. But not entirely hopeless.'

He could not risk adding any details.

'I have received you once more,' the *Geheimrat* said to him some time later, 'to let you know that I do not take your opposition in bad part. You will be going now to Washington. There you will have a new field of activity—far from the firing line.'

In such fashion had *Geheimrat* von Holstein pursued his dream of a Franco-German understanding since the entry of M. Rouvier into office as Prime Minister of France. The Chancellor had followed suit. The French Premier, however, gave the Russians the most definite of assurances that France had not the slightest intention of entering into any alliance in company with Germany. He had had enough of German statecraft and German approaches since the day when he had let Delcassé fall for the sake of the peace of Europe, and had received for that action not so much as a word of acknowledgment, to say nothing of any concession. Every step taken by Germany had brought some fresh vexation. The sacrifice of the Foreign Minister had been a humiliation, and the forcing of French assent to the Conference another; the fresh difficulties which Germany had constantly been making over agreeing on a programme for this unlucky Conference before it assembled had been one long chain of humiliations. Even though the treaty of Björkoe was not formally and juridically in conflict with the Franco-Russian alliance, France gave emphatic expression to her concern at her ally considering any close association with a Power that showed afresh every day that there could be no forgetting of the past.

So the treaty of Björkoe fell through, mainly through the policy pursued towards France by Chancellor Prince Bülow and his principal adviser. Only statesmen of their intellectual calibre could have imagined it possible to bring into being an alliance with Russia that depended in the first place on the France whom they were so mishandling. Emperor William had proceeded to the agreement on the strength of the efforts which he had made towards a Franco-German reconciliation. His instructions to the Ambassador in Paris, Prince Radolin; his enlistment of the assistance of the Prince of Monaco; his plain and repeated expressions of his own desire for an understanding to be brought about in spite of every difficulty—all this had been by way of preparation. Now the Russians were proposing that the first point in the treaty of Björkoe should be rescinded for the time being—the obligation to give armed assistance if either of the allies was attacked. That would bring matters back to the position before the signature of the treaty: the whole agreement would be empty and purposeless.

Naturally the whole course of events was painful for the Tsar. At last, simply as a matter of form, just in order to make a better retreat, he had the suggestion conveyed to the Kaiser that an addition should be made to the treaty, on the strength of which it would be possible to leave the existing text unaltered. In reality the effect of the addition was to cancel the first article:

'In view of the difficulties in the way of the immediate adhesion of the French Government to the defensive alliance signed in Björkoe on July 11-24, 1905, —an adhesion contemplated in Article IV of the said treaty—it follows naturally that Article I of this treaty has no validity in the case of a war with France, and that the mutual obligations by which France and Russia are bound remain in force up to the moment of coming into existence of a triple alliance.'

With that proposal Count Lambsdorff repaid the German Cabinet for the treatment which it had accorded to his own advances in the preceding autumn. And with it France launched the first blow at Germany in return for her part in the struggle over Morocco. The treaty of Björkoe was destroyed. Chancellor von Bülow had first tried to upset it from the German side. Later, when he himself took up the agreement again, he found that it had already been torpedoed by his own policy in East and West. The league of the nations faded out of existence. This much had become clear, that there was no possibility of creating a coalition of the Continental Powers, either against Britain or for any other purpose.

But this also was clear: Emperor William's policy, steadily adhered to, in spite of every variation in the method pursued, for fifteen years past, had arrived, so far as that period in German history was concerned, at complete and final failure. He had pursued it along two lines. He had tried but failed to secure the alliance with Britain, though he had worked for it with more conviction than for the alliance with Russia. Britain had not been induced to come over to Germany's side either by the friendship towards her that the Kaiser had shown or by concern when he seemed to be becoming Russophil. Ultimately the only possibility had seemed to be the winning of Russian friendship. The Kaiser had thought out plans of a Continental alliance by way of a spell to

333

exorcise Britain's aloofness; he had then made them his positive aim, but Russia had abandoned him precisely as Britain had done.

In East and West alike his statesmen had wrecked his aspirations. If it was blameworthy to suffer betrayal at the hands of those statesmen, to have one's plans secretly frustrated, then the Kaiser was to be blamed. Under his rule Germany's wealth and strength and prestige had visibly increased, and he himself could take credit for three big achievements—he had acquired Heligoland, had secured Cecil Rhodes's pledge for the acquisition of Samoa, and had assured to Germany the Bagdad Railway and her influence in Asia Minor. Against his better judgment he had twice complied with demands made by his Chancellors and forced on him by the claim that they had the support of the Reichstag and the nation. He had been reminded of his duty as a constitutional ruler, and he had done as his advisers requested. The first demand had been for the despatch of the telegram to President Kruger; the second, for the visit to Tangier. Visit and telegram alike had brought disaster. At last he had determined to act independently in Björkoe; but once more disaster had resulted. He had to bear the judgment of the onlooking nation if he failed to break through constitutional bonds in order to safeguard Germany's future. He had to bear the nation's verdict if he made up his mind to yield to his better judgment and break through those bonds.

This last, in actual fact, he had never done; although by a strange and depressing ordinance of

Fate he had been the only one—alone among his advisers—to follow definite lines of political thought, and the only one who had seen the right course. His weakness had been to show superficial signs of absolutist inclinations, in incautious gestures and in oratorical slips, although there was no trace of absolutism when he came to think out and put into practice any big decision. In the end he had always been firmly loyal to the Constitution, and this had saved him from serious complications in home politics. In Germany's foreign policy his reliance on his advisers had brought disaster. In reality it was not he who ruled over Germany but the decision of the nation, represented by its spokesmen. Germany's fate in these years had been determined by two men at the helm—Chancellor Prince Bülow and the mysterious figure of the juggler-calculator Holstein. Blind themselves, they carried the Reichstag on their backs. The calculator went on with his manipulations behind the scenes; the Prince stood forth to gather the plaudits of the crowd.

So it came that on the eve of the Morocco Conference, on the eve of the year 1906, the Kaiser began slowly to suspect that the Chancellor's invariable smiles and his clouds of verbiage were no more than a mask and a symbol of the actual nothingness which was the outcome of his statesmanship so far. After Björkoe, after the awakening from the shock that had seemed to make life impossible without Prince Bülow, the Kaiser considered for the first time whether to part from the Chancellor.

He felt that a long chapter in the history of his Empire had come to its end. Germany was sinking into isolation. London and Björkoe had revealed it. All that the German statesmen could do to promote this isolation, they had done. From then on the Powers would reap its fruits to the full. On all her frontiers they stood, menacing.

The encirclement of Germany had begun.

LIST OF AUTHORITIES

[All personal statements, memoranda, and materials of every sort, and unpublished documents, which served as basis of the work, are indicated by asterisks.]

CHAPTER I

THE UNRAVELLING OF THE ALLIANCES

P. 1. *Moltke and Caprivi*: Communications from Emperor William II.*

P. 2. *The Navy and the 'Stoschites'*: Communications from Emperor William II.*—*Caprivi strange to the navy*: Communications from his niece, the wife of General von Müller.*—*Caprivi's services to the navy*: Communications from Emperor William II.*

P. 3. *Caprivi's resignation from the Admiralty*: Communications from the wife of General von Müller, confirmed by the Kaiser.*— *Caprivi's personality; his reading*: Wife of General von Müller.*

P. 4. *Bismarck's recommendation of Caprivi*: 'Gedanken und Erinnerungen,' p. 75.—*Caprivi's sensitiveness and 'obstinacy'; his outlook on the world*: Communications from Emperor William II.* —*Caprivi's room in the Chancellor's residence*: Wife of General von Müller.*

P. 5. *Bismarck's meeting with Caprivi in March* 1890: 'Gedanken und Erinnerungen,' pp. 114-5.—*The new fact of a secret treaty with Russia*: Communications from Emperor William II.*—*Count Herbert Bismarck's pressure on the Kaiser*: Count Lambsdorff's diary, critically discussed and related to the Reinsurance Treaty by Professor Hans Uebersberger, 'Kriegsschuldfrage,' 1927, no. 10.

P. 6. *Alleged order to Shuvalov to negotiate only with Prince Bismarck*: 'Die Grosse Politik der Europäischen Kabinette 1871-1914' (German Foreign Ministry's collection of diplomatic documents), vol. 7, no. 1366.—'*This manœuvre' of Count H. Bismarck's*: Count Lambsdorff's diary, central archives, Moscow (in the original: 'manevr etot').—*Emperor William's note, 'Why?'*: 'Grosse Politik,' 7, no. 1367.

P. 7. *Shuvalov and Emperor William*: MS. note by Emperor William II.*

Y

P. 8. *Bismarck's support of the Mediterranean Agreement*: Erich Brandenburg, 'Von Bismarck zum Weltkriege,' p. 12.

P. 9. *Alexander III's moods*: Count Lambsdorff's diary.—*Bismarck's belief in the Tsar's trust in him*: Communications from Emperor William II.*

P. 10. *Tsar's note on Bismarck*: Count Lambsdorff's diary, p. 173, central archives, Moscow. The original runs: 'Opyat' chto to za levaet etot oder-skot, a nam khochet ot vecti zhaza istoriei s amerikantsami iz za Samoa. Naivno!'—*Tsar's suspicion of Bismarck*: Communications of Emperor William II.*—*Disraeli's triumph*: Disraeli's 'Letters' to two sisters.—*Tsar's hostility to the secret agreement*: Count Lambsdorff's diary.—*Tsar, Russian people, and Germans; Peter Shuvalov's initiative; Tsar and France; the differences between the Tsar and Giers*: Count Lambsdorff's diary.

P. 11. *Giers, the 'poor old man'*: 'Grosse Politik' 7, no. 1657.—*Giers' varying views*: 'Grosse Politik' 7, no. 1656, and 9, no. 2084.

P. 12. *Russia's isolation*: 'Grosse Politik' 7, no. 1369; and Count Lambsdorff's diary.—*Katkov and Grand Duke Vladimir*: Count Lambsdorff's diary.

P. 13. *Alexander III demands secrecy over the treaty*: Count Lambsdorff's diary.

Pp. 13-17. Jules Hansen, 'L'Ambassade Mohrenheim à Paris.'

P. 17. *Germany's obligation to place corps along the Russian frontier*: letter from Valfrey to Hansen, January 13, 1888.—*Secret treaty to be known only to the signatories*: Lambsdorff's diary.

P. 18. *Morier and Ignatiev*: Communications from Count Monts.* Cf. Freiherr von Eckardstein, 'Lebenserinnerungen.'—*Prince Lobanov's knowledge of the secret treaty*: Communications from Count Monts concerning his conversations with Prince Lobanov.*—*Ignatiev a liar*: Communications from an eminent British statesman.* [1]

P. 19. *Lord Salisbury; Bismarck; Count Hatzfeldt's conversations*: 'Grosse Politik' 4, 926, 930.—*Lord Salisbury and Germany's relations with Russia*: Communications from an eminent British statesman.* Cf. Eckardstein, 'Lebenserinnerungen,' p. 154.—*Russia's doubtful neutrality*: 'Grosse Politik' 5, pp. 116 *sqq.*

[1] The British statesman whose information has been availed of for the present work holds at the time of writing one of the crucial positions in the guidance of British affairs of state. It will therefore be impossible to give his name until a later edition of this work appears.

Pp. 20-22. *Count Berchem's memorandum*: 'Grosse Politik' 7, 1368.

P. 22. *Baron Holstein's urgency*: Uebersberger, 'Abschluss und Ende des Rückversicherungsvertrages,' in 'Kriegsschuldfrage,' 1927, no. 10.—*Baron Holstein's register*: Communications from Prince Hatzfeldt, Duke of Trachenberg.*

P. 23. *Holstein's hatred of Bismarck; Bismarck a Wallenstein*: Communications from an eminent British statesman.*—*Holstein and the possibility of Bismarck's return*: 'Grosse Politik' 7, 1369 Note.

P. 24. *The secret treaty with Italy*: Minute by Baron Holstein, May 20, 1890, 'Grosse Politik' 7, no. 1374.

Pp. 25-27. *Raschdau and the secret treaty*: Minute by Raschdau, May 20, 1890, 'Grosse Politik' 7, no. 1377.—*Bismarck 'alarmed' over his own treaties; Prince Reuss and Count Kálnoky; Russia, Austria, and Serbia; the march through Roumania*: Communications from Herr Raschdau, Minister of Legation.*

P. 26. *Bismarck's doubts whether the secret treaty could be carried out; its destruction by continual modifications*: Raschdau in Schmidt-Pauli's 'Denkunwürdigkeiten des Fürsten Bülow.'

P. 27. *Holstein's general and personal grounds for urgency*: 'Briefwechsel des Botschafters General von Schweinitz,' p. 265; Muschler, 'Philipp zu Eulenburg,' p. 242.

P. 28. *Caprivi and peoples' alliances, 'war of aggression,' and casus foederis*: 'Grosse Politik' 7, 1379.—*Marschall's appointment and the Grand Duke of Baden*: Communications from Emperor William II.*

P. 29. *General von Schweinitz on the Reinsurance Treaty*: Communications from Emperor William II.*—*Caprivi and Schweinitz*: 'Briefwechsel des Botschafters von Schweinitz,' p. 266.

Pp. 29-30. *Emperor William's thoughts concerning Russia and the Tsar's reply*: Communications from Emperor William II.*

P. 30. *Lambsdorff and the Tsar's reply*: Count Lambsdorff's diary.—*Alexander III's preparation for an alliance with France; Bismarck's ingratitude*: Hansen, 'L'Ambassade Mohrenheim.'

P. 31. *Emperor William's decision*: Communications from Emperor William II.*—*Eulenburg's telegram*: Communications from Emperor William II* and Muschler, 'Philipp zu Eulenburg.'— *The breakaway from the treaty; the plenary powers; the indifferent Tsar*: Count Lambsdorff's diary.

P. 32. *Schweinitz's conversation with Giers*: Schweinitz to Caprivi, 'Grosse Politik' 7, 1370.—*The Russian statesmen's attitude and the proposal in regard to the substituted protocol*: Lambsdorff's diary.—*Giers on the 'exchange of notes'*: Minute by Caprivi, 'Grosse Politik' 7, 1379.

Pp. 32-33. *The Russian anarchists and the Tsar*: 'L'Ambassade Mohrenheim.'

P. 33. *'Preserving the essentials'; the Tsar's resistance*: Lambsdorff's diary.—*The standpoint of William II*: Communications from Emperor William II.*—*Letter from William II to Emperor Francis Joseph*: Secret State archives, Vienna.

P. 34. *Tsar's marginal note; the last attempt*: Lambsdorff's diary.

P. 35. *Raschdau's delaying tactics*: 'Grosse Politik' 7, 1377; and Raschdau in Schmidt-Pauli, 'Denkunwürdigkeiten.'

P. 36. *Caprivi and General von Werder*: 'Grosse Politik' 7, 1651.

P. 37. *Bismarck, 'the Englishwoman'; Queen Victoria and the British Court*: Communications from Emperor William II.*

FURTHER SOURCES FOR CHAPTER I

Manuscript commentary by Emperor William II on Prince Bismarck's 'Gedanken und Erinnerungen,' vol. 3; and on Professor Hans Uebersberger's 'Abschluss und Ende des Rückversicherungsvertrages.'*

Reports from the Austro-Hungarian Ambassadors in Berlin, St. Petersburg, London, Paris, and Rome, and from the other Ministers of Legation, to the Minister of Foreign Affairs in Vienna, Count Kálnoky; from the secret State archives in Vienna.*

CHAPTER II

THE WOOING OF ENGLAND

Pp. 39-40. Communications from an eminent British statesman.*

P. 41. *Bismarck's 'ten per cent'*: Communications from an eminent British statesman.*

Pp. 41-47. *Sketch of the Prince of Wales*: Communications from Emperor William II.* Communications from an eminent British statesman,* from Prince Max Egon Fürstenberg,* from Count Monts, Ambassador.*

P. 43. *Queen Victoria and Prince Edward's political views*: 'The Letters of Queen Victoria,' 1886-1901 (Osborne, January 3, 1888).

Pp. 46-47. *Correspondence between the Prince of Wales and Prince Christian*: 'Letters of Queen Victoria.' Count Kálnoky to Count Deym, Ambassador in London, April 1, 1889. Secret Court and State archives, Vienna.*

P. 48. *Reception of the Prince of Wales in Berlin*: Sir Edward Malet to Queen Victoria, March 31, 1890, in 'Letters of Queen Victoria.'—*Emperor William's Anglophil feeling*: Communications from the Kaiser.* Brandenburg, p. 30.

P. 49. *Caprivi, blockade, and a war on two fronts*: Caprivi's speeches on the army bill on December 10, 1891, and November 23, 1892. Johann Ziekursch, 'Das Zeitalter Wilhelms II.' Hammann, 'Der Neue Kurs,' p. 27.—*Caprivi, Heligoland, Zanzibar*: Communications from Emperor William II.* Friedjung, 'Das Zeitalter des Imperialismus.' Bismarck, 'Gedanken und Erinnerungen.'

P. 50. *Attacks on Caprivi*: Memorandum by the Chancellor for the Reichstag on the Heligoland treaty. Friedjung, 'Zeitalter des Imperialismus,' p. 129.

P. 51. *The Prince of Wales and Heligoland*: Communication from Prince Hatzfeldt.*—*Queen Victoria and Heligoland*: Communications from Emperor William II.—*The Queen and the Kaiser's foibles*: 'Letters of Queen Victoria.'

Pp. 51-52. *Queen Victoria proud of the Kaiser*: Communication from an eminent British statesman.*

P. 52. *The Attitude of Empress Frederick*: 'Briefe der Kaiserin Friedrich,' Berlin 1929.—*Rudini and France*: 'Grosse Politik' 8, 1724. Brandenburg, p. 33.—*Britain's colonial troubles*: Communications from an eminent British statesman.* Friedjung, 'Zeitalter des Imperialismus.'

P. 53. *Constantinople and the Ottoman Bank*: Harold Nicolson, 'Sir Arthur Nicolson, Bart., first Lord Carnock: a Study in the Old Diplomacy.'

Pp. 53-56. *Salisbury and Marschall*: 'Grosse Politik' 8, 1724, and 9, 2111. Cf. Brandenburg, 'Von Bismarck zum Weltkrieg,' p. 33.—*Marschall's character*: Communications from Emperor William II, and from an eminent British statesman.*—*The impression he made on Salisbury*: Report from Count Deyms, Ambassador in London, to Kálnoky, July 15, 1891. State archives,

Vienna.*—*Marschall and diplomacy*: Briefwechsel Schweidnitz, p. 302.

Pp. 57-59. *Hatzfeldt*: Communications from Emperor William II, from Count Pückler, Minister of Legation, from Prince Hermann Hatzfeldt. Alfred Dumaine, French Ambassador, 'Choses d'Allemagne,' Paris 1924.

P. 60. *French Colonial and Eastern policy*: Friedjung, 'Zeitalter des Imperialismus.' Nicolson, 'Sir Arthur Nicolson, Bart.'

P. 61. *Siam*: Communications from an eminent British statesman.*—*Metternich's report*: 'Grosse Politik' 8, 1754. Comments by Friedjung and Nicolson.—*The Quadruple Alliance*: 'Grosse Politik' 8, 1749.

Pp. 61-63. *Holstein's attitude*: 'Grosse Politik' 8, 1750.

Pp. 63-64. *Rosebery and the telegram from Bangkok*: Metternich's report, 'Grosse Politik' 8, 1754.—*Queen Victoria and William II*: Communications from Emperor William II.*—*Emperor, Kiderlen, and Rosebery*: Communications from Emperor William II.*

P. 65. *The pushing of the Quadruple Alliance and Hatzfeldt's proposal to present it in plain terms*: 'Grosse Politik' 8, 1753. Cf. Brandenburg, 'Von Bismarck zum Weltkrieg.'—'*Bierphilisterpolitik*': Communications from Emperor William II.*

P. 66. '*The best beginning of the next war*': 'Grosse Politik' 8, 1753.

P. 67. '*Anatolian Company' and the railway concession*: Nicolson, 'Sir Arthur Nicolson, Bart.'

Pp. 67-74. Communications from Emperor William II. Communications from an eminent British statesman.* 'Grosse Politik' 8, ch. lii, liv, 'Auf dem Wege zur Quadrupelallianz' and 'Die Bedeutung der Kolonialfragen für die Gruppierung der Mächte.' Friedjung, 'Zeitalter des Imperialismus.' Nicolson, 'Sir Arthur Nicolson, Bart.'

CHAPTER III

GERMANY SETTING HER HOME IN ORDER

P. 75. *Eulenburg on particularism*: Muschler, 'Philipp zu Eulenburg.'—*Caprivi on the Bismarckian heritage*: Count Szögyény to Count Kálnoky, August 19, 1893. Secret State archives, Vienna.*

P. 76. *Conditions in the army*: Communications from Emperor William II.*

342

P. 78. *Caprivi and Britain*: Communications from an eminent British statesman.*—*Emperor William's telegrams en clair*: Muschler, 'Philipp zu Eulenburg.'

P. 79. *Hinzpeter's attitude*: Hinzpeter's letters to Emperor William II, Hohenzollern archives, Berlin.*—*The retailed sayings*: Count Széchényi to Count Kálnoky, May 14, 1892. State archives, Vienna.*—*The Kaiser's 'mental trouble'*: Denkwürdigkeiten des Feldmarschalls Graf Waldersee.—*The American Ambassador's Court uniform*: Communications from Emperor William II and from Countess Scheel-Plessen.*

P. 80. *French views of the Kaiser; the company on board the Hohenzollern*: Reports from Count Zichy, from Paris, to Count Kálnoky, August 5 and 6, 1891. Secret State archives, Vienna.*

P. 81. *William II's speeches and their reading aloud*: Communications from Emperor William II.*

P. 82. *The entry in the Munich visitors' book*: Communications from Emperor William II and letter from Count Széchényi to Count Kálnoky, December 18, 1891. Secret State archives, Vienna.*

P. 83. *Caprivi and the Kaiser*: Caprivi to Count Széchényi, March 1, 1891. Secret State archives, Vienna.*—*Bismarck's gloom over William II*: Communications from Countess Scheel-Plessen.*

Pp. 84-85. *Count Herbert Bismarck's journey to London*: Communications from Emperor William II.*

P. 85. *Bismarck's persecution mania*: Communications from Emperor William II*; F. Philipp, 'Bismarck Vertrauliche Gespräche.'

P. 86. *Kaiser, Caprivi, and Bismarck's visit to Vienna*: Communications from Emperor William II.*

P. 92. *The two years' military service period*: Communications from Emperor William II.*

Pp. 94-96. *The labour question*: Communications from Emperor William II.*

P. 100. *Bebel on the anarchists*: Letter from Bebel to Engels, in archives of the Social Democratic Party, Berlin.*

Pp. 103-106. *William II and Bismarck*: Communications from Emperor William II.*

P. 105. *The Conversation in the Lustgarten*: Communications from Major-General von Seeckt.*

Pp. 115-118. *Caprivi's fall*: Communications from Emperor William II.*

FURTHER SOURCES FOR THIS CHAPTER

Manuscript notes by Emperor William II on the Army Bill.* Manuscript commentary by Emperor William on Egmont Zechlin's 'Staatsstreichpläne unter dem Fürsten Bismarck und Wilhelm II.'* Emperor William's commentary on Bismarck's references to Caprivi in 'Gedanken und Erinnerungen.'* Private letter from Count Kálnoky to Count Szögyény on Count Philipp Eulenburg's communications concerning Caprivi's fall (Appendix).* The reports of the Austro-Hungarian Ambassadors in Berlin, London, St. Petersburg, Paris, and other capitals (1890-1894) to Count Kálnoky, Foreign Minister in Vienna: Secret State Archives, Vienna.*

'Caprivi's Entlassung,' in Erinnerungen des Majors von Ebmeyer, 'Deutsche Revue,' 1922.

Johannes Haller: 'Aus dem Leben des Fürsten Philipp zu Eulenburg-Hertefeld.'

Johannes Haller, 'Aus fünfzig Jahren Erinnerungen des Fürsten Philipp zu Eulenburg.'

Otto Hammann: 'Der Neue Kurs.'

Freiherr Lucius von Ballhausen: 'Bismarcks Erinnerungen.'

R. C. Muschler: 'Philipp zu Eulenburg.'

Ferdinand Philipp: 'Bismarck Vertrauliche Gespräche,' with comments by Emperor William II.*

Friedrich Thimme: 'Die Kanzlerkrise von 1894 und die Kölnische Zeitung.' Kölnische Zeitung, August 1930.

Briefwechsel des Botschafters General von Schweinitz.

Generalfeldmarschall Alfred von Waldersee: 'Denkwürdigkeiten,' with comments by Emperor William II.*

Kaiser Wilhelm II: 'Ereignisse und Gestalten.'

Johannes Ziekursch: 'Das Zeitalter Wilhelms II.'

CHAPTER IV

THE PARTITION OF THE WORLD

P. 121. *Prince zu Hohenlohe*: Communications from Emperor William II.*—*Eulenburg's report*: Muschler, 'Philipp Fürst zu Eulenburg.'

P. 122. *Letzlingen, the toast and the elections*: Communications from Emperor William II.*

P. 124. *The manœuvres at Rohnstock*: Communications from Emperor William II, from Major-General von Seeckt, and from Cavalry General Baron von Gebsattel.*

Pp. 125-126. *The old gentleman as Chancellor. Prince Hohenlohe, Britain, France, and Russia*: Communications from Emperor William II.*

Pp. 127-128. *The Tsar's betrothal*: Manuscript notes by Emperor William II.*

Pp. 128-131. 'Grosse Politik,' vol. 9. Friedjung, 'Das Zeitalter des Imperialismus.' Brandenburg, 'Von Bismarck bis zum Weltkrieg.'

P. 132. *Tirpitz and Kiaochow; Formosa*: Communications from Emperor William II.*

P. 133. *Holstein, Hatzfeldt, Kimberley*: 'Grosse Politik' 9, 2223. —*The pressure on Nicholas II*: Communications from Emperor William II.*

P. 134. *Holstein and the Dual Alliance*: Communications from Count Monts.*—*Holstein's sharp tone*: Nicolson, 'Sir Arthur Nicolson, Bart.'—*Japanese intentions on Port Arthur*: 'Grosse Politik' 9, 2239.—*Port Arthur, a new, Japanese Gibraltar*: Brandenburg, p. 52.

Pp. 134-135. *Attitude of von Gutschmidt*: Reports from Gutschmidt, 'Grosse Politik' 9. Brandenburg, p. 56.

Pp. 136-137. *Emperor William and the 'Yellow Peril'*: Communications from Emperor William II.* 'Grosse Politik' 9, 2321.

Pp. 137. *Assurance for the Tsar*: Letter from Emperor William II to the Tsar, April 26, 1895. In Walter Goetz, 'Kaiser Wilhelms Briefe an Nikolaus II.' Brandenburg, p. 49.

Pp. 137-138. *The Continental Alliance, the Kaiser, and Count Schlieffen; Britain's reminder*: Communications from Emperor William II.*

Pp. 138-139. *The Tsar's support in the Far East*: Reply from Nicholas II to the letter of April 26, 1895. Brandenburg, p. 60.

Pp. 139-140. *The Boers' railway line; President Kruger's toast*: 'Grosse Politik' 11. Friedjung.

P. 140. *Queen Victoria; Lord Salisbury*: Communications from Emperor William II.*

Pp. 141-142. *Conversation between Emperor William and Lord Salisbury*: Manuscript communications from Emperor William II.*

Pp. 142-143. *Lord Salisbury, the anecdotes, and the Queen*: Communications from Emperor William II.*

P. 143. *Lord Salisbury's flight to London*: Communications from an eminent British statesman.*

P. 144. *The Balkans under a glass shade. The* coup *against Constantinople*: Rektor Professor Dr. Hans Uebersberger, 'Die Dardanellen als Schicksalsfrage Russlands,' inaugural address delivered in Vienna University on September 30, 1930. Count Witte, 'Erinnerungen.'

P. 145. *Emperor Francis Joseph and the Vatican*: Communications from Emperor William II.*

P. 147. *Colonel Swaine, Emperor William, and Britain*: 'Grosse Politik' 11, 2579.

Pp. 148-151. Communications from an eminent British statesman.* Also Friedjung.

P. 151. *Count Hatzfeldt and his passport*: 'Grosse Politik' 11, 2590.

P. 152. *Count Münster's inquiries in France and the Notes in connexion with the Jameson Raid*: 'Grosse Politik' 9.

Pp. 152-156. *The Kruger telegram*: Communications from Emperor William II. Notes by Emperor William on the origin of the Kruger telegram, house archives, Doorn.* Notes by Marschall, Baron von Senden, and others in Friedrich Thimme's study 'Die Entstehung der Krüger-Depesche,' in 'Europäische Gespräche' 1924, no. 3; and commentary by Emperor William II in 'Chlodwig Fürst zu Hohenlohe.'*

P. 157. *The idea of dismissing Marschall; first prospects of Bülow's succession as Secretary of State*: Communications from Emperor William II.*—*British steps against the participants in the Jameson Raid*: Communications from an eminent British statesman.*

Pp. 157-158. Nicolson, 'Sir Arthur Nicolson, Bart.'

P. 158. *Police and Kurdish soldiery*: Communications from Dr. Richard von Kühlmann, formerly Secretary of State.*

Pp. 159-161. *The Armenian massacres, Queen Victoria, the 'red coats'*: Communications from Emperor William II.*

Pp. 162-163. *Rumely Hiszar and the Armenian students*: Communications from Dr. R. von Kühlmann.*

Pp. 164-165. Communications from Emperor William II.*— *Crete: the suggestion of the King of the Belgians*: Communications from Emperor William II, in opposition to Prince Bülow's 'Denk-würdigkeiten.'*

Pp. 167-173. *Count Muraviev*,' Le droit du premier mouillage'; *Admiral Hollmann*: Communications from Emperor William II.* Manuscript comment by Emperor William II on Nicolson's 'Sir Arthur Nicolson, Bart,' and on Prince Bülow's 'Denkwürdig-keiten.'*

CHAPTER V

TWO ROAD BUILDERS

P. 179. *Egypt; the Soudan; Chamberlain on the French*: Communications from an eminent British statesman.*

Pp. 180-181. *Salisbury and Chamberlain*: Communications from an eminent British statesman.*—*Chamberlain and the Russians in the Far East; his overtures to Germany*: Brandenburg, p. 95.

P. 182. *Hatzfeldt's conversations in London*: 'Grosse Politik' 13, 3407 and 3410; 14, 3709.—*Collaboration 'somewhere in the world'; Britain's unimportant battleships*: Brandenburg, p. 93.

P. 183. *Holstein and 'the gamble of a treaty'*: Brandenburg, p. 96.

P. 184. *Chamberlain's hint of an approach to France and Bülow's reception of the idea*: 'Grosse Politik' 14, 3792, 3793.

Pp. 184-188. Communications from Emperor William II.*

P. 188. *Letter from Emperor William to the Tsar*: Prof. Dr. Walter Goetz, 'Briefe Wilhelms II an den Zaren.'

P. 189. *Chamberlain's intentions*: Communications from an eminent British statesman.* Communications from Lord Haldane.*

P. 190. *The Portuguese colonies*: 'Grosse Politik' 14, 3817; 19, 3829 *sqq.*

P. 191. *The 'whole bundle of things' and Lord Salisbury*: 'Grosse Politik' 14, 3796, 3797.

P. 192. *Importance of the British proposal*: Communications from Emperor William II.

P. 193. *The Kaiser not to meet the British*: 'Grosse Politik' 14, 3867.—*The Portuguese treaty*: 'Grosse Politik' 14, 3872.

P. 194. *Bülow's reports to the Kaiser*: Communications from Emperor William II.*

P. 195. *No British offer of alliance to Russia*: Communications from an eminent British statesman.*—*Lord Salisbury, China, Sir N. O'Connor and Count Muraviev*: 'British Documents on the Origins of the War 1898-1914,' vol. 1, ch. 1 (ii), 'The direct British overture to Russia.'

P. 196. *The impression made on the Kaiser*: Communications from Emperor William II.*—*Fashoda*: Communications from Emperor William II.*

Pp. 197-199. *The cruise in the East and the visit to Abdul Hamid*: Communications from Emperor William II.*

P. 199. *Abdul Hamid's request for a secret code*: Communications from Herr von Eckart, Minister of Legation.*

Pp. 199-201. *The early history of the Bagdad Railway*: Communications from Dr. von Kühlmann, formerly Secretary of State.*

Pp. 201-202. *Abdul Hamid gives the concession for the Bagdad Railway*: Communications from Emperor William II.*

Pp. 202-203. *The unrest in Samoa*: Friedjung.

P. 203. *The proposal to recall Count Hatzfeldt*: 'Grosse Politik' 14, 4049.—*Hatzfeldt's advice*: 'Grosse Politik' 14, 4059, 4060, 4062.—*Lord Salisbury and the Samoa conflict*: 'Grosse Politik' 14, 4073, 4074, 4076, 4077.

P. 204. *The Volta delta*: Eckardstein, 'Lebenserinnerungen.' Brandenburg, p. 113.—*Admiral von Tirpitz's attitude*: 'Grosse Politik' 14, 4107.—*The National Post Office*: Brandenburg, p. 118. —*Chamberlain's annoyance, his talks with Hatzfeldt, his troubles*: 'Grosse Politik' 14, 4105, 4106, 4109.

Pp. 205-206. *Rhodes in Berlin*: Communications from Emperor William II.*

Pp. 206-211. *Narrative of Rhodes's audience*: Manuscript account by Emperor William II.*

P. 211. *Bülow's admiration*: Communications from Emperor William II.*

P. 213. *The Boers and the punishment of the participants in the Raid*: Communications from an eminent British statesman.*—*The British and the Boer War*: Communications from an eminent British statesman.*

P. 214. *The reception of Emperor William II in London*: Communications from an eminent British statesman.*

Pp. 214-215. *Morocco, Sir Arthur Nicolson and the French*: Nicolson, 'Sir Arthur Nicolson, Bart.'

348

Pp. 215-216. *Chamberlain, Lord Londonderry, Balfour*: Communications from Emperor William II.*

Pp. 216-217. *Chamberlain and Bülow*: Asquith, 'The Genesis of the War.'

Pp. 217-219. *Chamberlain's speech*: Reuter.

P. 220. *The 'explanation'*: Brandenburg, p. 123.—*Bülow's heirdom to the Chancellorship as explanation*: Communications from Count Monts, Ambassador, concerning the motive stated to him by Bülow.*

P. 221. *Count Hatzfeldt on Bülow*: Communications from an eminent British statesman.* Cf. Chamberlain to Eckardstein, December 28, 1899, in 'Lebenserinnerungen.'—*Chamberlain to his friends*: Communications from an eminent British statesman.*

Pp. 221-234. *Study of Bernhard von Bülow*: Communications from Emperor William II,* King Ferdinand of Bulgaria,* an eminent British statesman,* Prince Max Egon von Fürstenberg,* Prince Hermann Hatzfeldt,* Chancellor von Bethmann-Hollweg,* Count Monts, Ambassador,* Count Wedel, Ambassador,* Count Brockdorff-Rantzau,* Dr. von Kühlmann, formerly Secretary of State,* Herr von Treutler, Minister of Legation,* Herr von Eckart, Minister of Legation,* Herr von Berg, head of the Civil Cabinet,* Count Ernst zu Rantzau, Chamberlain,* Admiral von Tirpitz,* Field Marshal Count Conrad von Hoetzendorf,* Cavalry General Baron von Gebsattel.* Also: Bernhard Fürst von Bülow, 'Denkwürdigkeiten,' with manuscript commentary by Emperor William II;* 'Deutschland und die Mächte,' Dresden 1929, with manuscript commentary by Emperor William II;* Report from Admiral von Grumme, formerly A.D.C., on Prince Bülow to Emperor William II.*

P. 234. *Tirpitz and the confiscated ships; Caprivi and naval organization*: Communications from Emperor William II.*

P. 235. *Tirpitz's advice on Kiaochow*: Communications from Emperor William II.*

P. 235-236. *Tirpitz in the Straits Settlements*: Communications from Admiral von Tirpitz.*

P. 236. *The propaganda for the navy*: Communications from Emperor William II and from Admiral von Tirpitz.*

P. 237. *Tirpitz and Bülow*: Communications from Admiral von Tirpitz.*

Pp. 238-239. *The 'risk theory'*: Communications from Emperor William II and from Admiral von Tirpitz.*

P. 239. *Chamberlain and the naval plans*: Brandenburg, p. 122.

Pp. 239-240. *Salisbury's discontent with Germany*: 'Grosse Politik' 15, 4456, 4471.

Pp. 240-241. *Queen Victoria and the advice for the campaign in South Africa; the Russo-French intervention proposal; the telegram from Heligoland; Bülow's disapproval*: Communications from Emperor William II.*

Pp. 243-245. *The Boxer rising; Japan's proposal; Baron von Ketteler; the 'Generals accustomed to victory'*: Communications from Count Wedel, Ambassador.*

P. 244. *Baron von Ketteler's daring and death*: Communications from Emperor William II.*

P. 245. *The suggested 'step to please the Kaiser'*: Paul von Schwabach, 'Aus meinen Akten.'

Pp. 245-246. *The steps that led up to Waldersee's appointment*: Communications from Emperor William II and from Count Wedel.*

P. 246. *Viscount Aoki; Emperor William's telegram; Holstein's complaint*: Communications from Count Wedel.*

P. 247. *Emperor William's speeches; the deleted sentence*: Communications from Dr. Friedrich Trefz (Munich).—*Bülow's assent to the speeches*: Communications from Emperor William II.*

P. 248. *Waldersee in China*: Communications from Baron von Gebsattel.*—*His military ability*: Communications from Emperor William II.*

P. 249. *The Japanese divisions in Peking*: Communications from Emperor William II.*

Pp. 249-250. *Waldersee's realization of the struggle for spheres of influence in China; his military activities; Prince Engalitchev and the railway line*: Waldersee, 'Denkwürdigkeiten.'

P. 251. *Policy of the 'open door'*: 'Grosse Politik' 16, 4712.

Pp. 251-252. *The Yangtze treaty*: 'Grosse Politik' 16, 4732-4739. Brandenburg, p. 134.

P. 253. *Marquis Ito and the outline of the Anglo-Japanese agreement*: Communications from Count Wedel.*

P. 254. *Emperor William's exultation*: 'Grosse Politik' 17, 4982.

P. 255. *'Between two stools'*: Communications from Emperor William II.* Brandenburg, p. 130.

Pp. 255-256. *Holstein and Britain's adhesion to the Triple Alliance*: 'Grosse Politik' 17, 5007. Brandenburg, p. 146.

Pp. 256-260. *The story of the Japanese offer*: Communications from Count Wedel.*

P. 261. *Japan in 'good political society'*: 'Grosse Politik' 17, 4998.

P. 263. *Chamberlain and the 'entirely new grouping in the world'*: Communications from an eminent British statesman.* Communications from Lord Haldane.* Eckardstein, 'Lebenserinnerungen,' vol. 2, p. 301.

CHAPTER VI

GERMANY AT THE ZENITH OF HER PSEUDO-POWER

P. 267. *Britain's turn away from Germany and towards France*: Communications from an eminent British statesman.*—*The negotiations with Paul Cambon*: Nicolson, p. 167.

P. 268. *Japan as field of enterprise; Count Lambsdorff's proposal*: 'Grosse Politik' 17, 5048-5063.

P. 269. *An end of friendship with Britain*: Communications from Emperor William II.*—*Italy, Tripoli, the Triple Alliance; nothing to endanger France*: Pribram, 'Die Dreibundverträge,' vol. 1, p. 247. Brandenburg, p. 165.—*Reval*: 'Grosse Politik' 18, 5416. Walter Goetz, p. 86.

P. 270. *French negotiations with Spain; King Edward in Paris; France, Egypt, and Morocco*: Nicolson, p. 169.

P. 271. *'Time is working for us'*: 'Grosse Politik' 18, 5421.—*'No reason to panic'; the Queen of Spain; compensation*: 'Grosse Politik' 17, 5199-5203.

P. 272. *The Yalu forests and the cordon*: Communications from Emperor William II.*

P. 274. *The recognition of Bülow's error; his consolation in the Russo-Japanese war*: Communications from Emperor William II.* 'Grosse Politik' 20, 6379.

Pp. 275-278. *The Russo-Japanese war; the Dogger Bank*: Communications from Emperor William II.*

P. 278. *Nicholas II's diary entries*: Michael Freiherr von Taube, 'Die russische Politik der Vorkriegszeit und das Ende des Zarenreiches.'

Pp. 278-280. *Further story of the Dogger Bank incident*: Communications from Emperor William II.*

P. 279. *The entries in the logs*: Michael Taube.

P. 280. *The new possibility of a Continental alliance*: Communications from Emperor William II.* W. Goetz, pp. 133, 146.

Pp. 280-281. *The draft agreement; the Tsar and his advisers*: 'Grosse Politik' 19, 6124-6126.

P. 281. *Britain and the coal supplies; the question to Russia*: Communications from Emperor William II.* 'Grosse Politik' 19, 6077-6099. Brandenburg, pp. 191-2.

Pp. 282-283. *The Mediterranean cruise; Bülow and Tangier; the departure*: Communications from Emperor William II.*—Note by Emperor William II: 'Tangier,' in the Doorn House Archives.*

Pp. 284-288. Communications from Dr. von Kühlmann, formerly Secretary of State.*

P. 288. *Bülow, Holstein, and France*: Brandenburg, p. 199.

P. 289. *Baron von Mentzingen's report; Consul Vasal*: 'Grosse Politik' 20, 6539-6562.—*Bülow as Sphinx*: 'Grosse Politik' 20, 6573.

Pp. 289-292. *The visit to Portugal; the Chancellor's telegrams; public opinion*: Communications from Emperor William II.*

Pp. 292-298. Communications from Emperor William II and from Dr. von Kühlmann.*

Pp. 298-299. *The arrival in Gibraltar and the meeting with Bülow*: Communications from Emperor William II and from Dr. von Kühlmann.*

P. 300. *Delcassé's offer*: Communications from Count Monts, Ambassador; also communications from Count Monts to Baron von der Lancken, then Secretary of Embassy, at Fossanova on May 1 and 2, 1905, repeated to him at Camaldoli in the summer of 1905, and attested by a note from Count Monts to Baron von der Lancken in the summer of 1930.*—*The idea of a conference*: Communications from Dr. von Kühlmann.*

Pp. 301-302. *Holstein and Count Schlieffen*: Communications from Baron von der Lancken, Minister of Legation.*

P. 302. *Casablanca, the concessions in Asia Minor, the further open offer*: Communications from Count Monts, confirmed by his letter to Baron von der Lancken.*

Pp. 303-304. *Delcassé's fall*: Communications from Dr. von Kühlmann.*

Pp. 304-306. *The activities of Prince Albert of Monaco; the instructions to Prince Radolin*: Communications from Emperor William II.*

352

CHAPTER VII

ISOLATION

APPENDIX

VIENNA, *April* 12, 1890.

MY DEAR FRIEND,

You will have learned already from General Count Wedel how greatly the mission entrusted to him pleased me. I read every line of your lucid account of almost incredible occurrences with the liveliest interest, and not until I reached the end of it did I realize what deep thanks I owe you for your unreserved demonstrations of confiding friendship and for all the trouble you have taken on yourself in order to strengthen me in the conviction that in the given circumstances you could have done nothing else in the end but, at the bidding of higher considerations, adopt the firm resolution to set a limit to your magnanimous complaisance, your patience and endurance. Now that I have gained a closer acquaintance with the real conditions of the situation, I am able to gauge and to feel with you how hard it must have been for you to come to this resolution, what bitter hours you had to go through from the beginning of the crisis. Sharing with you the deep regret for the necessity of letting things go so far, I lament none the less that so great a man, and one who has performed such services to Prussia, Germany, and peace, should have been able to let himself be carried away into activities against his Emperor and master for which in their final causes it might be easier to find an explanation than an excuse. The thought that in loosing the tangled knot you were obeying an inescapable necessity of state, will bring you complete peace of mind. I am convinced that in the present endlessly difficult period you will control the helm at home and abroad with a firm hand, with calm circumspection and consideration, supported by the new Chancellor, whom you have certainly been entirely right in recognizing as the right man, and whose acquaintance I shall be glad to make. I see a special guarantee for the future in the fact that under the guidance of a wise impartiality and a clear judgment you have chosen General von Caprivi, although on a former occasion a difference of opinion had arisen between you and him.

Looking forward to seeing you again in Silesia in the autumn, and with the most cordial thanks for your kind visit to the Empress in Wiesbaden, I assure you once more that you may continue for all time to count on the most loyal friendship of

> Your
> Most sincerely devoted friend and brother
>   FRANZ JOSEPH.

MANUSCRIPT LETTER FROM EMPEROR WILLIAM II TO EMPEROR FRANCIS JOSEPH

VIENNA, *April* 14, 1890.

MY DEAR FRIEND,

Major General von Bolfras has just brought me your kind letter, which has done me infinite good. I hasten to thank you once more most warmly for the expression of your trust in me. I was anxious above all—considering the high honour in which I hold your exalted person—that you should not be in the slightest doubt and not suffer in the least from any appearance of inadequacy of information in regard to conditions here. Above all I was sure of what shines so warmly from your lines—that you were able to feel what that time meant for me and how infinitely hard and bitter the struggle and the decision were for me. But it is better so, and better also for our relations with one another, as in view of the independence and with it the secretiveness of the Prince, I should, unhappily, not have been in a position to know, quite freely, what courses he might be entering on in our foreign policy

355

without my knowledge, and how these could be justified to my allies.

I was so grateful for the Empress's permission to visit her. She looked well, was satisfied with her cure, and was infinitely kind and gracious to me, and I am glad to be able to send you this report from Wiesbaden. The young couple were radiant with happiness and contentment.

With 1000 greetings and looking forward to the pleasure of another meeting,

Your true friend

WILHELM.

COUNT KÁLNOKY, MINISTER OF FOREIGN AFFAIRS, TO VON SZÖGYÉNY, AUSTRO-HUNGARIAN AMBASSADOR IN BERLIN

(Private letter.)   VIENNA, *November* 14, 1894.
Secret.

HIS EXCELLENCY HERR VON SZÖGYÉNY, BERLIN.

Count Philipp Eulenburg returned to his post a few days ago, after several months' absence, and sought me out at once. He was, naturally, still wholly under the influence of the fall of Count Caprivi, effected in Liebenberg, and the retirement of the Prussian Prime Minister; he said that he had been commanded by Emperor William to communicate 'with the utmost candour,' not only to me but especially to H.M. the Emperor, 'everything down to the smallest detail' concerning the causes and circumstances which produced this astonishing Cabinet change. Our most gracious master met this desire and gave Count Eulenburg an opportunity of discharging the mission entrusted to him, which he did in the amplest measure.

Count Eulenburg also told me the origin of the things that produced the catastrophe, in great detail. Without going more closely into these narratives, rather confused by the countless immaterial details and personal questions, I am able to state that the account sent to us in your despatch of November 10, when the crisis was not entirely over, in no way conflicts with

Eulenburg's, and is, indeed, substantially in agreement with it if one removes from the latter its peculiarly Eulenburgian embellishments. So much of the details communicated by Count Eulenburg as might serve to complete your reports has reference simply to circumstances of a more personal nature, and just to the points on which I could not admit Count Eulenburg to be an impartial narrator. Accordingly, in what follows I am confining myself to communicating to you in strict confidence a few indications of the impression which I gained from Eulenburg's account, simply for your personal information.

To begin with I want to mention that at the time of his arrival in Liebenberg Emperor William believed, quite *bona fide*, that his last effort at conciliation had been successful, that Count Caprivi was remaining in office, and that the Parliamentary campaign was going to begin. Thus it was in Liebenberg, where the Emperor was under the sole influence of the Eulenburg clique, that the plot, evidently long hatched, was ripe for execution. The levers available for its execution were Count Caprivi's attacks on Imperial German Ministers and members of parliament, with their echoes in the *Kölnische Zeitung* articles; these were interpreted as an unwarrantable cry of triumph over Botho Eulenburg—and Caprivi's increasing intimacy with the Left fractions and the Centre. I should doubt whether the gentlemen intended that Count Eulenburg, the Prime Minister, should also fall; it almost seems to me that Emperor William's prompt cutting of the knot by dismissing *both* of the rivals came as a surprise to the promoters of the intrigue. In his impatience of the perpetual annoyance from these personal incompatibilities—which, incidentally, showed plainly (1) that the two offices need to be combined again, and (2) that the indispensable Conservatives are implacably opposed to Caprivi—Emperor William brought the whole situation to an end by a decision which may have been all too precipitate, but of which the logical justification cannot be denied. There are, however, several circumstances which lend colour to the supposition that the clique was non-

357

plussed, and, as Philipp Eulenburg said, the Prime Minister, who was always ready for any sacrifice, accepted without hesitation the course chosen by the Emperor. No doubt the plan still held good up to then to place his cousin in the fat post in Strassburg that he had earned—but now that that has come to nought, the next thing is to find a place for Count Botho! In bringing down Caprivi the gentlemen have won a victory which they will certainly be able to turn to account, for they are assured of the thanks of the Conservatives, and it will be very interesting to follow their further operations.

The way Count Eulenburg spoke of the absolute necessity for Baron Marschall to remain at Prince Hohenlohe's side, for the sake of the great services he is able to render through his uncommon parliamentary gifts, showed that Baron Marschall is regarded as indispensable *in Parliament* and not at the Foreign Ministry. Perhaps the rumour will thus prove well founded that Herr von Boetticher will leave his post and make room for the new Minister of State, whose post could in turn be given to one of the gentlemen of the consortium.

The Kaiser is in the midst of this net, quite unaware that it is being spun round him—let us hope that the moment is coming when he will see through the game and cut his way out. General Caprivi was not smart enough for these gentry, he was too honest and too slow-going to comprehend these subtle intrigues; unfortunately he also failed to keep in with the young Emperor. All this business may yet work great mischief, and I see no hope of improvement unless the Emperor's sound sense and his good impulses forge a way out.

So far as specially concerns ourselves, or rather our relations with Germany, I have no fears, as Emperor William himself offers us the best guarantee in this regard. The great pains these gentlemen are taking to see that the events are viewed here in *their* sense shows how anxious they are lest our most gracious master should have cause for dissatisfaction.

Hammerstein, the new Minister of Agriculture, is so out-and-out an agrarian that I am prepared for not a few new hindrances and impediments in the way of our imports into Germany; though we must energetically defend ourselves against them.

Emperor William's caution in his dealings with the young Tsar shows that he is capable of going to work shrewdly and with reflection.

Yours, etc.

KÁLNOKY.

EMPEROR FRANCIS JOSEPH'S ABANDONED VISIT TO ROME

MANUSCRIPT NOTE BY EMPEROR WILLIAM II

After the accession to the throne of King Victor Emanuel of Italy, there came a perceptible alienation between Rome and Vienna. It filled Herr von Szögyény with deep concern for the future and the stability of the Triple Alliance.

One day he unburdened his troubles to me, closing with the question:

'What can one do in Vienna to combat the animosity in Rome?'

From my meetings with King Victor Emanuel I was aware of the true ground. He had never made any secret in speaking to me of the fact. Emperor Francis Joseph's *omission* to return in Rome the visit made to him by the King's *father*,—*Re Umberto*—was felt by Victor Emanuel as an insult, which he had *quasi* to 'avenge'! He had, he considered, to exact penance for the injury to the memory of his insulted father.

I replied to His Excellency's question by informing him of these facts.

The Ambassador nodded gloomily, remarking that he had feared as much. He had been brought into the secret discussions in Vienna on the question of the preparation for the return visit to *Rome*. All efforts to make any other place than Rome acceptable to Italy had failed, and there had been no choice but to face the necessity of approaching the Vatican

359

and negotiating with it for a settlement of the question of the prior visit which the Vatican demanded but to which the Quirinal refused to agree.

The Vatican insisted on receiving the *first* visit from the Emperor after his arrival in Rome; *after that* it would *permit* him to enter the Quirinal. The Quirinal, of course, declined that arrangement.

After describing these proceedings and expressing his regret that the Roman Curia by its intransigent attitude was helping to cloud the *political* relations between Rome and Vienna, His Excellency asked me:

'Whether I really knew of no means of disentangling this fearful knot, which threatened to produce regrettable consequences in the future.'

He admitted *sub sigillo* that during the negotiations in Vienna at which he had been present *Re* Umberto had been given the *express promise* that the Emperor's return visit should take place in *Rome*. Thus, he added, King Victor Emanuel had *formal justification* for being excited over Vienna's omission of the visit.

I thought for a considerable time over this very complicated case, viewing it from every side, and I was guided by the following considerations:

I. *Vienna* had *promised* the return visit to *Rome*, but had *not* carried it out.

II. The Quirinal had consequently felt *injured*, and *rightly*.

III. The *Vatican* had put forward conditions which *interfered* with the visit.

A. *Vienna's position.*

Vienna imprudently *promised* a return visit of H.M. the Emperor to *Rome*, before ascertaining the views of the Curia. That ought *eo ipso* to have been done first. On the other hand, the much younger King of Italy who later came to govern has so far *omitted* to make his visit on accession—in conformity with long-standing custom among the Monarchs of Europe— to the much older Emperor. That was a *mistake*. Reason: the abandoned return visit from the Emperor to *his father*. Accordingly, in conformity with the usage above mentioned between the European Sovereigns, the Emperor was not in a position to visit the younger Sovereign *before* his own accession visit to him.

The Emperor's visit to *Re* Umberto *was omitted* because the *Curia* demanded of the Emperor on his arrival in Rome the *first* visit *before* entering the Quirinal.

That postulate the Emperor refused—rightly—to fulfil, as it amounted to an insult to the House of Savoy. Accordingly he abandoned the visit to Rome.

This abandonment, however, visibly worsened Austro-Italian relations and endangered the Triple Alliance considerably more after the succession to the Italian throne.

Vienna ought thus to have declared to the *Curia*:

'The Curia is a spiritual power and as such one is bound to follow it *in rebus ecclesiae*. But the Curia must not intervene by action in the temporal sphere to the injury of the interests or relations of two peoples, by imposing postulates which the Sovereigns in question are not in a position to fulfil.'

If the Curia had shown continued opposition, Vienna ought then to have undertaken the visit 'as *necessary* for the cultivation of good relations and as *required* in fulfilment of a promise,' ignoring the desires of the Curia. The *political interest of a country*, it should have held, comes *before* a gesture of courtesy towards the Curia.

B. *Position of the Quirinal.*

The young King Victor Emanuel, filled with an uncommonly exalted pride and sense of the dignity of his 'House of Savoy,' felt the Emperor's omission to return *his father's* visit as an offence against his exalted house, which it was hard for him to bear. This was all the more dangerous since he was in the *right*. The King was well aware of the precise ground of the omission—the Curia's postulate concerning the first visit from H.M. the Emperor to it *before* entering the Quirinal. Outwardly at least he was stiffly hostile to the Curia, and he felt its intervention in the question of the visit as an *affront* to his house and his rights as Sovereign, so far as concerned Rome as his capital and that of his Kingdom of Italy. In this too the King was *right*.

He must, for all that, have been familiar with the Emperor's spiritual bonds with the Curia, and it should have been his duty to help to make the situation easier for the K. und K.[1] 'Apostolic' Emperor and King, or at least to make the attempt to do so. Undoubtedly unofficial private relations existed between Quirinal and Vatican. With the Italians' gift of discovering and effecting compromises, it could not well have been entirely unthinkable for a solution satisfactory to both parties to be found with a little goodwill.

Evidently the King of Italy did not enter on this course. Instead, he seized on the idea of *reprisal*. He, the younger 'colleague,' refused to make the *first visit on accession* due to his older 'colleague'—a visit which, once for all, was '*de rigueur*' among Sovereigns in Europe—and in this way put himself in the *wrong* with Vienna. From the standpoint of the etiquette of courtesies observed between the Sovereigns of Europe, he committed a *tactless* action and an undeniable *slighting* of the older Emperor, which Emperor Francis Joseph in turn was bound to feel as an *affront*. In this Vienna was *right*. The visit from King Victor Emanuel on his accession was beyond all question due to be made to the Emperor, who was entitled to demand it. Thus there was *right* opposing *right*.

C. Position of the Curia.

The Curia demanded of the Emperor, in the event of his coming to Rome, his *first* visit, *before* entering the Quirinal.

It imposed its recognized *ecclesiastical* authority, which for His Imperial and Royal 'Apostolic' Majesty carried *decisive* weight, in a question of purely *temporal* and political importance, thus applying *compulsion* to the Emperor, against the

[1]Imperial and Royal.

interests of Austria-Hungary. Into the purely political considerations which governed the preparations for the promised visit of the Emperor to Rome, it pushed its way disturbingly and with the claim to *authority*. That was, therefore, an encroachment.

To begin with it damaged the temporal power of Italy and the dignity of the royal house of Savoy in the most painful way by the postulate of the *first* visit, which was equivalent to an ignoring of the Kingdom and its ruler. This was an affront to King Victor Emanuel and his realm. For he was bound to perceive in it a public non-recognition of his dignity as King of Italy and as protector of the Constitution of the Kingdom. In that he was *right*. The Curia was wrong, all the more as what was involved here was a purely political, *temporal* question, which did not in any way directly concern the Curia.

Secondly, through its postulate to Vienna the Curia exercised political pressure in a direction which was bound to bring injury to the Austro-Hungarian Monarchy *pro futuro*. It also brought the Emperor inward struggles of conscience of the gravest nature, of which the anxiety expressed to me by his Ambassador was the reflexion. For the Curia *prevented* the Emperor's visit to Rome through an appeal to his feelings as 'an obedient son of the Roman Church.' It thus brought his religious feelings into conflict with his *conscience* as *guide of the State*. The considerations of the ruler demanded from him absolutely friendly relations with the house of Savoy and Italy, and therefore the visit to Rome. On the contrary, the Roman Pontifex tried to hinder or prevent the 'obedient son of the Church' from making his visit.

Conversely, it was bound to be known in Vienna that the house of Savoy regarded this postulate of the Curia as an affront, and to be known why it did so. If in spite of that Vienna accepted the postulate as justified and abandoned the visit, it put itself in the position of seeming to the Quirinal and to Italy to share the Curia's view, injurious as that was to the Quirinal. That was once more an affront to the King. Thus the attitude taken up by the Curia in the question of

Emperor Francis Joseph's visit to Rome was absolutely devoid of justification. It was bound to know that its intransigent insistence on the utterly *unjustified postulate* bore within itself *dangers* for the future of the two Monarchies and their ruling houses, for which the Church had not to bear the responsibility. It should have been its *duty* to yield to the representations of the venerable Emperor, in order that he might be able to fulfil his duty as ruler and representative of the *political* interests of his countries and carry out the visit. The Curia ought never to have disturbed or hindered the Emperor's temporal policy.

From the foregoing it thus follows that on the two sides there stood right facing right. Facts that were assessed by one side as an affront facing similar facts on the other side.

My proposed attempt at a solution

H.M. the Emperor should write a personal letter to the King of Italy—to some such purport as follows: he has grown old; with the passing of time long journeys are becoming no longer possible for him. He has now to think of the closing of his life's journey. There is one thing that weighs upon his conscience: the abandonment of his return visit to his friend and ally, the *Re* Humbert. The King who was so close a friend of his has, unhappily, in the meantime passed away. The Emperor is, nevertheless, desirous of honouring before his death his promise given to *Re* Umberto, and, as the latter is no longer dwelling among the mortals, of at least visiting his grave and laying a wreath on it. He therefore begs King Victor Emanuel to permit him to carry out this intention.

In the case of that being acceded to, the following programme for Rome might be sketched:

    I. Arrival: at the railway station a great reception, King, Princes, Ministers, guard of honour.

    II. Drive of the two Monarchs through Rome to the Pantheon.

III. Laying of the wreath on the grave of *Re* Umberto, H.M. the Emperor addressing the assembled members of the house of Savoy and corporate bodies:

'This is an act of friendship for the dead King, for the reigning King Victor Emanuel, for the house of Savoy and the whole Kingdom of Italy, towards whom H.M. hereby fulfils the promise he once made and pays to *Re* Umberto his formal return visit.'

Victor Emanuel's desire for the return visit to be made to *his father* would thus be fulfilled, and the injury done to his house by the omission so far to make it would be remedied. At the same time, the *first* visit—through the presence at *Re* Umberto's grave—would have been made to the royal house and to Italy. If the Curia still held to its postulate and if the Emperor regarded himself as bound to respect it, he could part from the King at the Pantheon and drive to the Vatican, as the King still owed him the first visit on accession. If the Emperor did not intend to pay attention to the Curia's objection, he would drive with the King to the Quirinal. Perhaps his subsequent visit from there to the Curia would be declined (?), perhaps, with tactful handling, it would not. Quirinal and Curia would each have to be informed of the programme, and meanwhile would be able to negotiate direct with one another.

When I had recounted and explained the reflexions and proposals set down in this document to Herr von Szögyény, he agreed with me fully and entirely. He too was a convinced 'true son of his Church,' but had not the slightest doubt concerning its attitude:

'If the Curia saw and were able to feel the depth of the Emperor's desire, it would reflect twice before administering to the venerable Kaiser, *coram publico*, a refusal which would absolutely bring all his subjects *of both confessions* into harness, and would be very sharply and disapprovingly judged by Italy and all the world. *It cannot slight the guest of the*

Kingdom of Italy.' He decided with great pleasure to send this attempt of mine as a proposal to H.M. in Vienna.

At the first opportunity I related the whole affair to my father's friend King Albert of Saxony, who was also a 'true son of the Roman Church.' He awarded me his full approval in every respect with the remark that I had 'rendered an inestimable service to Vienna and the Triple Alliance by this proposal, and also to the peace of the world.' For King Albert of Saxony—the *only* trusted friend of Emperor Francis Joseph—was also feeling anxiety over the increasing tension between Vienna and Rome. The King was also of the opinion that the solution proposed by me was, 'with a little goodwill,' entirely acceptable both for the Curia and for the Quirinal.

To make thoroughly sure, I put the *proposed programme* for Rome in strict confidence before an Italian friend of mine, who is devotedly loyal to the Triple Alliance. In reply to my question what would be the attitude of the '*Roman piazza*' to this programme, he exclaimed:

'The Romans will take the Emperor's horses out of the shafts and pull him along to the Pantheon, for as a man the venerable old gentleman is regarded with much sympathy by us Romans.' This statement too I had transmitted to Herr von Szögyény.

Months passed without my hearing anything about the affair. Finally the Ambassador came to me. I read no encouragement in his depressed appearance. With great and sincere regret he informed me that his report with my proposal had been *rejected* by the Emperor, 'since the Curia would not assent to it.'

The visit was abandoned. The tension grew. In the world war Italy fell away from her allies. Not until many years after did I learn from 'well-informed' National-Catholic quarters in Austria and Germany the real reason for the rejection of my solution, which the Ambassador's tactful discretion had withheld from me. Vienna had *not* preserved discretion in regard to the Curia as to the source of the solution. When the

Curia discovered *who* had made this proposal for a solution, it declared it unacceptable for that reason.

Emperor Francis Joseph submitted to the decision of the Church as final *against* the proposal of his *ally*.

By frustrating Emperor Francis Joseph's visit to Rome the Curia, instead of promoting peace among the peoples—which, as is well known, is the function of the Church on earth—had contributed consciously or unconsciously to the sowing of mistrust and discord between the princes and their peoples, and had thereby indirectly brought to its charge the downfall of Austria-Hungary.

> *Mulier taceat in ecclesiam!*
> *Ecclesia taceat in politicis!*

This note has been written because no consideration is to be found in any of the more recent historical works concerning Emperor Francis Joseph of this most important affair, which determined the fate of the Habsburg Monarchy.

Emperor Francis Joseph made the sacrifice of the political interests of his peoples to the interference of the Curia, damaging as it was to those peoples' political future; he lost his Italian ally, and his Empire fell into ruins.

Written from memory without documents

THE CONTROVERSY OVER THE THRONE OF LIPPE

MANUSCRIPT NOTE BY EMPEROR WILLIAM II

The old Prince of Lippe-Detmold had no children. In order to provide for the succession in the event of the death of a childless prince, the Prince of Lippe-Detmold had concluded a treaty with the Prince of Schaumburg-Lippe-Bückeburg at the beginning of the nineteenth century, providing that one of the latter's sons or brothers should succeed in the event of his death.[1]

[1] Mentioned in *Fürstin Pauline* v. *Lippe-Detmold* (published 1930).

When the throne became vacant, the Prince zu Schaumburg-Lippe designated his younger brother Adolf—the husband of my sister Victoria—as Regent for the time being, in accordance with the treaty. That was as agreed on. At the same time the succession was disputed by the lines of Weissenfeld and Lippe-Biesterfeld. My brother-in-law and his wife were given a hearty welcome on their arrival by the population, and they soon succeeded in so winning sympathies in the Princedom by their disposition and their activities that the population wanted them to remain permanently.

Meanwhile the Biesterfeld line especially moved heaven and earth to secure the succession in Detmold. The Bundesrat was mobilized and an arbitral judgment was demanded. As this was a controversy between princes the standpoint was taken up that the German Emperor was the proper authority to decide it. Accordingly I chose Baron von Marschall as my adviser. Who can describe my amazement when ultimately it was decided on a vote that not the head of the Empire but King Albert of Saxony should be chosen as arbitrator—'as he is the oldest German prince and helped to create the Empire and as a reigning prince has an older title than the Emperor's'!

In the controversy the succession of the Biesterfeld line was disputed by the Bückeburg house on the ground of the inequality of the former in birth, as one of its ancestors had married a lady of the lesser nobility, Modeste von Unruh, whose descendants were not entitled to succeed. Marschall then worked on the issue with the King of Saxony without further consulting or considering me, and elaborated a decision in favour of the Biesterfeld line, although the impression had become general that it could not succeed for the reason just given. Thus as a result of his *votum* my brother-in-law and my sister had to leave Detmold, in accordance with his plain decision, much to the grief of the whole population, which had no liking for the Biesterfeld house. The treaty was ignored.

I spoke rather sharply to Marschall about this turn in the affair; at first he became very excited, maintaining that the right had been undeniably on the side of the Biesterfeld line. When I cut him short by asking briefly: 'And Modeste von Unruh? Has she simply been left out of account?' he became silent and very embarrassed; finally he got out of his difficulty by saying that 'He had been unable to vote any other way; the award had had to be given so, as the King of Saxony had confidentially admitted to him when the two were alone that he had *pledged his word* to the old late Count of Lippe-Biesterfeld, before his death, to place his son on the throne of Lippe and to prevent the Bückeburgs from seizing it.'

I replied: 'Then H.M. the King of Saxony was a *party* to the dispute and should not have pronounced an award, and you too should at once have resigned your function.'

The affair was not correct. For in a decision on a purely constitutional issue personal motives had been introduced, with the support of the Secretary of State.

WILHELM I. R.

Index of Names

370

Index of Subjects

PRINTED IN GREAT BRITAIN
BY ROBERT MACLEHOSE AND CO. LTD.
THE UNIVERSITY PRESS, GLASGOW